THE ROMANTIC STORY
OF TEXAS

THE ROMANTIC STORY OF TEXAS

PETER MOLYNEAUX

THE CORDOVA PRESS, INC.
NEW YORK AND DALLAS
1936

To the Memory of
LOUIS J. WORTHAM
Who First Aroused My Interest
in the Story of Texas.

ACKNOWLEDGEMENT

It is hardly necessary to say that the author of this book is indebted to Dr. Eugene C. Barker, head of the Department of History at the University of Texas, more than to anybody else. No one who attempted to tell the story of Texas could possibly escape a similar indebtedness. But he is indebted also to so many others, including practically everybody who has published the results of original research in this field during the past quarter of a century, that an attempt to enumerate them would be certain to have an unsatisfactory result because of inevitable omissions. However, it should be said that his debt to Dr. Herbert E. Bolton, head of the Department of History at Stanford University, and to George Lockhart Rives, author of the exhaustive work, "The United States and Mexico: 1821-1848", is exceeded only by that which he owes Dr. Barker. He hereby makes grateful acknowledgement to these and to scores of others whose scholarly labors have made "The Romantic Story of Texas" possible.

PREFACE

I once heard Dan Moody, then the Governor of Texas, tell a Boston audience that whereas every school child in Texas knows about Lexington and Concord Bridge and Bunker Hill, and cherishes them as shrines of American liberty, very few people in Massachusetts know much about the Alamo, Goliad, and San Jacinto. He was not suggesting, he said, that these Texas shrines should be regarded as entirely on a parity with those of Massachusetts in relation to American history. But he insisted that the Texas story is an essential part of the story of America, in the same sense that the history of the Atlantic coast is part of that story, and that as such it ought to be familiar to all Americans.

It occurred to me at the time that while it is perfectly true that Americans outside the Southwest do not know much about the Texas chapter of the story of their country, there is sounder basis for complaint in the circumstance that so many of them believe so much with respect to it that is not true. For it is a fact that a vast majority of educated Americans, while having only a hazy idea of how Texas was separated from Mexico and annexed to the United States, are quite certain that there was something discreditable about it.

During more than a quarter-century as a Texas journalist, I have had occasion repeatedly to challenge the statement, made periodically by this or that distinguished American writer, that the United

States "took Texas from Mexico". It does not appear
that I have succeeded very often in convincing the
offending party that he was in error, but, as an inci-
dental result of this experience, it has been made
apparent to me that the story of Texas is almost completely unknown among Americans.

And that is why I have written this book. It is an
attempt to present in the form of a connected narra-
tive, between the two covers of a single volume, what
has been revealed by the most competent historical
research with respect to this subject. It is the story
of how Texas was settled, how and why it was separated from Mexico, and how finally it was annexed
to the United States. I have called it a "romantic"
story, and I think it is certainly that. But it is something more than that. Not only is it an important
chapter in the story of America, but there is a sense
in which it may be truly said to be part of the record
of the world struggle between democracy and despotism during the first half of the nineteenth century.

Aside from this, however, the Texas story is extremely interesting in itself. I have tried to tell it in
an interesting way, and I hope I have succeeded
sufficiently to justify this book from that standpoint,
if from no other.

PETER MOLYNEAUX.

CONTENTS

THE ROMANTIC STORY
OF TEXAS

CHAPTER I

TWO MEET ON THE PLAZA

In the single room of a little rock-walled house facing the plaza of the town of San Antonio de Bexar, in the Spanish province of Texas, there lived in the early years of the nineteenth century a man who called himself Baron de Bastrop. He lived alone, and many regarded him as something of a man of mystery. San Antonio in those days was one of the most remote settlements in North America. It was the only community in the vast expanse of Texas and nearly a month's horseback journey through a wilderness from the Louisiana border. And yet this man, who claimed to be of noble birth, lived there for years in relative poverty, an exile among an alien people. Very little was known about him— nothing, in fact, except what he chose to tell. And what he told tended to make him appear even more mysterious rather than otherwise. For it failed altogether to explain the strangest thing about him: why such a man should bury himself in that isolated place, almost completely cut off from all contact with civilization.

Bastrop had come to San Antonio from New Orleans, probably some time after Louisiana was transferred to the United States in 1803, though the time is not certain. According to his own story, he was a native of Holland and had fled from that country in 1795, when an army of revolutionary France invaded it, following the Reign of Terror in Paris. His first appearance in New Orleans was in 1797, in which year the Spanish Governor of Louisiana made him a grant of land on condition that he colonize it. His experience as a colonizer apparently had not been very happy, for his grant was subsequently suspended, pending approval by the King of Spain, and he seems to have had some difficulty with New Orleans merchants over delayed payment for supplies. Meantime, Louisiana was ceded to Napoleon Bonaparte, who soon sold it to the United States, and while Bastrop managed to retain title to the land which had been granted him and even to make a start at settling it, he evidently had elected to remain a Spanish subject and had moved to San Antonio after the Americans took possession of New Orleans.

Bastrop had disposed of a portion of his Louisiana land, and this circumstance linked his name with the ill-fated conspiracy of Aaron Burr. When Burr started down the Mississippi in 1806 on the expedition which was suspected to be one of conquest against Mexico, his immediate destination was the Bastrop grant in Louisiana. The Bastrop grant, it was said, was to have been the base for Burr's operations in the Southwest. Burr's arrest and his subsequent trial for treason brought this scheme to naught, and there is no evidence that Bastrop himself was in any way directly concerned in the conspiracy. But the incident tended to add to the air of mystery about him.

Bastrop must have been about twenty-eight years old at the time of his flight from Holland, and though he lived to be sixty and on his own testimony had left a wife and five children in Europe, he never returned to his native country. His wife is believed to have died in 1811, sixteen years after his flight, and after that he seems to have ceased altogether to communicate with his relatives. In any event, near the end of his life he did not know whether his daughters were married, because, he said, it had been many years since he last received news from Holland. Evidently he had severed all ties with his past, and to his relatives he must have become as one dead. Indeed, he might have passed completely from the memory of men, dying at last in his humble dwelling, unnoticed by the great world he had left behind, but for an accidental incident which occurred on the plaza two days before Christmas in the year 1820.

Bastrop was then fifty-three years old, and a quarter of a century had passed since he had fled from his native land. Situated as he was, life could not seem to hold very much for him in the future, and certainly it would not have been thought that any act of his could affect in the slightest degree the affairs of the great world from which he was now so remote. But on that December day, through an accidental meeting on the plaza with a man he had not seen in twenty years, this lonely exile was transformed into an instrument of destiny.

The man whom Bastrop met on the plaza was Moses Austin, an American, then fifty-nine years old, who had also been a colonizer in a limited way in the Spanish province of Louisiana. It does not appear that they had been more than casual acquaintances, for while Austin's Louisiana grant was dated only a month earlier than that of Bastrop, his operations were in the upper province, near St. Louis, and he seldom went to New Orleans, which was then Bastrop's headquarters. Nevertheless, Bastrop had known Austin well enough to recognize him instantly when he encountered him unexpectedly, after two decades, in that out-of-the-way place.

Austin had arrived in San Antonio that very day, after a horseback journey of hundreds of miles through the Texas wilderness, with the object of laying a proposal before the Spanish authorities. The province of Texas was then ruled locally by a "Governor", which was rather a grand title to bestow upon an official whose constituents numbered no more than three thousand persons. The Governor was under direct authority of the Commandant of the Eastern Interior Provinces of New Spain, and the Commandant at this time was Gen. Joaquín de Arredondo. The Governor was Antonio Martinez, and he was under strict orders from Arredondo to keep Americans out of Texas. Only the previous year it had been necessary to drive out an invading party of American filibusters, commanded by Dr. James Long, which had taken possession of East Texas, and even at the very moment of Austin's arrival at San Antonio, the American buccaneer, Jean Lafitte, was established on Galveston Island, from whence he was making war on Spanish ships. Americans, therefore, were extremely unwelcome in Texas and it was Martinez's duty to keep them out. It was before Martinez that Austin had come to San Antonio to lay a proposal, and that proposal was the preposterous one that he be granted permission to settle Americans in Texas!

Martinez, as was natural in the circumstances, declined to entertain such a proposal. In fact, he refused even to listen to Austin and ordered him to get back across the American border without delay. Austin had counted heavily on his ability to persuade the Spanish authorities that his proposal was feasible. Failure in this would mean for him an intolerable outlook, for the panic of 1819 in the United States had found his affairs in an involved condition and had completed his ruin. Years before, as a younger man, he had made a new start as a Spanish subject in Louisiana, and now he proposed to become a Spanish subject again, this time in Texas, with a similar object in view. In colloquial parlance, Austin was "broke" and hopelessly in debt. And, to use his own words, he was impelled to go to Texas because "to remain in a country where I had enjoyed wealth, in a state of poverty I could not submit to." Failure to convince Martinez meant the end of all his high hopes. And evidently he had failed. Austin had just left Martinez, and already had "determined to quit the place in an hour, being much disgusted and irritated by his reception", when, crossing the plaza, he came face to face with Bastrop.

Chance often plays an important part in men's lives, and even in history. Both Austin and Bastrop must have regarded this meeting as almost providential. For each was suited to the other's need. Each of these men was sorely under the necessity of mending his own fortunes, and each must have recognized at once that the other could help him greatly. But what neither of them could have guessed at the time, and what their contemporaries of the great world never knew, was that the moment of their encounter on the plaza of San Antonio de Bexar, two days before Christmas in the year 1820, was the precise moment of the beginning of the history of modern Texas.

CHAPTER II

A PRICE OF THE COMPROMISE

WHILE Moses Austin was making his trip to Texas
with the object of becoming a Spanish subject again,
and of obtaining from Spain permission to colonize
the province, some very interesting things were happening in the United States. The Legislature of the
sovereign State of Kentucky was adopting a resolution declaring that Texas belonged to the United
States and instructing the State's two Senators to vote
against ratification of the treaty which ceded it to
Spain. This treaty, under the terms of which the
United States "renounced forever" all its "rights,
claims, and pretensions" to Texas, had been signed
nearly two years before. It had been promptly ratified by the Senate, but inasmuch as it provided that
ratifications must be exchanged within six months
and Spain had permitted this time limit to expire
without acting on it, another ratification by the
United States would be necessary.

The Kentucky resolution represented the view of
Henry Clay, who had introduced a similar resolution in Congress the previous April. Clay contended
that the treaty was "illegal" on the ground that it
attempted to transfer territory of the United States
to another nation without the approval of both houses
of Congress. No action had been taken by Congress

on his resolution, but it had afforded him the opportunity to deliver an impassioned speech in the House castigating President Monroe for negotiating such a treaty. Clay used a statement of Monroe's as a text. Several years before, Monroe, as a diplomatic representative of the American Government, had stated in a communication to the Spanish Foreign Office that the evidence in hand convinced the United States that it had as good a title to Texas as it had to New Orleans. Monroe had formed a different opinion in the meantime, but Clay dug up this old statement, quoted it as his authority, and demanded to know by what right the President had presumed to "give away" such a rich region, which, according to his own official word, belonged to the United States. In the same treaty Spain had ceded Florida to the United States in consideration of the assumption by the American Government of the claims of American citizens against Spain up to five million dollars. Clay called it a bad bargain to give Texas and five million dollars in exchange for Florida. Besides, he said, the Latin American republics (which Clay contended the President ought to recognize) would soon drive Spain from the Western Hemisphere forever, and in that event, as certain as ripe fruit falls, Florida would become United States territory.

Clay was not striking at Monroe alone in this speech. He was aiming also at Monroe's Secretary of State, John Quincy Adams, who had negotiated the treaty and who was regarded as a candidate for the Presidency. Clay had similar aspirations of his own, and he used the Spanish treaty as the text of a political tirade.

This speech of Clay's was widely discussed throughout the country, for such views had already been gaining currency among the people. As Spain continued to withhold approval of the treaty, after an unsuccessful attempt to obtain as a condition of favorable action the promise of the United States not to recognize the independence of revolting Spanish colonies, the impression began to spread that Spain would never ratify it. People began to say that it was just as well, that Clay was right when he said that Texas was too much to give for Florida. This opinion was expressed by no less an elder statesman than Thomas Jefferson, who had been Monroe's mentor in both law and politics.

Jefferson was then seventy-seven years old and was living in retirement at Monticello. He put in much of his time writing letters on questions of the day to his political friends, among whom, of course, was the President. And he wrote to Monroe about the treaty on May 14th, 1820, six weeks after the delivery of Clay's speech. "I confess to you," Jefferson wrote the President, "I am not sorry for the non-ratification of the Spanish treaty. . . . The province of Texas will be the richest State in our Union, without any exception . . . . Florida, moreover, is ours. Every nation in Europe concedes it such by right. We need not care for its occupation in time of peace, and, in war, the first cannon makes it ours without offense to anybody." The treaty, he said, had had "the valuable effect of strengthening our title to Texas, because the cession of the Floridas in exchange for Texas imports an acknowledgment of our right to it." Jefferson concluded by saying that once

Mexico is independent of Spain, Texas would join the United States, "a measure to which their new government will probably accede voluntarily."

Such a communication from Jefferson was not to be treated by Monroe with the same indifference he assumed toward a political tirade by Henry Clay. So he replied to it in a long personal letter, taking great pains to explain his position and writing nearly a thousand words in doing so. And the whole purport of his letter was that he did not dare to annex Texas to the United States, not because of Spain or its colonies or any European power, but for reasons that were entirely domestic in character.

Monroe agreed with Jefferson on the probabilities of the situation. "I am satisfied we might regulate it in every circumstance as we thought just and without war," he wrote, "that we might take Florida as an indemnity and Texas for some trifle as an equivalent. Spain must soon be expelled from this continent, and with any new government which may be formed in Mexico it would be easy to arrange the boundary in the wilderness so as to include as much territory on our side as we might desire. No European power could prevent this if so disposed."

The difficulty, Monroe explained, did not proceed from such sources. "It is altogether internal," he said, "and of the most distressing nature and dangerous tendency." And to make clear the character of this internal difficulty, Monroe reminded Jefferson how the Federalist partisans had opposed every move to extend the boundaries of the United States from the first. They had attempted in 1785 and 1786, through the means of a treaty with Spain, to have the Mississippi River closed to navigation by the people of Kentucky and Tennessee. "This was not a question with Spain in reality," he pointed out, "but among ourselves, in which her pretensions were brought forward in aid of the party at the head of the project. It was an effort to give such a shape to our Union as would assure dominion over it by its Eastern section." It was expected, he said, that the closing of the river would be followed by the secession of the region west of the Allegheny Mountains. "The Union then consisted of eight navigating and commercial States, with five producing States, holding slaves; and had the river been shut up, the division would always have been the same. . . . It was foreseen by these persons that if the Mississippi should be opened and new States be established on its waters, the population would be drawn thither, the number of the productive States be proportionately increased, and their hope of dominion, on that contracted scale, be destroyed. It was to prevent this that the project was formed."

Happily this project had failed, wrote Monroe, and the progress of the United States since then in an opposite direction had been rapid and wonderful. The river had been opened and all the territory dependent upon it acquired. Eight States had already been admitted to the Union and another was on the point of entering. "This march to greatness has been seen with profound regret by them," he continued, "but it has been impelled by causes over which they have had no control."

Monroe pointed out that several attempts had been made to impede this process and that the latest had been the opposition to the admission of Missouri into the Union. The object of this, he said, was to obtain power by uniting all the non-slave-holding States on that question alone, regardless of other differences and conflicts of interest. "Since 1786," wrote Monroe, "I have not seen so violent and persevering a struggle, and, on the part of some of the leaders in the project, for a purpose so unmasked and dangerous. They did not hesitate to avow that it was a contest for power only, disclaiming the pretext of liberty or humanity." They were willing to risk the Union on the measure, he declared, if indeed dismemberment was not the principal object.

Complete success of the scheme was prevented, he continued, "by the patriotic devotion of several members of the non-slave-holding States who preferred the sacrifice of themselves at home to a violation of the obvious principles of the Constitution and the risk of the Union." The arrangement arrived at was most auspicious for the Union, in his opinion, since "had the conflict been pursued, there is reason to believe that the worst consequences would have followed."

"From this view," Monroe concluded, "it is evident that the further acquisition of territory to the west and south involves difficulties of an internal nature which menace the Union itself. We ought, therefore, to be cautious in making the attempt. Having secured the Mississippi and all its waters, with slight exception only, and erected States there, ought we not to be satisfied, so far at least as to take no step in that direction which is not approved by all the members, or at least a majority, of those who accomplished our revolution?"

This letter, expressing the innermost thoughts of the President of the United States to his closest political friend, gives a graphic idea of the difficult position in which Monroe found himself. Less than three months before this Monroe had signed the "Missouri bill", undoubtedly with a sigh of relief, for it had brought to a close a whole year of bitter and violent controversy which had raged in every section of the country. Hardly a State Legislature had been free of debate on the question or that did not adopt some kind of a resolution bearing on it one way or the other. The newspapers had vied with one another in the use of extreme invective in discussing it. It is a significant fact that the amendment which had set off the explosion was introduced in the House on February 13th, 1819, just nine days prior to the signing of the Spanish treaty. This amendment had been presented by Representative Tallmadge of New York and it proposed as a condition of admitting Missouri into the Union that "the further introduction of slavery or involuntary servitude be prohibited, except for punishment of crimes whereof the party shall have been duly convicted, and that all children born within the said State after the admission thereof into the Union shall be free, but may be held to service until the age of twenty-five years." That is what started the fireworks and from that point the country was in turmoil for a year. All other national questions were forgotten—the tariff, internal improvements, the currency, even the panic, all became secondary. A historian records that "the patient, imperturbable Monroe was confident that a compromise could be found, but few of our leading statesmen were so optimistic."

A compromise was indeed found at last. Missouri was admitted without restrictions with the understanding, having the force of law, that slavery should be excluded from all States formed in the future from the Louisiana Purchase territory north of a line running west from the southern boundary of Missouri. Monroe's letter to Jefferson, written less than three months after that understanding had become law by the affixing of his signature, reveals how deeply the incident had affected him. It reveals also his private opinion of the motives of those who had precipitated the controversy and who had refused to the last to compromise. In the House the compromise had been finally passed by the narrow margin of three votes, and the switching of two votes would have reversed the result. Monroe realized, as his letter shows, that the addition of any new territory *south* of the compromise line would undoubtedly reopen the whole bitter struggle. And most of the vast expanse of Texas was south of the line. That was why he did not dare to annex Texas and why he wanted Spain to ratify the treaty.

It would have been a simple matter to anger Spain into rejecting the treaty entirely. Recognition by the United States of the independence of a single Spanish colony would have turned the trick. Consequently Monroe did not dare to adopt a program of recognition until the treaty should be safely out of the way, ratified by Spain and ratified by the American Senate. Henry Clay expended all his matchless elo-

quence in denunciation of the despotic colonial system of Spain in America. "The most stupendous system of colonial despotism that the world has ever
seen," he called it. And he scathingly criticized the
hesitating policy of the United States in relation to
the struggle of the people who were attempting to
free themselves from this despotism. Monroe no
doubt felt the sting of Clay's invective keenly. However, he had no choice but to bear it, for he dared to
do nothing which would even indicate a definite
change of policy with respect to the revolutionists
of Spanish America until Spain had ratified the
treaty and Texas was safely outside the boundaries of
the United States for good. The compromise on the
Missouri question must not be upset in any circumstances.

And so during the years 1819 and 1820 Monroe
played a game of patient waiting with Spain, in spite
of all criticism. How well he managed the extremely
difficult situation is evident from the circumstance
that in the fall of 1820 he was reelected President
without opposition, a distinction which only Washington had attained before him and which no other
President has attained since. And at last the tidings came that the Spanish Government had ratified
the treaty. This was among the items of news, incidentally, that Austin had to tell Bastrop. Monroe
still had to obtain another ratification of the treaty
from the Senate, but he had no fears about that. The
resolution of the Kentucky Legislature did not disturb him. That was some more of Clay's politics.
Monroe felt that the Senate would ratify the treaty
promptly in the spring, and then the danger would

be past. Texas would be "renounced forever" by the United States and the compromise on the Missouri question would be safe.

If Monroe had known about it, he would have attached no significance whatever to the accidental meeting of two obscure men on the plaza in far-off San Antonio two days before Christmas. And these two men, Austin and Bastrop, probably would have shared this attitude with respect to their meeting, so far as the affairs of the great world were concerned. Nevertheless their meeting was big with portent for the future.

CHAPTER III

UNDER DOMINATION OF BARBARIANS

THE argument between the United States and Spain over the question of which of them owned Texas had lasted more than fifteen years. The United States had contended that it had bought Texas, as part of Louisiana, from Napoleon Bonaparte; Spain had retorted that Texas had never been part of Louisiana and was never Napoleon's to sell. Meanwhile, the people who lived in the province, and whose wishes in the matter were of little consequence to either party to the dispute, had been compelled to huddle together in the lone settlement of San Antonio because of the hostility of the Comanche and Apache Indians. These Indians, of course, had been among the original inhabitants of the country, and they objected to the presence of white men of any kind.

Most of the people of San Antonio, though of European descent, were not in fact Europeans. They were Texans. They were born in the province, Texas was their home, and they wished only for peace and security. For many years, because of Spanish neglect, they had had very little of either. They were a simple, frontier folk, and for the most part they were very poor. Their situation was not unlike that of a shipwrecked crew on an island of savages, who

greatly outnumbered them, for San Antonio was isolated from the rest of Mexico and the nearest settlement across the Louisiana border was nearly four
hundred miles away. Great considerations of empire
had placed their ancestors in this remote wilderness
a hundred years before, and then they had remained
because it was their home. If the truth could have
been known, it is probable they would have welcomed annexation to the United States, for this would
have meant a more rapid settlement of the wilderness that surrounded them and a brighter hope of
relief from the ever-present menace of the Indians.
But while Spanish pride impelled insistence on every
jot and tittle of real or fancied territorial rights,
Spain had been too greatly occupied by troubles of
its own in the great world to give attention to the welfare and safety of a handful of colonial provincials
in the American wilderness.

About five weeks prior to Moses Austin's sudden
appearance at San Antonio this unhappy plight of
the people of Texas had been set forth at length and
in detail in a document drafted by the *ayuntamiento*
or council of the town for the instruction of the deputy who was to represent the province in the Spanish
Cortes or parliament. Word had come to them in that
far-away outpost of civilization that a revolution had
occurred in Spain and that the King had been compelled to agree to a constitution. And they had hastened, so they asserted in this document of instruction, to seize "the happy moment" which offered
"national freedom" to make their desperate situation
known in the Spanish capital across the sea. If that
"happy moment" were allowed to pass, they said,

they would be "submerged in the confused, abnom-
inable, and horrible chaos of forgetfulness and abandonment."

As a matter of historic fact, that moment was passing even while they were drafting the catalogue of
their woes, for the monarchs of Europe, now that
Napoleon Bonaparte was safely a prisoner in St.
Helena (where he died on May 5th, 1821), had decreed an end to constitutions and they had no intention of permitting such republicanism to get a foothold in Spain or anywhere else in the Old World.
On the contrary, they had plans, as shall be seen,
for extending their system of absolute monarchy to
the New World. And besides, the colonial ruling
classes in Mexico had ideas of their own with respect
to this matter. So the hope of the people of Texas for
relief through the agency of the Spanish Cortes was
a vain one. The document they drafted was labor
lost, except as it serves today to give a vivid picture
of their unhappy condition in 1820.

The chief boon the people of San Antonio desired
their deputy to obtain for them was a military force
capable of carrying out a successful campaign against
the Indians, and then the establishment and maintenance of a line of forts along the northern frontier.
There were three thousand persons in the province,
they said, practically all of them at San Antonio,
with a few at the *presidio* of Bahía del Espíritu
Santo, near the mouth of the San Antonio River.
"The remainder of this extensive, immense, and spacious region composing the entire province," they informed their deputy, "is occupied by the different
tribes of barbarous Indians, who, at all times, have

been masters of the possessions and lives of the unfortunate inhabitants."

They complained that the troops then in Texas,
and which had been maintained there during the
previous seven years, were "useless for performing
the active services of their calling" which conditions
in the province demanded, and that they had been
"only a certain means of consummating the ruin of
its inhabitants." "For the soldier, finding himself
unmounted, unclothed, and without supplies—what
service can he perform and how can he exist with
only two *almudes* of corn which he receives every
fortnight, unless, in order to maintain himself, he
lays hands upon someone's cow which he kills in the
fields, now upon things which he steals from the
cornfields, and now by other excesses, such as necessity forces him to commit?" Either these troops
should be provided with suitable and sufficient rations, they declared, or they should be withdrawn
from Texas, in spite of the urgent need of them and
the good which might result from their service, were
they in condition to perform it instead of being
forced to maintain themselves or live at the expense
of the people of the province.

What was needed, they said, was a force of two
thousand men, commanded by "officials hardened to
an active life, familiar with the country, and experienced in the methods of making war against this
kind of an enemy." And these men must have "full
pay and other necesssary supplies." If such a force
should carry out a successful campaign against the
Indians and then be established in a line of frontier

forts, this would "attract to the settlements all kinds of people useful in these lands."

With this latter object in view, they asked for other things also—the opening up of a port on the coast, the establishment of regular communication and trade with the Spanish settlements in New Mexico, the distribution of vacant lands among the inhabitants, including the lands of the abandoned missions, the right to round up wild horses every winter, and other "reforms", the mere enumeration of which but disclosed their desperate situation.

This situation was due primarily to the practical failure of the Spanish effort to settle Texas, but it had been aggravated during the previous twenty years by a number of causes. First, the withdrawal of the Spaniards from Louisiana, after the cession of that province to Napoleon Bonaparte and its sale to the United States, had suddenly converted Texas from an interior into a border province. This had been followed shortly by the establishment of a neutral region between Texas and Louisiana, a region over which no nation had exercised authority for fourteen years and which had become the rendezvous of fugitives and outlaws of all kinds. And finally and especially, Texas since 1810 had become a battle ground of the revolution against Spain, because of the ease with which forces recruited by revolutionary *juntas* in the United States could invade the province. One such revolutionary force, composed chiefly of American volunteers, had operated in Texas for two years between 1811 and 1813 and had actually occupied San Antonio during four months of the latter year. Arredondo had completely annihiliated this

revolutionary army at the "battle of Medina," fought
near San Antonio in the summer of 1813, and had
dealt summarily with residents of San Antonio suspected of being sympathizers with the revolutionists.
Many old residents of Texas had fled to the United
States at that time and had not returned. One of the
things for which the people of San Antonio petitioned, now that they believed constitutional government had been established in Spain, was that these
exiles should be permitted to return and their confiscated property be restored to them.

This was not the first time, however, that appeals
had been made in behalf of the people of Texas. Less
than a year before this a military officer, Juan Antonio Padilla, had made a report on the province,
describing its vast and abundant natural resources
and the complete ascendency of the Indians over it,
and recommending among other things that the lands
of the abandoned missions be offered to settlers. This
report, too, set forth that the province was inhabited
by "the barbarians and wild beasts, with the exception of the people of San Antonio de Bexar and the
presidio of Bahía del Espíritu Santo, the only settlements of Spaniards, and they are small." The report
waxed almost enthusiastic over the "spacious and extensive territory", declaring that "irrigable and non-
irrigable lands are afforded to the admiration of all
who have seen them, but all under the domination
of barbarians."

Padilla described the ruins of the four missions
still standing near San Antonio almost pathetically,
referring particularly to the "former splendor and
riches" of one of them, but he made practical sug-

gestions as to their future use. "These four missions", he said, "are in a state of decadence for lack
of repair of the buildings. Each of them, at small
cost, would support a settlement of Spaniards if the
lands, water, and ruined buildings were divided
among those who would voluntarily present themselves as the first settlers. None of them has any
Indian settlers, the principal object of their establishment. If there are any, they are but few in number and changed into casts by mixture with the
settlers of Bexar . . . From the settlement of these
missions, there would follow the advantage of increasing the population of that deserted province.
The troops would have better means for securing the
supply of things they use, and the settlers would secure advancement. They would aid each other mutually in their work for the preservation of the missions and in the defense against the barbarians."

Padilla estimated that there were more than twelve
thousand Indians in Texas, divided into more than
a score of different tribes or "nations," nearly half
of whom were implacable enemies of the people of
San Antonio and in constant war with them. His
description of the "friendly" tribes revealed San Antonio's economic isolation, for he set forth that these
Indians, most of whom practiced some form of agriculture, resided chiefly in the region between that
place and the Louisiana border and that they went
to Natchitoches in Louisiana to trade instead of going to San Antonio. He piled up an appalling array
of adjectives in writing of the hostile Indians. "The
Comanches, who are the most numerous and who
cover the greater part of the vast region toward the

north," he declared, "are treacherous, revengeful, sly, untrustworthy, ferocious, and cruel, when victorious; and cowardly and low when conquered." The Apaches, on the other hand, he said, "unite all the vices of the Comanches with those peculiar to themselves—the quality of being very astute and daring in their hostile expeditions."

The conditions described in these two documents, one of which had been drafted within a few weeks of Moses Austin's arrival at San Antonio, were plainly such as would grow worse instead of better, if nothing were done to improve them, and tend to become unendurable. Bastrop had been living in the midst of these conditions for many years and undoubtedly he recognized the pressing necessity of doing something about them. Indeed, there is reason to believe that he saw an opportunity in this very necessity, but alone he was in no position to grasp it. This circumstance made his accidental meeting with Austin seem strikingly opportune.

CHAPTER IV

ONLY BY MEANS OF THE PLOW

To say that the Spanish effort to colonize Texas had failed does not tell the whole story. The truth is that Texas was never particularly inviting to the Spaniards and they went there in the first place almost reluctantly and because they felt compelled to go. And they were never altogether happy there. The Spaniards were never quite happy in any part of the New World where profit was to be had only as the reward of their own labor. They were not natural colonizers and developers like the English, nor traders and diplomats like the French. They were conquerors and rulers and exploiters. For this reason they were never comfortable in the neighborhood of hostile Indians. They could fight, to be sure, and they even enjoyed fighting; and they could endure almost unimaginable hardships if there was something at stake which they valued. But the establishment of trade or the opportunity to till the soil or to raise livestock in a region were not among such desirable things in Spanish estimation. If a region offered only such things then there had to be natives to do the work. Texas was such a region, but the natives were hostile, and so it was not the most desirable place in the world from the Spanish point of view. In spite of all the terrible adjectives which Padilla

25

used to describe the Comanches, probably nothing he said about them was worse in the judgment of his superiors than the statement that "they love their liberty so much they will not bear servitude."

At no time during their long occupation of Texas was the region profitable to Spain. On the contrary, it was always unprofitable and even expensive. Texas was a wilderness when the Spaniards first heard of it and three hundred years after the first Spaniard set foot on its soil it was still a wilderness. During nearly two-thirds of that time they remained away from the region altogether and it is close to the precise truth to say that it was only when somebody else showed an interest in Texas that the Spaniards valued it at all.

To all this one general exception must be noted. The Spanish padre, filled with sincere zeal for the salvation of souls, was interested in any region where there were heathen Indians to be converted. And though in nothing was the Spanish failure in Texas more evident than in the ruins of the missions, the Spanish priests never lost interest in the Texas Indians. In spite of enormous handicaps and repeated setbacks, they never accepted defeat. Indeed, the ultimate failure of the missionary effort in Texas was due in no small measure to purely secular causes. It was due to a lack of continuing secular Spanish interest in Texas, to handicaps which the acts of secular Spaniards placed upon the labors of the missionaries, to inadequate secular support, and finally to actual secular opposition. In short, it was due to the failure of the secular effort in Texas.

The first news of Texas that the Spaniards had ever received was uninviting. In the spring of 1536, Cabeza de Vaca, who had been the King's treasurer of an expedition to Florida in 1528 and had long been given up for dead with the rest of that company, suddenly returned to Mexico out of the northern wilderness with a tale of seven years of slavery among the Texas Indians. He published an account of his adventures, telling of a life of privation among tribesmen who spent most of their waking hours in search of food of the meanest kind and also relating stories he had been told of golden cities somewhere in the northwest. The Spaniards were impressed chiefly by what he had heard instead of by what he had seen. They set out to verify the imaginative stories the Indians had told him and showed no inclination to visit the scenes he had actually beheld. Coronado went in quest of the Seven Cities of Cíbola and found the villages of the Pueblo Indians in New Mexico, and De Soto sought for the Land of Golden Helmets and found a grave in the muddy waters of the Mississippi. Coronado did cross the plains of the Texas Panhandle, because an Indian guide had been bribed to lure him there with lies and lose him. And the survivors of De Soto's company did journey into northeast Texas and probably as far as the Brazos before deciding it would be better to attempt to get to Mexico by water instead of by land. But other than this, no Spaniard visited the region between the Pecos River and the Gulf of Mexico for more than a hundred and fifty years after Cabeza de Vaca had left it. And when the Spaniards came at last they came looking for Frenchmen. For

the intrepid LaSalle, the same who had navigated
the Mississippi to its mouth and had given to the
region along its banks the beautiful name of Louisiana, was already resting in an unmarked grave in the
Texas wilderness, thus establishing a French claim
to the region.

LaSalle landed on the Texas coast in December,
1684. He had come from France with the object of
planting a colony at the mouth of the Mississippi
and had somehow lost his way. He raised the French
flag on the shores of Matagorda Bay, built a fort
with timbers from one of his wrecked vessels and
established a colony around it, and then went in
search of the Mississippi. He did not find it because
he had no idea of how much too far to the west his
fleet had sailed. Soon the members of his little colony were facing starvation in the very region where
Cabeza de Vaca had grubbed for edible roots on
the seashore, and in desperation LaSalle resolved to
attempt to make his way overland to one of the
French posts of the north and bring them relief. He
started on this hazardous journey, but he never
reached his destination and he never returned. Somewhere in the wilds of Southeast Texas, on the 19th of
March, 1687, four of his men, because of some trivial
circumstance which they had magnified into a wrong,
enticed LaSalle from camp and waylaid and murdered him. A few of his party finally reached Can-
ada, but the members of the little colony, except for
nine persons found later among the Indians, all per-
ished. When the Spaniards finally located the site
of the French fort, which they did in April, 1689,

a full two years after LaSalle's murder, it was deserted.

But it was this "French menace" that aroused Spanish interest in Texas, though not for long. In the spring of 1690 the Spaniards established a mission in East Texas, near the Neches River, leaving it in charge of three Franciscan friars and guarded by five soldiers. It lasted only about three years and a half and was then abandoned because of the hostility of the Indians. One of the three friars, Father Francisco Hidalgo, continued to be interested in the Texas Indians while laboring south of the Rio Grande, and he made many unsuccessful attempts to obtain permission to return. But for more than twenty years after this the Spaniards did not move again to occupy Texas. And when they did move again it was practically at the invitation of the French. For it was not until 1716, after a French post had been established at Natchitoches on Red River, that the Spaniards returned to East Texas and set up missions there, one of which was within fifteen miles of the French. And the first Spanish colonization party was conducted into the country by the Frenchman, St. Denis, founder of the Natchitoches post, who went boldly to Father Hidalgo's mission south of the Rio Grande for the purpose of inviting them.

This was the beginning of the Spanish settlement of Texas. In 1718 a *presidio* and a mission were established at the site of San Antonio, and this soon became the chief Spanish center. Three years later, after temporarily withdrawing from East Texas because of a war in Europe between France and Spain,

the Spaniards built a *presidio* opposite the French
post at Natchitoches and established another on the
site of LaSalle's old fort on Matagorda Bay. The
latter, which was twice moved to new locations, was
the Bahía del Espíritu Santo of 1820 and was later
to be known as Goliad. At this time it was decreed
by the Spanish Government that four hundred families should be introduced into Texas, but not until
1731 did anything come of this and then only fifteen
families, consisting of fifty-two persons from the
Canary Islands, were settled at San Antonio. At different times missions were established at other points
in Texas, only to be moved later to San Antonio because of the hostility of the Indians. This contributed toward establishing San Antonio more firmly,
but it tended to leave the rest of the vast province a
wilderness.

In 1764 France ceded Louisiana to Spain to keep
it from falling into the hands of the English at the
close of the Seven Years War, and it is a significant
fact that the King of Spain at first refused to accept
the gift and then consented to do so rather reluctantly. But it was not until 1770 that Spanish authority
was completely established over all of Louisiana,
and three years later the Spanish Government ordered all settlers in East Texas to move to the neighborhood of San Antonio. This was fifty-seven years
after the establishment of the first Spanish mission
in East Texas and by that time a good portion of the
settlers were natives of the region. But so little value
was placed on the colonization of the territory that
these people were compelled to abandon their homes
and begin again in a region three hundred miles

away, in the protective shadow of San Antonio. The
"French menace" had been removed by the establishment of Spanish authority over Louisiana and
the Spanish Government saw no reason for continuing the expense of maintaining a military force in
East Texas merely for the protection of the settlers
against the Indians. Some of these people returned
to East Texas in 1779 and took up residence in "the
depopulated mission of Nacogdoches". Forty years
later, in that document which the people of San Antonio drafted in 1820 for the instruction of their
deputy, this settlement was mentioned as "the advanced and deserted *pueblo* of Nacogdoches on the
frontier of the United States toward the east."

The idea of a "French menace" in East Texas was
largely a figment of Spanish imagination, for the
truth was that the Spaniards were able to remain in
East Texas during most of the time chiefly because
the French wanted them there. French influence
among the Indians of East Texas, as among the Indians nearly everywhere else that Frenchmen went
in America, was practically complete, and these Indians drew a sharp distinction between Frenchmen
and Spaniards. Indeed, after the Spaniards took possession of Louisiana it became necessary for them to
keep Frenchmen in their service on the frontier in
order to maintain peace with the Indians. This policy was even carried to the extent of appointing a
Frenchman to the office of Governor of Texas in
1779.

The condition of Texas in 1820, therefore, was
due not merely to the circumstance alone that the
Spanish effort at colonization had failed, but rather

to the fact that this effort had never been more than half-hearted because the Spaniards had no great relish for the job. Texas was not the kind of territory best adapted for the exercise of Spanish abilities. It could be redeemed from its wilderness state only by means of the plow, and Spaniards were not especially talented as plowmen. Yet the necessity of settling Texas had now become greater than it had ever been in the past. For in addition to the ever-present domination of the Indians, the old "French menace" had been reincarnated in another form, for the Colossus of the North had advanced to the Texas border. How could this necessity be met? The two men who met on the plaza, Moses Austin and Bastrop, knew a probable answer to that question.

CHAPTER V

A NEW CHANCE

In the light of its consequences, the accidental meeting of Moses Austin and Bastrop has an aspect of immense significance. But at the time it had no such aspect. Austin's only object in coming to Texas was that of making a new start. And there is no reason to think that Bastrop's ready interest in his proposal was due to a less personal motive. For Bastrop did take an interest in the proposal immediately. There is no record, of course, of what passed between them. But it is entirely clear that they reached an understanding. It is recorded that Bastrop took Austin to his one-room house and that there they talked the matter over. As a result, Bastrop obtained a stay of the order for his immediate departure and arranged for a hearing before Martinez, held the same day, which enabled Austin to establish his status as a former loyal subject of Spain. The record of this hearing shows that Austin answered Martinez's questions "through the Baron de Bastrop, who had promised well and truly to discharge the duty of interpreter."

In the record of this hearing there is no mention of any proposal to settle Anglo-Americans in Texas. Replying to the question as to what his object was in entering Texas, Austin is recorded as saying that "he

33

came to the province for the purpose of applying to the Government for authorization to settle himself in it with his family" and that it was "his intention to provide for his subsistence by raising sugar and cotton." He presented a copy of a passport issued to him by the Spanish minister at Philadelphia on July 13th, 1797, and he explained that he had become a Spanish subject in Louisiana in that year, that he had worked lead mines near St. Louis, but that under the American Government he had "lost all the benefit of his labor," and that "now, in view of the new system of government adopted in Spain, he resolved upon applying for authorization to settle in this province."

Austin gave such information as was in his possession with respect to the movements of Dr. Long and Jean Lafitte, saying that he had heard at Natchitoches that most of Dr. Long's men had deserted him and that an American frigate had compelled Lafitte to leave Galveston Island. He stated also that he had "read in American newspapers a treaty made by Don Luis de Onis, Spanish Minister, with the American Congress, which treaty was already signed by the King and approved by the Sovereign Congress of the Cortes."

This was two days before Christmas. But the day after Christmas, Austin filed with Martinez a formal petition, doubtless drafted by Bastrop, for permission to settle three hundred families in Texas, whose object would be to see the desires of his majesty the King fulfilled and "to defend the Spanish Government against the Indians, adventurers, or other classes of enemies." This petition was approved by the *ayuntamiento* of San Antonio at once and it was dispatched without delay to Arredondo, the Commandant at Monterrey, with the urgent recommendation that it be granted. And from that day forward Martinez and other leading men of San Antonio became ardent advocates of the policy of colonizing Texas with Anglo-Americans.

This reversal of attitude seems to have been due chiefly to the influence of Bastrop. Evidently he succeeded in convincing them that this was the only practicable way to improve the unhappy conditions then existing in Texas and to promote the growth and prosperity of the province. But whatever the cause, the change of attitude was complete. Martinez and the leading men of the province became warm partisans of the project of a man of whom they had never even heard only a week before. But this was not merely showing favor to an individual who had won their confidence. They had become advocates of a new policy, a policy that had never before been contemplated for Texas. For it was not long until Martinez himself was writing his superiors on "the actual condition of Texas", declaring that "it is absolutely necessary that the nation make some effort to populate it" and that "admitting foreigners would be the easiest and less expensive way, offering them advantages that would induce them to come to this province." Without some such policy, he affirmed, "peace will never be seen" in the province, "commerce will never prosper, nor agriculture flourish."

Austin did not wait in San Antonio to learn whether his petition would be granted. He left everything in Bastrop's hands and started homeward, filled with enthusiasm for the new project. "If you can obtain a permit for me to land with my property at the place I have requested, say the mouth of the Colorado," he wrote to Bastrop before reaching Natchitoches, "and permission is given to establish a town and settle 300 families, one year will make a change in the state and condition of San Antonio beyond anything you can believe. I have full confidence that a town at the mouth of the Colorado in three years would become of the utmost consequence and an interest in this town would give some thousands of dollars to the friends of this establishment without any violation of confidence or injury to the Government." He promised to return in May with a sufficient number of persons to begin farming and insure defense against the Indians. "The Governor was pleased to say that if I returned I might depend on his friendship," he continued. "On my part, I assure you that I shall make use of every exertion in my power to promote the interest of the Government that gives me protection." He was conscious of his debt to Bastrop and hoped that he would pardon the liberty he had taken in thus calling upon his friendship. "I trust the day will arrive," he wrote, "when I shall have it in my power to make full and *satisfactory* compensation."

In another letter to Bastrop, also written before reaching Natchitoches, Austin said that he had heard from some citizens of Arkansas whom he met at the Sabine that the action of the American Government in moving certain Indians from the Tennessee River to the headwaters of the Arkansas was interfering with a great many families, evidently "squatters", who already had settled on the land and who had been given until the end of May to move. "They might be very available," he wrote, "if they could be allowed to settle in the Province of Texas. However, there are several families concerned who will neither wait nor apply for authorization, but will settle on their own authority. The Government ought to be on its guard against them; they may prove to be dangerous."

Austin sent Bastrop all the newspapers containing any information that might be of interest to him that he could collect, and he called particular attention to an account of the action of the Kentucky Legislature condemning the Spanish treaty. "Although the Legislature have instructed their representatives in Congress to oppose the treaty between Spain and the United States," he wrote, "yet it is the most general belief that it will be accepted . . . War will not take place with the United States and Spain unless some of the Western States have power to rule the Union. The Eastern and Middle States are in opposition to extending the limits of the United States and war with Spain."

This was written on January 26th, 1821, and within less than a month, on February 19th, the United States Senate ratified the treaty. Three days later ratifications were exchanged between representatives of the American and Spanish Governments at Washington and thus the treaty fixing the boundary between the United States and New Spain at the Sabine River became "the supreme law of the land." Meantime, even before Austin's letter was written, on January 17th, Arredondo had notified Martinez

that, with the approval of the Provincial Deputation at Monterrey, the petition to settle three hundred families in Texas had been granted. And then
on February 24th, only two days after the exchange
of ratifications of the treaty between the United
States and Spain, Augustín de Iturbide, in the far
southern part of Mexico, promulgated the "Plan of
Iguala", declaring Mexico independent of Spain forever.

Austin's return trip through the Texas wilderness
had been one of privation and great hardship, and
while he was writing such confident letters to Bastrop he was being delayed by illness at McGuffin's,
about half-way between the Sabine and Natchitoches, where he was compelled to remain for three
weeks before undertaking to return to Missouri. He
made the homeward trip by way of Natchez, where
he took a steamboat for St. Louis. He reached home
on March 23rd, and though his illness had left him
in a much weakened condition, he set about at once
to adjust his muddled business affairs as best he might
and to prepare for the move to Texas. He wrote enthusiastic letters about the project to his two sons,
both of whom were away from home, and bade them
to look cheerfully to the future. He busied himself
also in spreading the news of his "grant" and in picturing the great opportunities offered in Texas. In a
short time the report that he was about to open Texas
to colonization was one of the leading topics of talk
all over the western country, and he was besieged by
applicants for places in his colony. He appealed to
his elder son, Stephen, who was in New Orleans, to
try to find someone in that city who would take a

financial interest in the project and provide a vessel
to transport a party of settlers to the mouth of the
Colorado.

To his younger son, James E. Brown Austin, who
was away at school and much embarressed by pressing debts, he sent a ninety-day draft for $150 on
Stephen (who was having financial troubles of his
own) in the hope that he could use it to get himself
released by his creditors and return home. He promised to send him "fifty dollars more in Kentucky
money" if he could obtain it, but nearly two weeks
later he wrote he had been unable to obtain it and
would "continue making exertions until I can obtain as much as will relieve you." Two weeks after
this he was writing from St. Louis to his son-in-law,
"I am in a most unpleasant situation, without a dollar to get a shirt washed," and the next day he wrote
to him again urging that he make a little exertion to
send something to the younger son, Brown. "Fifty
dollars," he wrote, "will now release him from debt
and return him home." He added that his own wife
"is recently distressed for common necessaries, she is
out of flour and meat."

In spite of such annoyances and even greater ones
having to do with his efforts to settle his differences
with business creditors, Austin kept cheerful. He
waxed eloquent in writing his younger son about the
town he proposed to lay out in Texas near the mouth
of the Colorado, "a spot of country desirable to behold, overflowing with wealth and *health*." "In this
situation," he added, "I shall soon reinstate myself in
property. I have already offers to fill up the families
which will bring me about $18,000." In another let-

ter he told him that if he would look at Melish's map
of the United States he would find the Bay of St.
Bernard and the Colorado River, "at the mouth of
which I calculate to lay out the town of *Austina,*
which will be in a few years equal to New Orleans
in consequence if not in wealth."

Conscious, no doubt, of how his misfortunes had
interfered with his younger son's education and wish-
ing to reassure him, he made him a proposal. "You
are a Spanish subject born," he wrote him, "and were
baptized by a Roman priest and are recorded as such
at the Church of St. Genevieve. I shall obtain a
record of this fact and if you will go with me I can
get you introduced to the college at Monterrey, a
large city about 500 miles south of San Antonio. At
this place I shall be able to support you a year or
more and you will learn the Spanish language which
will be of more consequence to you than you can now
conceive of . . . The college at Monterrey or Royal
Mountain has now 400 students from every part of
the Spanish provinces, by which means you will have
an opportunity to visit the City of Mexico and become acquainted with the young men of first families
of that country."

Austin was full of plans for the future which this
new start was making possible. And he sought to
divert the members of his family from their existing
troubles by picturing the better things ahead. As late
as May 22nd, he wrote to Stephen at New Orleans in
this strain. "Raise your spirits," he advised. "Times
are changing. A new chance presents itself. Nothing
now is wanting but concert and firmness." A new

chance! That was the dominant thought in his mind. For that was what Texas meant to him.

When he had left Natchitoches on his homeward journey from Texas it was his intention to be back by the beginning of May, but by the middle of that month he was not yet ready to start. Meantime, Martinez had sent commissioners to Natchitoches to meet him and conduct him and his party into the new promised land. Austin was within a few days of settling his affairs finally when he received news of their arrival, and he was making preparations to join them when he was stricken with pneumonia. And then on June 10th, 1821, a little more than six months after his accidental meeting with Bastrop on the plaza at San Antonio, he died at the home of his daughter at Hazel Run, Missouri.

Moses Austin had been a pioneer of frontiers most of his life. Born in the colony of Connecticut, fifteen years before the adoption of the American Declaration of Independence, he founded the town of Austinville on the western frontier of Virginia in 1791, when he was thirty years old. He moved across the Mississippi into the Spanish province of Upper Louisiana in 1798, and established one of the first settlements in what is now Washington County, Missouri. And he was facing a new frontier in Texas when he died. He was truly of the race of pioneers that planted civilization in the American wilderness. And his elder son, into whose hands his Texas enterprise now passed, was also of that race, for he was born in the Virginia settlement, Austinville, and he was reared on the Missouri frontier.

CHAPTER VI

A CAREER BEGINS

UNTIL a few weeks prior to Moses Austin's last illness, his elder son, Stephen Fuller Austin, who was then twenty-seven years old, apparently had had no intention of taking any part in his father's Texas venture. Some time in the fall of 1820, Stephen had gone to New Orleans to seek employment. He was penniless and deeply in debt, for he had been involved in his father's business failure and his own affairs had been greatly affected by the prevailing hard times. He had had some idea earlier in the year of attempting to make a fresh start in the newly-organized Territory of Arkansas and had even obtained appointment as a circuit judge there, but evidently his debts proved so embarrassing and the prospects so uncertain that he had been compelled to give this up. He was well educated according to the standards of the frontier, he had been a member of the territorial legislature of Missouri several terms, and he had had considerable business experience for a man of his age. Nevertheless, his situation was such that he went to New Orleans fully resolved to accept any kind of work he could find.

"I offered to hire myself out as a clerk, as an overseer, or anything else," he wrote to his mother, "but business is too dull to get into business. There are hundreds of young men who are glad to work for their board."

The devastating effects of the universal hard times were reflected in the letters which passed between Stephen and members of his family at this time. He received news at New Orleans that his sister and her husband, James Bryan, were in straightened circumstances as a result of the collapse of the latter's mercantile business, and this troubled him with the thought that he might appear to be running away from it all. "My heart bleeds for their troubles," he confessed in a letter to his mother. "If I can be of service to you or them let me know it, and I will go home; I will do anything that is right. My reputation is *all* I have on earth, if *that* is destroyed I can be of no use to you or anyone else, and there will no longer be a necessity of my remaining either in this country or any other."

Stephen believed, however, that it would be better for him to remain in New Orleans and to devote his energies to the task of getting on his feet gain. He had managed to obtain a little work helping to edit a newspaper, the *Louisiana Advertiser,* and a lawyer had given him some employment in his office. But he earned very little. He wrote to his mother in grateful terms about this lawyer, James H. Hawkins. "He is a man who in every respect is an honor and an ornament to the human race," he wrote. "He has kindly advanced me money enough to purchase a few groceries for you and sister, which I have shipped. . . . I will send $10 in a letter by the boat toward paying the freight. This is all I can do now. When I earn some more I will send another supply and will try to keep you and Bryan's family supplied with sugar and coffee at least."

Hawkins offered to permit Stephen to study law in his office and to provide him with board and lodging in exchange for such services as he might render, meantime lending him money for clothes until he could begin practice on his own account. Stephen wrote his mother that he would like to accept this offer and intended to do so, but there were two obstacles in the way. "One is that I shall earn nothing to help you with for at least eighteen months," he wrote; "another is that perhaps those I owe in Missouri may prosecute me here; it will do them no good, I have nothing—all the property I had in Arkansas, I gave to Father. If I am left alone a few years I may get up and pay all off; it will take me eighteen months to become acquainted with civil law which is in force in this country and learn the French language. That once done I then shall have the means of fortune within my reach. I am determined to accept Hawkins' offer."

Stephen wrote this on January 20th, 1821, at which time his father was at McGuffin's on his way back from San Antonio. He had heard from a cousin, he wrote, that "Father had arrived at San Antonio and was to be back at Natchitoches by the 15th of February." But he added, "I know nothing as to my father's objects or prospects."

From all this it seems clear that at that time Stephen was not contemplating the taking of any part in his father's enterprise. Certainly he had no intention then of going to Texas. And yet, such were the far-reaching results of Moses Austin's trip to San

Antonio and his accidental meeting with Bastrop, that Stephen changed his plans completely. When illness prevented his father from going to Natchitoches to meet the Spanish commissioners, Stephen went in his place. Not only this, but before leaving he induced Hawkins to take a financial interest in the project to the extent of his ability. And when, just before entering Texas, he received the sad news of his father's death, Stephen went on to San Antonio to request that he be recognized as his father's successor, fully resolved to assume the immense responsibility of carrying the project to a successful conclusion.

It was Moses Austin's dying wish that Stephen should see to it that the start he had made to restore the family fortunes should not be frustrated by his death. In a letter which reached Stephen at Natchitoches, his mother told him of this. "He called me to his bedside," she wrote, "and with much distress and difficulty of speech, begged me to tell you to take his place and if God in his wisdom thought best to disappoint him in the accomplishment of his wishes and plans formed for the benefit of his family, he prayed Him to extend His goodness to you and to enable you to go on with the business in the same way that he would have done had not sickness, and . . . perhaps death, prevented him from accomplishing."

Awaiting Stephen at Natchitoches were Josef Erasmo Seguin and Juan Martín de Berrimendi, both natives of San Antonio and both enthusiastic over the new policy which offered prospect of a change in Texas. They had been waiting patiently for Moses Austin more than a month, and they welcomed his son cordially. Seguin was the official representative of Governor Martinez and brought with him a letter from the Governor to Moses Austin, which contained a transcript of Arredondo's approval of the colonization petition, and was in the nature of an official notification. Berrimendi also had with him a letter for Moses Austin, which he delivered to the son. In this letter Moses Austin was informed that Berrimendi "will advise with you and will do everything that lies in his power to serve you and I am in hopes that you will do the same with him." It gave the assurance that Berrimendi was "a gentleman of veracity" and added "anything that he tells you, I pledge myself for the performance of it." This missive was signed "El Baron de Bastrop."

Stephen had left New Orleans with a delegation of "eight or ten" men who wanted to look over the country with the intention of becoming interested in the project, and at Natchitoches he was met by others who had come in the expectation of meeting his father there. So it turned out to be quite a party that assembled at the old French town and that Seguin and Berrimendi were to conduct into Texas. Seguin hastened to get word off ahead to Martinez that there would be sixteen men to be entertained on their arrival at San Antonio, and that they seemed to be men of substance. He felt that it was important that the Governor should be forewarned so that the proper arrangements could be made to impress them favorably.

Here indeed was something new under the sun! The bare idea of the Spanish authorities in Texas welcoming a delegation of visiting Americans must

have seemed so novel as to have left not the slightest doubt in the mind of anyone that a new day had
arrived in that province. But there was no mistake
about it, for on their arrival at San Antonio, after a
not unpleasant four weeks of travel and camping, the
Americans were given a royal reception. No modern
Chamber of Commerce ever put itself to more trouble to make visitors think well of a community than
Governor Martinez and the leading people of San
Antonio did on that occasion.

Meantime, things had been happening in Mexico.
As has already been recorded, Augustín de Iturbide
had proclaimed the so-called Plan of Iguala on February 24th, 1821, declaring Mexico independent of
Spain. This movement, which had been already under way secretly when Moses Austin was in San Antonio the previous December, was not a republican
movement. On the contrary, it was anti-republican
and royalist in character and had its inception in the
circumstance that republicanism was making too
much headway in Spain, in the opinion of the privileged classes of Mexico. The Spanish Cortes (parliament) was controlled by republicans, and the King,
Ferdinand VII, was practically a prisoner, obeying
the leaders of the Cortes because he had no other
choice. The Cortes had embarked on a radical program with respect to the privileges of the Church
and had decreed the sequestration of church property, and this program was intended to apply to the
Spanish colonies in America as well as to the home-
land. So while the people of San Antonio had been
hailing the restoration of the Constitution in Spain
as a new birth of "national freedom," the Spaniards,

native royalists, and higher clergy at Mexico City had been considering ways and means of preventing that Constitution from going into full effect in Mexico. And the way they had finally decided upon was that of independence.

The revolutionary activities of the previous ten years in Mexico, which had been republican in spirit, were now completely crushed. Hidalgo, Morelos, and other leaders had been captured in turn and put to death, and by 1820 only one small force, under Vicente Guerrero, was still in the field. But now the leaders of the privileged classes became advocates of independence. And they chose Iturbide to attain it. Ostensibly for the purpose of pursuing and capturing Guerrero, Iturbide obtained a command from the Viceroy, but he formed a junction with Guerrero instead and the basis upon which they reached an agreement came to be known as the Plan of Iguala. Its objectives included (1) independence for Mexico, (2) the maintenance of the clerical privileges, and (3) equality of Spaniards and native Mexicans. These were called "the three guarantees". It was further agreed that the form of government should be monarchial and that the throne should first be offered to Ferdinand himself, but in the event that he should not be available it should then be offered to some other Bourbon.

Iturbide's revolt was in progress while Stephen Austin and his companions were journeying from the Sabine to San Antonio. As a matter of fact it had reached a point where its triumph was foreshadowed before the party had left Natchitoches, for on July 6th, yielding to pressure in Mexico City, the

Viceroy, Juan Ruiz de Apocada, had resigned, surrendering his powers to General Pedro Novella. News of this event reached San Antonio in due course, and early Sunday morning, August 12th, messengers from that place roused Austin's camp with the tidings that Mexico had attained its independence. This was not strictly true, but it was hailed with unfeigned rejoicing by Seguin, Berrimendi, and the other Texans of the party. It is doubtful that they comprehended the real objects of those behind the move, but there was no mistaking their sentiment with respect to independence. And this sentiment evidently extended to the entire population of San Antonio, for when the Americans arrived there later the same day the whole town was celebrating the attainment of Mexican independence.

Bastrop was on hand to greet Stephen at the moment of arrival. Indeed, when the sad news reached him that Moses Austin was dead and that the son was coming to take his place, Bastrop had sent a letter to Stephen by messenger, welcoming him. So it was with Bastrop as well as Seguin that Sephen called upon Governor Martinez. He notified the Governor in formal fashion of his father's death and asked to be recognized officially as his successor. There was no hesitancy in agreeing to this nor in working out other details of the terms upon which lands would be granted to settlers. And it was the opinion of all of them that the impending change of government would not affect the matter adversely. The fact was, of course, that so far as the leaders of San Antonio were concerned, Stephen would have

found it difficult to formulate any reasonable demand
to which they would not have acceded readily. For
they were now warm partisans of the plan to settle
Americans in Texas. So Stephen was received as his
father's successor and royally welcomed and entertained. The relations which Bastrop had established
with Moses Austin were also promptly effected with
the son. Indeed, Seguin seems to have been brought
into the circle, for before Stephen departed from
San Antonio, after a very busy ten days, these three
discussed a plan of obtaining for themselves jointly
an exclusive franchise to trade with the Indians.

Leaving San Antonio, Austin and his party set out
on an expedition of exploration in the region of the
lower Colorado and Brazos Rivers, after first visiting La Bahía, near the mouth of the San Antonio
River. It was October 1st before they were back in
Natchitoches, where Austin found nearly a hundred
letters from prospective colonists awaiting him. They
had been in Texas two and a half months, and meantime far-reaching events had been going forward in
Mexico. On August 24th, while Austin and his party
were on their way to La Bahía, Iturbide and Juan
O'Donojú, a new Viceroy who had arrived from
Spain on July 30th, signed a treaty at Córdova which
embodied the Plan of Iguala, with the exception that
it was not required that the monarch should be a
Bourbon. And then on September 27th, while Austin was hurrying to complete the last lap of his journey back to Natchitoches, Iturbide entered Mexico
City in triumph, loudly acclaimed by the populace as
"the Liberator".

CHAPTER VII

INTEGRITY OF INTENTION

Stephen Austin lost no time in getting his settlers moving into Texas. Within six weeks after his return to the United States the first contingent had started overland from Natchitoches for the banks of the Brazos, and a schooner, the *Lively,* loaded with equipment and supplies, had sailed from New Orleans for the mouth of the Colorado. The spring of 1822 found more than a hundred men at work cutting down trees, clearing land, building cabins, and doing a dozen and one other things incident to getting a human habitation started in the wilderness. There were difficulties from the beginning, not the least of which resulted from the failure of the *Lively* to arrive at an appointed rendezvous, which left the settlers short of tools and seed for the first crop. But such annoyances may be borne cheerfully by men who know they are laying the foundations of homes for themselves and their children. It was a good land into which they had come and it required only industry and patience to make it a fruitful land as well. Austin had chosen his first settlers with some care, and there was no great doubt about their being able to overcome whatever difficulties might arise.

Then like a bolt from a clear sky came the news that the authorities at Monterrey had refused to ap-

prove the arrangements Martinez had made with
Stephen Austin relative to the distribution of lands
and that inasmuch as the new Government at Mexico
City was considering a uniform colonization policy
for Texas and California the whole thing was up in
the air. Austin first learned of this situation when he
went to San Antonio early in March to report to
Martinez the progress he had made. It was quite as
much a blow to Martinez and the leading men of
San Antonio as it was to Austin and his colonists, and
immediately there was much conferring as to what
might be done about it. The conclusion finally
reached was that Austin should go to Mexico City
and make an effort to have his grant confirmed.
There seemed nothing else to do, for new colonists
were arriving almost daily along the Brazos and the
Colorado and unless all doubt as to the terms upon
which they were to receive land could be removed
without much delay the whole project might end in
disaster. So, after appointing one of his colonists,
Josiah H. Bell, to take charge of the settlement during his absence, and with the assurance that Bastrop
would keep an eye on matters from the San Antonio
end, Austin started for the Mexican capital. He left
San Antonio on March 13th, and six weeks later,
after a thousand-mile journey on horseback, he arrived at Mexico City on April 29th, 1822.

"I arrived in the City of Mexico," Austin wrote
later, "without acquaintances, without friends—a
stranger in a city where until very recently foreigners
were proscribed by the laws and discountenanced by
the people from prejudice—ignorant of the language, of the laws, the forms, the disposition and

feelings of the Government, with barely the means of paying my expenses for a few months, and in fact I may say destitute of everything necessary to insure success in such a mission as I had undertaken but the integrity of my intentions."

Austin found himself in the midst of a maze of confusion and intrigue when he arrived at Mexico City. One of the first actions of the *Junta* of five members which had been created by the terms of the treaty between Iturbide and O'Donojú had been to provide for the electon and assembling of a Congress which should determine the future of the government. This Congress had been in session two months when Austin arrived. It was charged with the duty of deciding the form of the government and of drafting a constitution. Everything was unsettled, party spirit ran high, and intrigue was to be encountered on all sides. Some wanted a Bourbon for King, some wanted Iturbide for Emperor, some wanted a republic. Iturbide, while proceeding cautiously, was not unwilling to mount the throne, but in the Congress sentiment for a republic was growing. The advocates of a republic were divided into Centralists and Federalists, but for the moment they worked together against the monarchists.

Governor Martinez had transmitted all the papers concerning Austin's project to Mexico City, and both the *Junta,* prior to the convening of the Congress, and the Congress itself had discussed the matter of a general colonization law for Texas and California. Other Americans seeking land grants in Texas, some of them of great influence, had filed petitions, and the capital was crowded with such favor-seekers.

But practically no progress had been made at the
time of Austin's arrival. The truth was that the
Junta and the Congress found much more important
matters to occupy their time and attention than that
of settling the vacant lands of the domain they were
expected to provide with a new government.

Three weeks after Austin's arrival at the capital a
crisis was reached in the controversy over the form
of the government. On the night of May 18th, a
nondescript mob, composed of private soldiers and
civilians, and headed by "sergeants and corporals,"
paraded through the streets of the city crying *vivas*
for Iturbide and demanding that he be made Emperor. And the next day, without a quorum present,
the Congress, surrounded by bayonets, bowed to the
demand of the rabble and solemnly declared the
throne to be vested in Iturbide. This slowed up everything else until the Emperor could be formally installed, but finally on July 21st, at a ceremony which
was almost a burlesque of the coronation of Napoleon, Iturbide was crowned as Augustín I. Meantime, the Congress remained in session, tinkering
away at a constitution and sporadically discussing
the proposed colonization law. But intrigue continued, and on the night of August 26th fourteen of
the leading members of Congress were seized in their
beds and thrown into prison. Nevertheless, the Congress made headway on the colonization law and it
had completed all but one section of it when on October 31st Iturbide issued a decree dissolving the Congress, which decree he put into effect by a show of
force. Then he vested the legislative power in a smaller body, the members of which were appointed by the

Emperor himself. However, this smaller body continued to work on the colonization law and at the end of two months completed its enactment. It was approved by the Emperor and was promulgated on January 4th, 1823.

All this time Austin had labored constantly for the enactment of a colonization law and for the validation of his contract. As soon as the law was promulgated, therefore, he filed a petition under its terms and urged that it be granted without delay. The Council of State approved this petition on January 14th and then, after another month's delay, Iturbide issued a decree on February 18th granting it.

By this time, however, Iturbide had run his course and it was becoming clear that his brief reign as Emperor was nearing its close. Revolutionary activity and sentiment against him had become so widespread that he was compelled to take notice of it. And in desperation he reconvened the Congress which he had dissolved by force only four months before. But it was too late, and collecting such troops as he believed to be loyal to him, Iturbide left the capital, determined to defend his power to the last. His cause was hopeless, however, for he found that he could not trust even the small remnant of adherents still around him and, being pursued by a superior force, he agreed to a truce, pending the decision of the Congress. The Congress convened on March 29th, promptly abolished the executive power which had existed under Iturbide and vested the executive authority in a new tribunal, composed of three members, which it designated as "the Supreme Executive Power." And finally, on April 8th, 1823, less than

eleven months from the day on which Iturbide had
been declared Emperor, the Congress decreed that
his coronation had been an act of violence and
force, and was null and void, and that all the acts of
his Government of whatever character were illegal
and subject to be revised, confirmed, or revoked, as
the newly established Supreme Executive Power
might decide. Iturbide was banished from Mexican
soil forever, under penalty of death, but he was
granted a salary of twenty-five thousand pesos a year,
provided he would reside in Italy.

Austin had foreseen that something of this kind
was likely to happen and that in the event of Iturbide's fall the acts of his Government would be annulled. This would include, of course, the colonization law and the grant of his petition under that law.
So Austin had not hurried away from the capital after Iturbide had granted his petition, but had decided
to stay on awhile to see how things would turn out.
When Iturbide's acts were annulled, he found himself, in theory at least, back where he had started a
year before. But really it was not as bad as that, for
his patient labors during the year had borne fruit. By
that time the one matter on which practically all the
factions were agreed was Austin's petition. They all
agreed that it should be granted without further delay in order that he might return to his colonists.
So, within a week after Iturbide's acts had been annulled, the Supreme Executive Power revived the
erstwhile Emperor's colonization law long enough to
grant Austin's petition again under its terms, and
then the law was suspended permanently. Austin's
petition was the only one granted under the law,

though there were many others pending. Indeed, it was the only contract for introducing settlers into Texas that was ever granted by the national Government of Mexico.

Austin had now been away from Texas more than a year and in the meantime many of his settlers had returned to the United States and the whole enterprise had been given a bad name throughout the Southwestern States. It turned out to be time well spent, however. For the young man who had come to Mexico City a stranger, left it the most influential American in the land. He had become intimately acquainted with the political leaders of the country, and had made firm friends of many of them; he had learned the language, and he had won universal respect and confidence through his demonstrated ability and undoubted good faith. What he called "the integrity of his intentions" had proved his best asset, for in the estimation of the earnest men who were seeking sincerely to lay the foundations of a new nation this quality set him apart from the great number of favor-seeking Americans and adventurers who had flocked to the Mexican capital immediately upon the attainment of independence. Austin from the very first had shown himself concerned to insure the best interests of the country he proposed to adopt as his own. "From the day of my arrival on Mexican soil," he afterwards explained, "I bid an everlasting farewell to my native country and adopted this, and in doing so I determined to fulfill rigidly all the duties and obligations of a Mexican citizen." He was already accepted as such a citizen by many of the Mexican leaders when he left the capital for Texas.

CHAPTER VIII

REPUBLICAN OR BOURBON

During the spring and summer of 1823, while Austin was returning to Texas from the capital, all Mexico was in a condition of political ferment. The Congress which had dethroned and banished Iturbide had refused to assume the responsibility of drafting a constitution, but had called an election for a new Congress to perform this important task. The campaign of this election was in progress as Austin travelled northward.

Austin recognized fully that the form of government which Mexico would ultimately adopt was a question of vital importance in relation to his colonization plans. Consequently he took keen interest in it from the first. Even while Iturbide was at the height of his power and when it seemed that Mexico was destined to be a monarchy, Austin drafted a model constitution in which he sought to adjust the monarchial form of government to the needs of Mexico as he saw them. Before he could present it, however, it became evident that Iturbide's fall was imminent, and he set about at once to draft another, which provided for a federal republic, and which he proposed to present to the Congress which convened to deal with Iturbide. He completed it on the very day that the Congress assembled, and was very much disappointed to learn that it was the purpose of a majority of the members to postpone the consideration of a constitution until another Congress could be elected and convened. Austin declared that the Federalists "jeopardized all" by this action, but he decided, nevertheless, to place his model constitution before the leading Federalists. So he called on several important men and presented them with copies of his draft.

Notable among these was Ramos Arizpe, who had been one of Mexico's representatives in the Spanish Cortes and who was just then emerging as the outstanding leader of the Federalist Republicans. Austin conferred with Arizpe at Monterrey, where he was compelled to spend several weeks settling certain matters connected with the question of the character and limits of his authority in Texas, and the Federalist leader approved the draft heartily, ordered it printed, and told Austin he would send copies of it to his friends. This draft subsequently had much influence in giving unity of intention and direction to the Federalist party.

To appreciate fully the character of the task which the republicans of Mexico had before them immediately following the fall of Iturbide, it is necessary to know that at that time the whole conception of free government had been given a set-back by the aftermath of the French Revolution and the final defeat and confinement of Napoleon Bonaparte. Outside the United States, republicanism was widely regarded with very much the same kind of suspicion and abhorrence that many people felt with respect to Bolshevism during the period following the World

War. There was a strong reactionary movement in every country in Europe. It had been a temporary triumph of the constitutionalists in Spain that made the revolution of Iturbide possible, but now the Spanish constitutionalists were being subdued completely by a French army, headed by a Bourbon prince, which had invaded Spain with the object of rescuing the captive king, Ferdinand, and setting him firmly on his throne as an absolute monarch. This intervention in the internal affairs of Spain had the approval of the so-called Holy Alliance, a league of European nations which had been founded by the Russian Czar, Alexander I, though it was frowned upon by England, which country had steadfastly held aloof from the Czar's alliance. At the very time that Mexican leaders were discussing the matter of the future form of their government, the question of the hour in Europe was what should be done to check the spread of republicanism in Latin America.

The question of the future status of the Spanish colonies had been one of the important subjects of international discussion for several years. As early as April, 1818, Alexander had warned the powers in a confidential communication, the text of which has come to light only since the fall of the Romanoffs, that the United States could bring a "whole republican world" into being if it should adopt a policy of recognizing Latin American republics.

"The popular party in the United States, much strengthened of late," Alexander wrote the powers assembled at the Congress of Aix-la-Chapelle, "is preparing to make a strong effort to secure recognition of the independence of Buenos Aires during the

next session of Congress. Consideration of their actions reveal their ambitions to make the American continent one Grand Confederated Republic at the head of which will be found the United States. In the actual state of affairs, the United States centralizes all its efforts in developing its resources and population. It is directed by a moderate policy and does not offer a menace to Europe. This would not continue to be the case should a large portion of South America adopt its institutions. A whole republican world, young, ardent, and enriched by the production of every climate, will then set up in opposition to an old monarchial Europe, overpopulated and shaken by thirty years of revolution. This is a prospective worthy of the earnest consideration of all European statesmen. The consequences of all this might be incalculable."

Alexander advised that steps be taken to bring the United States into European counsels, with the idea of inducing its statesmen to take a like point of view with respect to recognizing the revolutionary governments in Latin America and to cooperate in bringing about a "reconciliation" of the former Spanish colonies with the mother country. Definite action at Aix-la-Chapelle was prevented by the British Foreign Minister, who took the position that England could not cooperate in any kind of intervention other than "friendly offices." Whereupon Alexander began a protracted campaign to induce the United States to accede to the pact known as the Holy Alliance. But John Quincy Adams, Monroe's Secretary of State, remained impervious to all the blandishments of the Czar's ministers.

Recognition of the Latin American republics by the United States, as we have seen, was withheld for the time being, in spite of Henry Clay and what the Czar had pleased to call "the popular party", but this was because of the unsettled condition of relations between Spain and the United States. The real attitude of the United States at this time is revealed in instructions given by the State Department to the American minister at St. Petersburg on the eve of the Congress of Aix-la-Chapelle. A sentence from those instructions sums up this attitude as follows: "We cannot participate in, and cannot approve of, any interposition of other powers unless it be to promote the total independence, political and commercial, of the colonies."

All this was in 1818. By 1822 the situation had changed in the important respect that it was generally recognized in Europe that the reunion of the colonies with Spain on anything like the basis which existed prior to 1810 was out of the question. The question was no longer one of reuniting the colonies with Spain. It was now a question of checking the spread of republicanism and of promoting "legitimacy" in Latin America. If Spain's former colonies were to be independent, then they must be converted into monarchies, with Bourbon princes on their thrones.

The chief convert to Alexander's ideas at this time was Chateaubriand, the "poet statesman," who for the moment was the French foreign minister. It was Chateaubriand who had won over Louis XVIII of France to intervention in Spain to restore absolute power to Ferdinand, and he proposed that this should be followed by a series of "restorations" in Latin America. Chateaubriand conceived himself in the rôle of restorer of the Bourbons and he proposed to accomplish this by placing princes of that royal house on the thrones of a whole galaxy of petty monarchies in Latin America. There can be little doubt that he was intimately concerned in some of the intrigue that was to be noted in Mexico City shortly after Stephen Austin's arrival there in April, 1822.

Chateaubriand set forth his views on this question very clearly in a memorandum directed to a colleague, under date of May 28th, 1822, which, incidentally, was just ten days after Iturbide had had himself declared Emperor. "Peru," he wrote, "has adopted a monarchial constitution. The policy of Europe should direct all its efforts toward obtaining a similar result in all the colonies which declare their independence. The United States fears the establishment of an Empire in Mexico. If the New World ever becomes entirely republican, the monarchies of the Old World will perish."

Chateaubriand urged this view at the Congress of Verona, held in October and November of 1822, and the French intervention in Spain which resulted from the decisions of this Congress was regarded by him as a first step in putting his program into effect. For he proposed that the restored Ferdinand should become a party to this plan of "legitimatizing" the governments of Latin America.

In Mexico there were many able, well educated and patriotic men who conscientiously adhered to the cause of "legitimacy." They sincerely believed that the safety and welfare of their country would be best

served by the creation of a monarchy and the placing
of a Bourbon on the Mexican throne. Some of these
were among the best and most enlightened men in
Mexico, men who had been educated in Europe, who
looked upon Europe as the center of the world's culture and wisdom, and who regarded European institutions as the very embodiment of civilization.
Such men had a very low opinion of the institutions
of the United States and were violently opposed to
any imitation of those institutions in Mexico. They
viewed with sincere misgiving the activites of the republicans of Mexico, especially those of the Federalists, and they threw all the weight of their influence
against their efforts to create a federal republic.
These men, be it said, represented much of the wealth
of the country and their influence was very great.

In the face of this powerful opposition, the republicans of Mexico were divided into two camps: the
Centralists and the Federalists. The Centralists desired a republic with a strongly cestralized government at Mexico City. The Federalists desired a republic in federalized form, with the provinces converted into States with a measurable degree of local
self-government. Quite naturally Austin desired the
triumph of federalism. He believed that adequate
provision for local self-government for the provinces
was of fundamental importance, and he regarded the
alternate plan of a centralized republic, with all power centered at Mexico City, as even worse than a monarchy. He especially desired that Texas should be
given as great a degree of local self-government as
possible, for he felt that this would minimize friction
and tend to insure loyalty to Mexico among the

Anglo-American colonists he proposed to introduce.
He realized, however, that with its small population
Texas could not hope to be formed into a separate
State. Therefore he hit upon the plan of having it
combined, provisionally, with adjoining provinces
until it should possess sufficient population to become
a separate State. In his draft of a constitution he
provided for this in an article which read as follows:

"Congress may by law establish special deputations
(legislatures) in provinces which have less than 20,-
000 inhabitants, or may establish one deputation for
two or more provinces."

It is more than probable that he pointed out the
importance of this to Arizpe and other leaders. In
any event, the matter was very much on his mind,
and he was anxious that the Federalist leaders should
recognize its importance. But he felt that all this
should be decided by the Mexicans themselves, and
he was especially fearful lest the little group of
American settlers, waiting for him in Texas, should
express themselves on the question.

"I wrote to the settlers on the Colorado and
Brazos," he said in a letter to his brother, J. E. B.
Austin, written from Monterrey under date of May
20th, 1823, "that they ought not to meddle with politics, and to have nothing to do with any revolutionary schemes. I hope they have followed my advice.
They are as yet too recently established in the country to take an active part in its political affairs. If
any questions are asked them as to their opinion of the
Government they ought to answer that they moved
here to live under the Government which the nation
may establish. They can do themselves no good by

meddling in politics, and at such a time as this, when
the Government is not yet settled and the nation in a
state of political fermentation, it is embarking on a
doubtful voyage to embrace any party. As foreigners we have a good excuse for remaining neutral
without being liable to suspicions and this is the safe
course."

However, Austin did not hesitate to express to his
brother his own preferences and his hope that the
federal form would be adopted. "The Emperor has
deceived us all," he wrote. "I thought he would adhere to his oath, and govern according to law. But
on the contrary he has violated the one and trampled
on the other. Nothing therefore is more just and
more magnanimous than the spirit of indignation and
resentment which the nation has manifested and the
result I hope and confidently believe will be a confederated republic very similar to that of the United
States."

Ten days later he wrote again to his brother from
Monterrey in a similar strain. "The people of this
quarter are all in favor of a Federal Republic," he
wrote. "I hope Bexar is the same. A central republic is the worst government in the world. For all the
power will be in the hands of a few men in Mexico
(City) and instead of a republic it will in effect be
an aristocracy, which is worse than monarchy, for in
it we shall have one hundred tyrants instead of one.
. . . I do not wish to take an active part in politics,
but if I can do anything in favor of the confederate
system, I will do it with pleasure."

Austin already regarded himself as a citizen of
Mexico, with a right to take part in its politics if he

chose. But he recognized that his foreign birth and recent migration to the country made it advisable that a certain delicacy should attend his exercise of those rights. On every opportune occasion, however, he made profession of his loyalty to his adopted country. From Monterrey, for example, he wrote the governing *junta* at San Antonio, notifying it of his arrival at that place and of the confirmation of his colonization contract by the Supreme Government, and in this letter he took occasion to make such a profession. "I am proud of the honor of being ranked as a citizen of the great Mexican nation," he wrote, "a nation which has displayed traits of heroism and magnanimity in the late glorious revolution in the cause of true liberty which will excite the admiration of the world, and give Mexico a rank amongst nations which centuries of subjection to despotism could not have acquired. As an inhabitant of Texas, I cheerfully tender my services to the Government of that province in any manner in which they can be useful, and declare my entire subjection to its commands."

CHAPTER IX

A NEW WORLD EMERGES

Stephen Austin returned to Texas the possessor of
extraordinary powers. He was authorized not only to
create a colony, but also to be its civil and military
ruler. His powers included those of head of the local
militia, with the rank of Lieutenant Colonel, and
those of judge and law-giver in all but capital cases.
Austin took the precaution of stopping at Monterrey
long enough to obtain a detailed interpretation of his
powers from the Provincial Deputation and the Commandant of the Eastern Interior Provinces. The new
Commandant was Felipe de la Garza, whom Austin
had met at Mexico City and with whom he had established intimately friendly relations. He showed a
genuine interest in the new colony and was very help-
ful in the matter of having Austin's powers precisely
defined. In grateful acknowledgment of this help,
Austin named the first Anglo-American municipality
San Felipe de Austin, in honor of the Commandant's
patron saint.

The settlers on the Colorado and the Brazos had
been organized into two companies of militia during
Austin's absence and an *alcalde* had been elected for
each river. Bastrop had seen to this. He had gone to
the Colorado settlement in December, 1822, and,
gathering the colonists together, had administered

the oath of allegiance to the Emperor, Augustín I, as Iturbide was called during his brief reign. He had then held an election for *alcalde* and officers of the militia and authorized Josiah H. Bell to do the same for the settlers on the Brazos. In this way a semblance of organized government had been maintained among those settlers who had stuck it out during Austin's long absence.

Austin reached San Antonio in the middle of July (1823) and presented his credentials to the new Governor of Texas, Luciano García. The Governor at once appointed Bastrop to the office of commissioner for the colony, charging him with the duty of formally and publicly investing Austin with the powers of his office, and authorizing him to survey the lands of the settlers and to issue titles to them when all required conditions were complied with. Bastrop performed this first duty by going with Austin to the settlements and by reading a proclamation at two meetings of the colonists, one held on the Colorado and the other on the Brazos. After enumerating the powers bestowed upon Austin, Bastrop's proclamation concluded as follows:

"I, therefore, the Baron de Bastrop, commissioner duly appointed by the Government for that purpose, now, and in this public manner, invest him, the said Stephen F. Austin, with the before mentioned offices and powers and I charge the inhabitants to respect and obey him in everything relative to the good government and prosperity of the colony, and the defence of the nation to which he belongs, under the penalty incurred by those who disrepect and disobey an officer or magistrate of the Mexican nation . . . .

I cannot too strongly recommend to you the necessity of good order, industry, and obedience to the constitutional authorities, and that you should be governed in all things connected with public matters by the founder of this colony, Mr. Stephen F. Austin, a man whose former character in the United States and prudent and correct conduct in this country have acquired him the full confidence of the higher authorities of the Mexican nation."

Endorsed on the back of the copy of this proclamation that Bastrop read to the settlers on the Colorado, in Austin's handwriting, is the following:

"And the civil and militia officers and inhabitants having in due form acknowledged and recognized the said Austin as invested with the faculties and powers conferred on him by the Superior Government, he, the said Austin, entered upon the civil and military command of the colony on the 10th day of August, 1823, 3rd year of Independence and 2nd of liberty."

Invested with these extraordinary powers, Austin began the labor of putting his little colony in shape. Within two months after his return, the work of surveying lands was started, and before another year had passed, Bastrop, as commissioner, issued the first land titles to the settlers. New immigrants began to arrive, and in spite of the bad name which the delays of the previous two years had given the colony throughout the southwestern portion of the United States, it became plain that the limit of three hundred families would soon be reached. Austin exercised great care in admitting colonists, requiring them to give acceptable evidence of good character and industrious habits. From the first he sought to impress his colonists with the fact that they had become citizens of a new country and were no longer citizens of the United States. His good faith in this respect was beyond question, and he was particularly solicitous about his own status as a citizen. His attitude in this matter and his anxiety that the Mexican authorities should understand it, both with respect to his colonists and himself, are well illustrated by a letter which he wrote on January 20th, 1824, to the Minister of Relations, Lucas Alamán, a man who later became one of the most uncompromising opponents of the American colonization of Texas in all Mexico.

"I have made it a habit," wrote Austin to Alamán, "not to admit any settler who does not produce the most unequivocal evidence of good moral character and industrious habits, and I will vouch for those received by me that they will not prove undutiful or ungrateful citizens and subjects of the nation which has so kindly received them . . . . I expect to spend my life in this nation, and if the new Constitution does not declare all persons actually established in the nation at the time of its adoption citizens (as I presume it will), or if the grant made to my father to settle in this province, previous to the independence, and my own removal in the first year thereof, will not entitle me to the rights of citizenship, I should wish, if deemed worthy of that honor, to procure letters of citizenship . . . . I then close this long letter with the prayer that Your Excellency will be pleased to take this first effort of colonization within the Mexican nation since its glorious emancipation under your protection and patronage, and that you will have the goodness to assure the Supreme Executive Power of our good disposition toward the Government of our adoption, and that we are at all times ready and willing to aid all in our power in defending the independence and liberty of the Mexican nation."

Austin was granted full citizenship in March, 1824, and thenceforth he thought of himself and always referred to himself as a citizen and in the national sense a Mexican.

Meantime, the congressional election had been held and the new Congress convened on November 7th, 1823. Erasmo Seguin, native Texan and the commissioner who had met Austin at Natchitoches in 1821, was elected to represent Texas, and very appropriately the colonists contributed toward his expenses while in Mexico City. Ramos Arizpe, who had been elected from Coahuila, was made chairman of the committee charged with the task of providing a provisional constitution, which would fix the form of government and its general character, pending the drafting of the Constitution itself. This was on November 14th and within a week, on November 20th, Arizpe, as chairman of this committee, reported a Constitutional Act of Federation, which was proposed as a solemn act of the Congress, vested with the will of the nation. It declared the form of government to be a federated republic.

A working majority of the Congress favored this form of government, but there was a considerable minority opposed to it. And there were strong influences at the capital, outside of Congress, being ex-

erted to defeat it. Leaders among the old ruling class
still hoped for European intervention and assistance,
and some of these were inclined to regard the proceedings of the Congress with a tolerant disdain.
"What great difference does it make what they do?
In due course the forces of legitimacy will restore
sound government throughout Latin America." This
was the attitude of many. And there was basis for
this belief. For reactionary absolutism was completely triumphing in Spain at the very time that the
Mexican Congress was being elected. And on the
very day that Congress convened, November 7th,
Riego, leader of the constitutionalists in Spain, was
hanged. Other leaders whose death had been decreed
were in flight. The restoration of Ferdinand's absolute power had been accomplished through the
French intervention. On April 7th, 1823, a French
army under the Duke of Angouleme had crossed the
Spanish border and on May 23rd it had entered
Madrid. Restored to absolute power, Ferdinand embarked upon a campaign of vengeance against the
constitutionlists which even the French did not approve. But such events encouraged royalists and
"legitimists" in Mexico to think that the next step
would be a move to restore absolutism in Latin
America. It was still plausible and even natural to
believe that with republicanism on the run everywhere in Europe, its triumph in an erstwhile Spanish
dominion like Mexico could only be temporary and
of little consequence.

But the French intervention in Spain was not universally approved, even in Europe. England had
been opposed to it, and the chief reason that country

had not sent armed support to the Spanish republicans was that such action would have precipitated a world war, for Russia, Austria, and Prussia would have taken the field rather than permit such British assistance to succeed. But England was determined that there should be no European intervention in Latin America. In a note to Chateaubriand on the eve of the intervention in Spain, the British Foreign Minister, Canning, had intimated as much, and this had prompted the American minister at London, Benjamin Rush, to inquire quite casually whether this meant that England would not remain passive if France and the Holy Alliance should attempt to control Latin American destinies. Canning replied with a pointed question. What did Mr. Rush think would be the attitude of the American Government toward a proposal for England and the United States to go hand in hand in such a policy? Mr. Rush was not prepared to answer that question, but he promptly reported the conversation to the American Government.

At Washington, of course, the events in Spain had not gone unnoticed. On the contrary they had been the subject of much deliberate consideration by President Monroe and his ministers, especially by his Secretary of State, John Quincy Adams. Moreover, there was correspondence between the President and his friends, particularly Mr. Jefferson. But it was not merely the immediate situation that was considered, it was rather the whole question of American policy with respect to all matters affected by the relations between Europe and the Western Hemisphere. And this was hardly a question to be determined in consultation with England. All this, however, was under the surface. Little of it was generally known and the menace of probable European intervention was regarded as very real when Arizpe reported the Constitutional Act of Federation on November 20th.

Within a few weeks, however, all fear of anything of this kind was removed by a declaration of policy by the President of the United States. For in his annual message to Congress, on December 2nd, 1823, President Monroe made it very clear that the United States would not be indifferent toward a move by the European allied powers to control affairs in any Latin American country.

President Monroe observed in that message that Europe was still unsettled. "Of this important fact," he said, "no stronger proof can be adduced than that the allied powers should have thought it proper, on any principle satisfactory to themselves, to have interposed, by force, in the internal concerns of Spain. To what extent such interposition may be carried, on the same principle, is a question to which all independent powers, whose governments differ from theirs, are interested; even those most remote, and surely none more so than the United States . . . . It is impossible that the allied powers should extend their political system to any portion of either continent (North or South America) without endangering our peace and happiness; nor can anyone believe that our Southern brethren, if left to themselves, would adopt it of their own accord. It is equally impossible, therefore, that we should behold such interposition, in any form, with indifference. If we look to the comparative strength and resources of Spain and those new governments, and their distance from each other, it must be obvious that she can never subdue them. It is still the true policy of the United States to leave the parties to themselves, in the hope that other powers will pursue the same course."

This was the announcement of the "Monroe Doctrine" to the world, and it left no doubt as to the probable course of the United States if the allied powers should attempt to carry out the policy of promoting "legitimacy" in Latin American countries. "We owe it, therefore, to candor," said Monroe, "and to the amicable relations exisiting between the United States and those powers, to declare that we should consider any attempt on their part to extend their system to any portion of this hemisphere, as dangerous to our peace and safety."

The situation was changed completely by this declaration. For a time there were those who believed that war would result, but for the most part it was accepted as a final settlement of the question. Letters received by Austin from Americans at this time expressed both views. Writing from Natchez, Mississippi, on February 1st, 1824, for example, Judge Joshua Childs told Austin that war was expected. "There is at present prospect of war," he wrote, "in which France and Spain will combine to subjugate Mexico, in which case Great Britain and the United States will unite in support of the Mexican Republic." A more intelligent and accurate view was expressed by Charles Douglas of Murfreesboro, Tennessee, in a letter to Austin under date of February 26th, 1824. "It is difficult to say," wrote Douglas, "how the late unhappy change in Spain will affect you; but we have hope for the best and are anxiously looking to the British Government for her final decision upon this important question. Judging from the bold and energetic language of our President in his late message to Congress upon the subject of the presumed future conduct of the Allied sovereigns, relative to the subjection of the South American States, and from the tone of the English ministerial prints, we believe there is an understanding between us, not only in opinion, but also as respects our future conduct. . . . You have nothing to fear from foreign invasion, for I am certain that the naval power of the two governments united can effectually prevent them from ever disturbing your repose. I believe if England protests against the Allied powers interfering in the political affairs of your country and declares her determination to oppose every such plan, that this, together with our declaration, will be sufficient to prevent them from attempting to make any serious efforts."

This was the dominant view and it was widely expressed. It was expressed even on the floor of the British House of Commons, where Mr. Bougham declared that the question of the future of Latin America was now disposed of, or nearly so. "For," he said, "an event has recently happened, than which no event has ever dispersed greater joy, exultation, and gratitude over all the free men of Europe; that event, which is decisive on the subject, is the language held with respect to Spanish America in the speech of the President of the United States."

It was in the changed situation created by Monroe's declaration that the Mexican Congress finally reached a vote on the Constitutional Act of Federation. On the direct question of the form of government, the Congress decided in favor of a federated republic by a test vote of 20 to 13, and then the Constitutional Act of Federation, with a few immaterial changes in the draft reported by Arizpe, was adopted as a provisional constitution and was published to the nation on January 31st, 1824. Incidentally, it provided that the three provinces of Texas, Coahuila, and Nuevo Leon should constitute one of the States of the Federation.

Austin received a copy of the Constitutional Act of Federation from Seguin in February and he immediately started plans for a formal celebration of the event. Accordingly, on May 1st, 1824, the settlers gathered in a number of meetings at convenient points along the Colorado and the Brazos to take a public oath to support the new document. A translation of the Constitutional Act, together with a proclamation of the Political Chief putting it into effect, was read at each of these meetings and a formal oath was administered. In each case, the chairman of the meeting put the question: "You swear to observe and obey the Constitutional Act of Federation of the Mexican nation?" And the assembled colonists responded: "Yes, we swear."

Austin took advantage of this opportunity to issue a stirring appeal to his colonists. "The great Mexican nation is free," he said. "Rational liberty, with all its concomitant blessings, has opened to the view of the world a nation which despotism had hitherto enveloped in intellectual night. The Federal Republican system, that last and glorious hope of persecuted freedom, first established by the great fathers of North American independence on the ruins of British colonial oppression, and which soon raised a new-born nation to a degree of prosperity and happiness unequalled in the history of the world, now spreads its fostering arms over the vast dominions of Mexico. . . . I hope that you will repose with confidence under the authority that governs, being assured that the Government will always cherish and protect you, and that everything in my feeble power to do for your benefit will be cheerfully done, for . . . the greatest consolation I ever expect to derive from my labors in the wilderness of this province will arise from the conviction that I have benefitted many of my fellow beings, and laid the foundation for the settlement of one of the finest countries in the world."

CHAPTER X

A CALL TO THE LANDLESS

New rumors of European intervention in Mexico became current early in the summer of 1824. They were to the effect that Iturbide had obtained financial support in Europe for an expedition to Mexico with the object of regaining his throne. Austin received news of this in a letter from one of his colonists, Anthony R. Clarke, who wrote him of a visit he had made to Natchitoches.

"The latest news from Europe," wrote Clark, "is that Iturbide, the late Emperor of Mexico, has sailed from England in a private armed ship for Vera Cruz. The account that he published in England was that the people of Mexico had been continuously sending for him to come and take charge of the Government, as the inhabitants were not capable of governing themselves; that his object was to go and render all the assistance in his power. An officer of the United States Army informed me that he read an account in French from Paris which stated that he was appointed by Ferdinand as Viceroy of Mexico, and was going to take charge of the Mexican provinces for the Spanish Government. I give you the account as I hear it. I do not answer for the truth of it. You must judge for yourself."

The report was true at least to the extent that Iturbide had sailed for Mexico. He landed on the Mexican coast at Soto la Marina on July 14th, 1824. He was promptly arrested, and three days later he was shot in accordance with the sentence of the Congress which had banished him from Mexico forever under penalty of death. Evidently Iturbide had counted on the support of the royalists and "legitimists" of Mexico, expecting that they would rally to his standard the moment he landed. And something of this kind might have happened but for the changed situation which had been created by President Monroe's message to Congress and the attitude of England. For this had made any considerable European support of a movement in Mexico impossible, and the republicans were so firmly entrenched that the monarchists and the "legitimists" would not risk their necks on the issue. But thenceforth every advocate of monarchy in Mexico became a Centralist. The waning of the hope of European intervention crystalized all the anti-federalist elements into a strong party which was to labor without ceasing for the overthrow of the federal republic just coming into being. More than that, anti-Americanism became a leading tenet of the Centralist program and from this time forward the charge that the Federalists were under the thumb of the United States was one of the most effective weapons of the Centralists.

Meantime, however, with a safe majority in the Congress, the Federalists proceeded with the work of settling up the new government. State governments were organized under the provisions of the Constitutional Act and preparations were made for the first sessions of the State legislatures and for the Presidential election. Austin's colonists, 101 voters in all, held an election on April 20th to decide who they wanted to represent the Department of Texas in the State Legislature, and they voted unanimously for Bastrop. Meeting at four polling places, everyone eligible to vote signed a formal return to that effect.

Before the Legislature met, however, the Congress reached the section of the permanent Constitution relative to the status of Texas, and inasmuch as Nuevo Leon had protested against being joined to other provinces it was decided to include only Coahuila and Texas within the boundaries of the State adjoining the United States. It was provided, however, that Texas should be erected into a separate State as soon as it "possessed the necessary elements" and that the union with Coahuila was provisional and temporary. This action was taken on May 7th, so when the Legislature assembled at Saltillo on August 15th it represented the people of "the State of Coahuila and Texas."

The chief business before this first session of the Legislature of the new State was that of enacting a State colonization law. It had already been decided by the Congress that each State should have control of its public lands, though New Mexico and California were given the status of "federal territories" and colonization matters in those two provinces were to be administered at Mexico City. A national colonization law was completed by the Congress as the members of the Legislature of Coahuila and Texas were assembling at Saltillo and it was decreed the law of the land on August 18th, 1824. It empowered each State to enact its own colonization law, subject to certain restrictions. These restrictions were framed with an eye chiefly on Texas and they included a provision that no colony should be established within twenty leagues of a neighboring country or within ten leagues of the coast without the consent of the Federal Government. Other restrictions were that no persons residing outside the Republic could acquire land under the colonization laws and that the Federal Government was empowered to take such precautionary measures as it deemed expedient for the protection of the country with respect to foreigners who came to colonize. It was provided that immigration should not be prohibited prior to 1840, but that foreigners from any particular country might be excluded at any time.

The view of the Mexican citizens of Texas was that their prosperity and security depended upon the rapid settlement of the wilderness that surrounded them. Austin's contract for the introduction of three hundred families was soon completed and when he applied to the Federal Government for permission to bring in additional settlers his application had been referred to the State Government. Everything was at a standstill, therefore, until the State colonization law could be enacted. It was because of the importance of this measure that the people of San Antonio had joined Austin's colonists in electing Bastrop to represent them in the Legislature, and he toiled long and faithfully at the task of getting the right kind of a law passed. It required eight months to complete it, but it was finally promulgated on March 24th, 1825.

In effect the State colonization law was an urgent invitation to the land-hungry of the world, especially of the United States, to settle in Texas. "The Constituent Congress of the free, independent, and sovereign State of Coahuila and Texas," declared its preamble, "desiring by every possible means to augment the population of its territory, to promote the cultivation of its fertile lands, the raising and multiplication of livestock . . . have thought proper to decree the following law of colonization." It then proceeded in a "whosoever will" fashion to invite foreigners to settle in the State. "All foreigners," it declared, "who in virtue of the general law of the 18th of August, 1824, which guarantees the security of their persons and property in the territory of the Mexican nation, wish to remove to any of the settlements of the State of Coahuila and Texas, are at liberty to do so, and the State invites and calls them . . . . Those who do so, instead of being incommoded, shall be admitted by the local authorities of said settlements, who shall freely permit them to pursue any branch of industry that they may think proper, provided they respect the general laws of the nation and those of the State."

The law provided for a contract or *empresario* system, under which colonists could be introduced into the State by authorized contractors. A premium of 23,040 acres of land would be awarded the *empresario* for every one hundred families introduced up to the limit of eight hundred families. Each family would be granted a liberal allotment of land and all settlers established in the State under the law

would be exempt from taxation of all kinds for a
period of ten years.

Meantime, while the Legislature had been working on the colonization law, a Presidential election
had been held and the Federal Constitution had been
completed. Guadalupe Victoria, one of the revolutionary leaders, was inaugurated as President on October 10th, 1824, with Nicolás Bravo as Vice President. The completed Constitution was promulgated
as the fundamental and organic law of the land on
November 6th. The United States had formally recognized the independence of Mexico two years before, while Iturbide was still Emperor, and President Monroe had honored the Mexican minister at
a banquet on December 24th, 1822. But now the
United States of Mexico, a federated republic, sent
an envoy extraordinary and minister plenipotentiary
to Washington in the person of Parlo Obregon. And
the instructions given this minister set forth that the
chief object of his mission would be the negotiation
of a treaty of limits with the purpose of obtaining
from the United States an acknowledgment of the
boundary established in the Spanish treaty of 1819.

The authorities of the State of Coahuila and Texas
began awarding contracts under the new colonization
law three weeks after its enactment, and within another two weeks authority was granted for the introduction of 2,900 families. Each contract provided for
settlement within a specified region, the boundaries
of which were set forth, and the *empresario* was free
to locate his settlers on any vacant land within the
prescribed area, all unalloted land remaining the
property of the State. Austin was granted a contract

to settle three hundred additional families, which number was promptly increased to five hundred at his request. Later, by special arrangement, Austin was authorized to introduce families beyond the limit of eight hundred.

Most of the contracts awarded under the law were never carried into effect by the introduction of settlers, but one of them should be noted in particular because of its subsequent history. Haden Edwards of Mississippi, who had been one of the petitioners for a Texas grant during the reign of Iturbide and who had remained in Mexico City while the general colonization law was before Congress, was awarded a contract to settle the legal limit of eight hundred families in the extreme eastern region of Texas, including the land around the old town of Nacogdoches. This was the region in which the Spaniards had originally settled one hundred years before, a circumstance which occasioned complications later. But it was also the region nearest the American border, being separated from the boundary only by the twenty-league strip reserved from colonization.

This latter fact may have been significant. Three weeks prior to the awarding of Edwards's contract and on the very day the State colonization law was promulgated, the newly appointed American minister to Mexico had been handed his instructions by the Secretary of State, and they directed him to seek a revision of the boundary between the two countries, and, if Mexico should be agreeable, to endeavor to extend the territory of the United States to a line somewhere between the Colorado and the Rio Grande. Whether Edwards was aware of this or not, reports that the United States would seek such a revision of the boundary had been current for more than a year and it is reasonable to assume that this circumstance influenced him to choose for the site of his proposed colony an area which any such revision would be certain to place within the boundaries of the United States. Brown Austin had heard such a rumor at Natchitoches in May, 1824, and had written his brother about it. And only five days before the State Department framed its instructions on the subject, a correspondent at Fort Jessup, La., one J. Cable, wrote Stephen Austin that such a report was current in New Orleans.

"By Mr. Smith I send you a few newspapers," Cable wrote to Austin, "from which you will see the result of the election of President of the United States. Mr. John Q. Adams has been duly elected . . . There is great hopes of the United States becoming peaceable possession of the Province of Texas. By a letter Mr. Johnson received from his father in Orleans last Saturday, he advises his son to not sell his land claims in Texas, that in conversation with some gentleman in Orleans he states that our Minister to Mexico is about to conclude a treaty with the Mexican Republic for the Province of Texas—the Rio Grande to be the line between the two governments."

Reports of the kind referred to in this letter were certain to come to the ears of the Mexican minister at Washington and to be transmitted by him to his superiors at Mexico City. Mexican ministers at Washington early acquired the habit of transmitting every wild rumor to their Government. The practice, indeed, was started by that first Mexican minister who was honored at a banquet by President Monroe, for two days after this celebrated banquet he wrote to Iturbide's foreign office that he had discovered ambitions with respect to Texas among the Americans. "In time," he added, "they will become our sworn enemies, and foreseeing this we ought to treat them as such from the present day." This particular minister, to be sure, was a monarchist who expected Mexico to remain a monarchy. Obregon was a Federal Republican and his instructions included the admonition to do everything possible to promote friendly relations with the United States and even to ascertain what assistance Mexico might count on in the event of a European attack. And at the very outset of his mission he encountered a disposition on the part of the United States to covet Mexican territory.

Coming at the time that the State of Coahuila and Texas was issuing an official invitation to Americans generally to settle within its borders, this circumstance was a little embarrassing. And it was destined to become increasingly embarrassing alike to the Federal Republicans in their struggle to maintain a federated republic in the face of the intrigues of the Centralists and to Stephen F. Austin in his efforts to colonize Texas as a Mexican State.

CHAPTER XI

THE SEED OF SUSPICION

As soon as John Quincy Adams became President
of the United States he completely reversed the policy he had followed with respect to Texas as Monroe's Secretary of State. Monroe had contrived to
have the Spanish treaty ratified in spite of the campaign of criticism Henry Clay had waged against it.
He wanted to keep Texas outside the boundaries of
the United States because he feared the addition of
so much territory in the southwest would upset the
Missouri Compromise and reopen the violent controversy which that measure had served to allay. Adams
took the position that the "Missouri question" could
be "left to Providence" and one of his first acts as
President was to make Clay his Secretary of State.

The Presidential election of 1824 was a striking
contrast to that of 1820. Monroe had been reelected
without opposition, but the 1824 election resulted in
no choice among four candidates. With 131 electoral
votes constituting a majority, Andrew Jackson received 99, Adams received 84, William H. Crawford
of Georgia received 41, and Clay trailed all the
others with 37. But Clay occupied the powerful position of Speaker of the House of Representatives
and when the election was thrown before that body
for a decision Clay supported Adams. Adams was

elected and Clay's appointment as Secretary of State
followed in due course. The first fruit of the alliance
thus formed was a move to "recover" Texas through
negotiations with Mexico for a revision of the boun-
dry established by the Spanish treaty. Joel R. Poinsett of South Carolina, who was appointed minister
to Mexico by Monroe, but who did not leave on his
mission until after Clay was installed, was expected
to bring this about. His instructions, which Clay
handed him on March 24th, 1825, directed him to
communicate to the Mexican Government that while
the Spanish treaty was binding on both countries, it
might be desirable to establish a more logical and advantageous boundary beyond the Sabine and south of
the Red and Arkansas rivers "if the Mexican Government be not disinclined to fix a new line." This
might relieve Mexico of territory too remote from
its capital, leave to American jurisdiction the troublesome Comanche Indians, and prevent future difficulties and collisions which might result after extension
of settlements.

Poinsett was instructed also to impress upon the
Mexican Government the friendly attitude of the
United States, as expressed in its prompt recognition
of Mexican independence, to explain the purpose and
scope of the Monroe doctrine, to ascertain the Mexican attitude with respect to the future of Cuba, to
negotiate a treaty of commerce, and to express ap-
preciation of the compliment implied in Mexico's
copying the American Constitution so largely, and
"to show on all occasions an unobstrusive readiness
to explain the practical operation and the very great
advantages which appertain to our system." With re-

spect to Cuba, he was directed to say that the position of the island "proclaims that it should be attached to the United States" in preference to any other American State.

The idea that an independent Mexico would consent to almost any boundary the United States might desire was a very popular one among American leaders of all parties during the first three decades of the nineteenth century. When Monroe wrote Jefferson in 1820 that "with any new Government which may be formed in Mexico, it would be easy to arrange the boundary in the wilderness so as to include as much territory on our side as we might choose," he expressed a widely prevailing opinion. Jefferson believed this and so did Adams, and Clay, and Jackson. Poinsett, who had much special talent for his task, being a polished gentleman, widely travelled, familiar with several languages, and well acquainted with Latin Americans, may not have been quite so sure of it. But it did not require long for him to discover, after two or three interviews with Lucas Alamán, the Mexican Minister of Relations, that this idea was an illusion. He presented his credentials on June 1st, 1825, and by July 25th, less than two months later, he was writing to Clay that it would be necessary to play for time in the matter of revising the boundary.

"It appears to me," wrote Poinsett, "that it will be important to gain time if we wish to extend our territory beyond the boundary agreed upon by the treaty of 1819. Most of the good land from the Colorado to the Sabine has been granted by the State of Texas and is rapidly peopling with either grantees or squatters from the United States, a population they will find it difficult to govern and perhaps after a short period they may not be so averse to part with that portion of that territory as they are at present."

What had happened was that Alamán, who was more than a match for Poinsett both in education and experience, had welcomed the suggestion for a reexamination of the whole question of the boundary, but with the object of fixing the line more accurately in accordance with ancient landmarks and the history of the region. Alamán was familiar with the negotiations between the United States and Spain on this matter and was convinced that the line fixed in the treaty of 1819 left a strip of territory on the American side which properly belonged on the Spanish side. He was glad, therefore, that the United States would not insist upon the line fixed in the treaty, and he proposed that a joint commission be set up by the two countries to examine all the facts pertaining to the ancient boundary between Louisiana and New Spain. Poinsett had backed away from the proposal of a joint commission, but he could not object, of course, to an investigation of the question by a Mexican commission. And so the matter rested for the moment.

But Poinsett's report to Clay on conditions in Texas showed that he had small understanding of the real situation. It was not true that "most of the good land from the Colorado to the Sabine" had been granted by the State Government. Very little land had been "granted" at that time. A contract to settle a given number of families within a certain described area was not a "grant" of that area. It was merely

authority to the contractor or *empresario* to introduce families into the region, the State Government
agreeing to grant each family a stated amount of
land, and to grant the *empresario* a premium of a
specified amount of land for every one hundred families introduced. In July, 1825, very few families had
yet been introduced by the contractors, for they had
been awarded their contracts scarcely three months
before and the machinery of the State colonization
law was just being put in operation. With few exceptions, the only "grantees" in Texas at that time
were those who had been introduced by Austin under
his original contract, and in their case there was no
justification for the opinion expressed by Poinsett
that the Mexican authorities would find them difficult to govern.

As to the "squatters," they had been in possession
of lands along the fringes of Texas, both on the Sabine and the Red rivers, for years before the attainment of Mexican independence. Bastrop reported to
the Federal authorities a colony of such invaders
at Pecan Point on Red River, which, he said, consisted of about three hundred families, and which
had been visited on more than one occasion by tax
collectors from the Territory of Arkansas on the
American side of the border who sought to require
them to pay taxes on lands which were clearly on the
Mexican side. Some of these might be desirable as
settlers, Bastrop said, but most of them ought to be
forcibly ejected from the country by Federal troops.
Such "squatters" were likely to cause controversy between the two countries, regardless of the national
policies of either, but their presence on Mexican soil

could hardly be expected to render the Mexican Government more willing to part with that soil, as Poinsett seemed to think. Incidentally, it was Bastrop's idea that each *empresario* should be made responsible for the area of his colony, so far as "squatters" and other undesirables were concerned. And in expressing this in a letter to Augustín de la Viesca, member of the Federal House of Deputies from the State of Coahuila and Texas, Bastrop took occasion to assure him that the militia organized in Austin's colony could be depended on to deal with such persons. "I do not hesitate in the least," Bastrop wrote Viesca, "to state that Don Esteban Austin, founder of the colony which bears his name, established between the Colorado and Brazos rivers, possesses all the qualities of an upright and honest citizen, a staunch supporter of the Government of the Mexican Republic, and capable enough to expel from the country all undesirable characters and vagabonds with the force of the national militia which he now has organized in his colony."

This letter of Bastrop's was characteristic of many he wrote during this period to Viesca and to José Manuel Ceballos, the member of the Federal Senate from Coahuila and Texas. These letters had to do with reforms which he felt were necessary to the welfare and prosperity of Texas, such as the establishment of adequate port facilities, the improvement of the mail service, an effective campaign against the Indians, the fostering of the growing of tobacco in Texas, and numerous other similar measures. He urged that there should be a provision in the treaties between the United States and the Republic of Mexico prohibiting trading with Indians across the border, so that the traffic in arms and ammunition in exchange for stolen horses might be stopped. "Also it would be wise," Bastrop wrote Viesca, "to stipulate in the treaties for the mutual delivery of fugitive negro slaves and perpetrators of atrocious crimes from both countries. This would make secure the boundary line between Texas and the United States, which at this time is overrun by desperate characters and vagabonds, whose trade is robbery and murder."

Poinsett's position in Mexico would have been an extremely delicate one even in ideal circumstances and even if his conduct at all times had been prompted by the utmost of wisdom and discretion. But the circumstances were anything but ideal and Poinsett at times was far from discreet. The Centralists, who now included the monarchists and "legitimists," were anti-American in spirit to begin with, and they were alert from the first to discover sinister and improper motives behind the policies of the United States. The proposal of a treaty of limits, with possible revision of the boundary, was just the kind of material they needed to arouse suspicion of American intentions with respect to Mexico and to create sentiment against the Federal Republicans as pro-American "traitors." However, if this proposal had stood alone and if it had been dropped as soon as its impracticability was disclosed, nothing very serious might have resulted. But it did not stand alone and it was not dropped.

Poinsett had been instructed, as has been seen, "to show on all occasions an unobtrusive readiness to explain the practical operation and the very great advantages which appertain to" the American system of government. And he interpreted this in a manner that soon involved him deeply in Mexican politics. He had found British influence on the Government in evidence shortly after his arrival, and this placed him at a disadvantage. And when he seemd to discover that the Masonic lodges of Mexico were centers of both anti-republicanism and anti-Americanism, he deemed it necessary to set some counter-influence in operation. The Masonic lodges were of the Scottish Rite, which had been introduced from Spain, in which country Masonry had been originally introduced from England. To offset the influence of these lodges, Poinsett suggested to the Federal Republicans that they set up York Rite lodges as a counter-influence, and he cooperated with them in obtaining charters in the United States. These two branches of Masonry were soon perverted completely to serve the purposes of opposing political factions, and Poinsett undoubtedly had much more to do with this development than was proper for a diplomatic representative in a foreign country. This ended in wrecking his mission, for in due course he became an "issue" between the factions and there were frequent demands that he be expelled from the country.

All of this, of course, was highly embarrassing to the Federal Republicans and placed them decidedly on the defensive with respect to everything concerning the United States. Nor did it tend to increase confidence in the colonization policy of Texas and Coahuila nor to allay suspicion of the intentions of the Anglo-American settlers in that State. On the

contrary, an idea began to get abroad in Mexico
about this time that the migration of Anglo-Americans into Texas was part of a deliberate policy of the
United States consciously aimed at the integrity of
Mexican territory.

And then came the so-called Fredonian War.

CHAPTER XII

THE FREDONIAN WAR

The Fredonian war was not a war at all. So far as actual fighting was concrned, it hardly attained the dignity of a riot. It consisted of an attempt by the *empresario* Haden Edwards and his brother, Benjamin F. Edwards, to instigate a revolt and it was confined to a small group of Anglo-Americans around Nacogdoches. It began in the middle of December, 1826, and it lasted scarcely a month. Nevertheless, it had far-reaching effects.

The merits of the quarrel of the Edwards brothers with the Mexican authorities depend largely upon the angle from which they are viewed. But viewed from any angle, the grievances were not of such public moment as to justify a revolt. The quarrel grew out of the circumstance that the area covered by the Edwards contract was that in which the Spaniards had originally settled and in which there were many old land titles. Added to this was the circumstance that there were a number of "squatters" in the region who had been in possession of land long enough to have improved it to a considerable degree. Controversies over land claims led to the lodging of complaints against Haden Edwards with the State authorities, and both of the brothers became involved in local political squabbles at Nacogdoches. Neither was a diplomatic person and their correspondence with the State authorities was conducted in a spirit which the Mexicans interpreted as insolent and arrogant. The upshot of the whole controversy was that the Governor peremptorily cancelled the Edwards contract and ordered the two brothers to leave Texas.

Evidently on the assumption that they had nothing more to lose, the Edwards brothers gathered a small body of their adherents around them, adopted a formal declaration of independence to apply to all Texas, set up what they gradiloquently called "the Republic of Fredonia," formed an alliance with the Cherokee Indians, and sent out appeals to Austin's colonists to join them. There were some skirmishes between the Fredonians and the "loyal" faction in the Nacogdoches district, but nothing that properly could be called a battle, and for a time the "Fredonian flag" flew over the town of Nacogdoches.

The "revolt" caused great excitement, both in Austin's colony and across the border in the United States. Austin himself had tried to caution the Edwards brothers with respect to the effect their methods would have on the whole *empresario* system in Texas, but his advice had produced no results. When they raised the banner of revolt, Austin did not hesitate a moment to display his loyalty to the Government, and his colonists followed his example. At a half-dozen or more "municipalities" in different sections of the colony there were mass meetings of the colonists, and ringing resolutions were adopted, condemning the revolt in unqualified terms and expressing absolute loyalty to the Government. Sentiment among them was unanimous. Austin induced the

State authorities to offer the "rebels" a general amnesty and an investigation of their grievances, including a review of the cancellation of the Edwards contract, if they would call the whole thing off in order to avoid bloodshed. Three of Austin's leading colonists were sent to Nacogdoches to present these terms, but Haden Edwards and his lieutenants rejected them. This delegation reported, however, that most of the people of the region were loyal. "There is scarcely one of the perverse party that has any property," they said. But they noted "many vagabonds and fugitives from justice, who have fled from the United States of the North."

When the first news of the "revolt" reached Austin he had immediately issued an address to his colonists calling upon them to rally to the support of the State authorities without waiting for orders to the militia. He said he was making no "official call" upon them, but merely was appealing to them "as men of honor, as Mexicans, and as Americans" to do their duty. "It is our duty as Mexicans," he said, "to support and defend the Government of our adoption, by whom we have been received with the kindness and liberality of an indulgent parent. It is our duty as men to suppress vice, anarchy, and Indian massacre. And it is our duty as Americans to defend that proud name from the infamy which this Nacogdoches gang must cast upon it if they are suffered to progress."

When the Fredonians rejected the offer of amnesty which Austin had obtained for them, he immediately issued a call to arms. "The persons who were sent on from this colony by the Chief of the Department

and the military commandant to offer peace to the
Nacogdoches madmen," Austin announced in a proclamation, "have returned without effecting anything.
The olive branch of peace that was so magnanimous-
ly held out to them has been insultingly refused . . . .
The people of the colony after a full understanding
of the pretended cause of complaint on the part of
the rebels, as well as of the mild and magnanimous
course of the Government in offering them a full and
universal amnesty and an impartial and public investigation of their alleged grievances, have unanimously, solemnly, and voluntarily pledged themselves in
writing to the Government to oppose the factionists
by force of arms. To arms then, my friends and fellow citizens, and hasten to the standard of our country."

When a force of Mexican troops arrived in Austin's colony on the way to Nacogdoches, therefore,
it was joined by a contingent of Anglo-American
militia, and with the assurance that reinforcements
would be available in the colony if they were needed,
this force proceeded to the "seat of war." At the same
time, the Political Chief of the Department of Texas
sent word ahead that full amnesty would be granted
to all who would abandon the revolt and submit to
the will of the Government. This had the effect
of ending the "war." When the Goverment troops
arrived at Nacogdoches, it was found that the leaders of the disturbance had fled across the American
border without waiting to give battle.

The whole Fredonian incident was of such opera
bouffe character that it would hardly be expected
to possess the slightest historical importance. But in

Mexico it was magnified into an attempt by the Colossus of the North to seize Texas and it was promptly connected in the public mind with Poinsett's alleged activities in Mexico. A great fear that the Republic was about to be invaded and dismembered
spread over the capital, and the Mexican Congress
immediately appropriated five hundred thousand
pesos to put the nation in a condition of defense.
The real lesson of the affair—the test of the loyalty
of Austin's colonists which it supplied—was lost entirely. That it tended to prove that the presence of
such adopted citizens in Texas was a guarantee of
the integrity of the national domain in that region
was completely overlooked in a wave of anti-Americanism that swept over Mexico.

It was at this moment that Adams and Clay decided to renew the proposal to revise the boundary,
and instructions were sent Poinsett, under date of
March 15th, 1827, that he might offer one million
dollars for a new boundary which would follow the
course of the Rio Grande. Clay prefaced this proposal with the observation that the numerous and extensive grants of land in Texas to Americans "authorized the belief that but little value is placed upon
the possession of that province," and that considering
the recent disturbances in Texas and the probability
of such disturbances in the future as a result of the
settlement of Americans in the province, the time
seemed auspicious to renew negotiations for a more
logical boundary. These instructions plainly took
their cue from the suggestion previously made in
Poinsett's dispatches, but Poinsett did not share the
view that the "time seemed auspicious" for such

negotiations and apparently he never made the direct offer of one million dollars for the Rio Grande boundary. He hinted privately that a money consideration might be obtained for a new boundary, and he was told by well-informed Mexican officials that neither the Mexican Government nor the Mexican Congress would consent to a sale or dismemberment of national territory, because anything of the kind would be a violation of the Federal Constitution.

But it was plain that the Fredonian disturbance appeared at Washington as a fulfillment of Poinsett's prophecy that the American colonists in Texas would be difficult for Mexico to govern. The action of the bulk of the Anglo-Americans in loyally supporting the authorities in putting down the "revolt" was as little understood at Washington as at Mexico City.

Poinsett, however, came to realize that he was wrong in supposing that trouble with Anglo-American colonists would have the effect of making Mexican leaders more willing to part with Texas. He had succeeded in negotiating a treaty of commerce with Mexico, but its ratification had been delayed in the Mexican Congress, and when it came up for discussion in the Chamber of Deputies in the midst of the excitement over the Fredonian affair angry deputies raised the question of why such a treaty should be concluded with the United States before the boundary fixed in the treaty of 1819 had been acknowledged. And so a resolution was adopted declaring that the Chamber would not give further consideration to the commercial treaty until an article should be added to it recognizing the validity of the boundary agreed upon between the United States and Spain.

When the Mexican negotiators, in accordance with this resolution, suggested that such an article be added to the commercial treaty, Poinsett agreed at once, but expressed a preference for putting it in a separate treaty. This was on January 8th, 1828, and within four days a treaty of boundaries, acknowledging the line fixed in the Spanish treaty, was drafted and signed. The United States, in the most solemn and formal fashion, again renounced all "its rights, claims, and pretentions" to Texas.

This did not settle the matter, however, for the Mexican Congress delayed action on the treaty until it was too late to exchange ratifications within the time limit. Poinsett believed that the demand for this treaty had been purely political, being made in the hope that he would refuse it. Whether this suspicion was justified, it is a fact that about the time the treaty was drafted, the Mexican commissioner who had been named to examine the ancient landmarks of the Louisiana border started for Texas to begin his investigations. This gentleman was Gen. Manuel de Miér y Terán. He arrived in Texas in March, 1828, and travelled leisurely to the Sabine. He took note of many things entirely unconnected with ancient landmarks, and he reached certain conclusions which were later to have much effect upon the affairs of Texas.

CHAPTER XIII

THE MAIN OBJECT

While there can be no doubt that Stephen Austin undertook the colonization of Texas originally as a business enterprise, conceiving it as a means of making a new start, likely to enable him to pay his debts and to win a competence for himself and family, the very character of the undertaking, as it developed, affected this motive to an extraordinary degree and in due course the means became for him an end in itself. His object grew to be that of "redeeming Texas from its wilderness state", regardless of personal advantage to himself and of everything else. This became literally the ruling passion of his life, determining his opinions and his attitude toward public questions, shaping his policies, and fixing the whole course of his career. Few men in history ever left so complete a record of themselves in letters and other documents as Austin did, and the evidence of this record on this point is overwhelming and unmistakable.

Almost from the outset Austin came to regard Texas as one of the richest undeveloped regions on earth. "Its fertility and resources," he wrote, "so far exceeding anything I had imagined, determined me to devote my life to the great object of redeeming it from the wilderness. It was a heavy undertaking for a young, inexperienced and very poor man. My first step was to study the character of the Mexicans and ascertain their ideas and views as to Texas. I found they knew nothing about it, and were profoundly ignorant of its real value, and also that they considered it next to impracticable to form a settlement in its wilderness without the aid of a very strong military force for garrisons to keep the Indians in check. I also discovered that strong prejudices existed against the North Americans owing to the conduct of some who were engaged in the revolutionary expeditions that had entered Texas at various times since 1811. I saw that all the efforts to get a foothold here by means of such expeditions had failed and ended in defeat and ruin, and I believed they always would fail. These observations convinced me that the only means of redeeming this country from the wilderness was by peaceful, silent, noiseless perseverance and industry, and that the axe, the plough, and the hoe would do more than the rifle and the sword. Under these impressions I began and have pursued the main object with a degree of patience and perseverance which nothing but its vast importance to the civilized world could ever have given me fortitude to continue through many years of hardships and amidst so many discouraging obstacles."

This determination of Austin's to "redeem Texas from the wilderness" at whatever cost was completely in harmony with the highest public interest in Texas, and even in Coahuila. And neither Austin nor the native leaders of Texas saw any conflict between this policy and the most vital interests of the republic itself. The well-being and security of the people of

Texas required that its vast wilderness be settled and its resources developed, and whatever interfered with or retarded immigration of desirable settlers was regarded by Austin and by the native leaders of Texas as against the public interest. This determined Austin's attitude on many public questions and was the guiding principle of his policies. And usually the native leaders at San Antonio (and frequently those at Saltillo as well) were in complete agreement with him.

One of the troublesome questions with which Austin had to deal from the first was that of slavery. And his attitude toward it was determined entirely by its relation to "the main object" of getting Texas settled. Austin apparently had no deep convictions one way or the other about slavery as an institution, and certainly he was in no strict sense an advocate of it. But the geographical situation of Texas and the character of its soil and climate made its rapid settlement by any except immigrants from the adjoining cotton-growing States across the American border highly impracticable. African slavery was an established institution in those States, slaves were property fully recognized by law and protected by the Constitution of the United States, and the more desirable settlers from any of those States were almost certain to be slaveholders. Austin, therefore, sought to have property in slaves given the fullest protection under the laws of the State of Coahuila and Texas.

Legal slavery did not exist in Coahuila and consequently most of the members of the Legislature which drafted the State Constitution were opposed to legalizing it. Texas had only one member in that Legislature, Bastrop, and he did everything in his power to have the provisions with respect to slavery made as liberal as possible. Brown Austin, Stephen's brother, remained at Saltillo during all the time this question was under discussion and labored in season and out to persuade the members that the absolute prohibition of slavery would destroy all hope of ever settling Texas.

Under the terms of Austin's original contract colonists had been permitted to bring in their slaves, and in one notable instance, that of Jared E. Groce, a large bonus of land had been granted in consideration of the fact that he brought with him about a hundred slaves and established a cotton plantation. Even under the State colonization law settlers were guaranteed the secure possession of whatever "property" they introduced into the State, and in practice this was interpreted as protecting the possession of slaves which were "property" in the States from which the settlers had come. There were several hundred slaves in Texas in 1826 when this matter was being considered and if the State Constitution had absolutely prohibited slavery hundreds of thousands of dollars of property would have been destroyed. Austin drafted a strong representation to the Legislature on this whole situation and urged that the introduction of slaves be permitted for a period of years in the future.

The result of all this was that the State Constitution, which was completed in March, 1827, while prohibiting slavery, provided that slaves already in the country, and those introduced within six months after the promulgation of the Constitution, should remain slaves, but that children born to slaves should be free from birth. The law putting this provision into effect required that one tenth of a master's slaves should be freed at his death if there were heirs and that all should be freed where there were no heirs. The slaves of a master who had been killed by a slave, however, were to remain in servitude. The trading in slaves, whether by importation or within the State, was prohibited.

Later Stephen Austin was able to obtain a further modification of the law so as to permit slaves to change masters, where the new master idemnified the old, thus permitting domestic trading in slaves. He also obtained other minor modifications. Then when Austin's benevolent rule came to an end through the establishing of constitutional government, which was instituted by means of the election of local officials throughout Texas in 1828, the first act of the *ayuntamiento* of San Felipe was the adoption of a petition to the Legislature requesting the enactment of a law guaranteeing the validity of contracts made by immigrants with their "servants" before entering the country. These contracts were of a character that bound the "servant" for life, thus evading the law against slavery. Fully understanding its object, the Legislature passed this law in due course.

Thus it will be seen that the Mexicans of the State of Coahuila and Texas sought to accomodate their laws to the needs of the new citizens from the United States. It was recognized that negro labor was important in the growing of cotton and that colonists from the cotton-growing States were necessary to the rapid settlement and development of Texas. It was for this reason that these concessions with respect to slavery were made.

Another question that was a little troublesome to Austin was that of the established religion. Just as in the United States most citizens at that time saw no incompatibility between a republican form of government and the institution of slavery, so the average citizen of Mexico saw no incompatibility between a republican form of government and an established religion, tolerating no other. Mexico had had an established religion longer than the institution of slavery had existed in North America, and it was hardly any more remarkable that the Mexicans did not find it essential to provide for religious toleration in their first republican Constitution than that the American people did not find it essential to provide for the abolition of slavery in their first republican Constitution. The Roman Catholic religion was the only one tolerated in Mexico and it was required that foreign settlers must either be Catholics or must become Catholics prior to entering Mexico. In practice, however, this requirement was ignored both by the settlers and by the Mexican officials. There was no great friction over this matter, except that public worship by any but Roman Catholics was prohibited. It was common knowledge among the Mexicans of the State of Coahuila and Texas that the American immigrants were almost all Protestants, but no official notice was ever taken of it.

Austin's determination to "redeem Texas from the wilderness", regardless of everything, is the key to an understanding of his attitude on this question. Any attempt to enforce the provision that all settlers should be Catholics would have retarded the colonization movement immeasurably and postponed the settlement of Texas almost indefinitely; therefore, from Austin's point of view, and from that of the native leaders of Texas as well, such an attempt would have been against the public interest. Consequently no such attempt was ever made. This question was different from that of slavery, because no property rights needing protection were involved, and so it could be safely ignored.

There seems little reason to doubt today that had things gone smoothly otherwise, the laws of the State of Coahuila and Texas would ultimately have been adjusted to the needs of the Anglo-American citizens to approximate completeness. Much credit for this situation during the sessions of the first Legislature was due to Bastrop, and it should be noted here that this interesting old man passed from the scene in 1827. He died at Saltillo in February of that year, as much of mystery about him at the end as there had been throughout the years he lived in Texas. It was necessary for the State Government to advance the money to pay for his simple funeral and it is of record that an old couple who nursed him during his last illness had to be content with the limited wardrobe of clothing he left as full compensation for their services. All of his possessions consisted of land which had little market value. Next to Stephen Austin himself, this man, who called himself a baron even with his dying breath, and may have been one for all we know to the contrary, affected the destiny of Texas more than any other single individual of that period. There is much reason to believe that it was in his brain, and not in that of Moses Austin, that the idea of colonizing Texas with Anglo-Americans was born. And it is certain that no one except Stephen Austin did as much as he did to bring that idea to reality. He was in the very truest sense one of the founders of modern Texas. During his final days he was full of plans for the development of Texas and he had every reason to believe that the colonization movement he had helped to start would continue without interruption until Texas became the most flourishing State of the Mexican Federation. And there is little doubt that this would have come to pass in due course had things gone smoothly otherwise.

But, as shall be seen in due course, things did not go smoothly in Mexico as a whole, nor with respect to the relations between Mexico and the United States. There were grave dangers ahead for the colonization policy. Bastrop's death was a serious loss to Austin in relation to all this, for it robbed him of his most able and devoted ally. And he lost another efficient helper when his brother, Brown Austin, also died in August, 1829. He was to feel the need of both of them sorely during the troubled years ahead.

CHAPTER XIV

A NEW MOVE TO BUY TEXAS

Guadalupe Victoria, the first constitutional President of Mexico, managed to serve out his full term, though he had been compelled to put down a revolt headed by the Vice President, Nicolás Bravo. In the election of 1828 the candidates for President were Manuel Gomez Pedraza, Victoria's Minister of War, and Gen. Vicente Guerrero, who had run an unsuccessful race against Victoria four years before. Pedraza received the votes of the Legislatures of ten States, while only eight voted for Guerrero, with one refraining from voting. Legally, Pedraza was elected, but he was not permitted to take his seat. Instead, there ensued the first of the successful revolts which have since become so familiar in Mexico, and Pedraza fled the country. Guerrero, who was head of the York Rite Masonic lodges which Poinsett was reputed to have had a hand in forming, was inaugurated as President on April 1st, 1829, and he began his administration under the onus of a strong suspicion that he was pro-American in sentiment. The new Vice President was Anastasio Bustamante.

Meantime, on March 4th, 1829, Andrew Jackson was inaugurated President of the United States. John Quincy Adams had reached the end of his term without accomplishing the proposed revision of the boundary between the United States and Mexico, which had been the pet project of his Secretary of State, Henry Clay. Indeed, even Poinsett's treaty accepting the boundary of the Spanish treaty had fallen through because of delay in exchanging ratifications, and Adams therefore bequeathed the whole question to his successor. Jackson did nothing with respect to it during the first five months of his administration, but when he did take it up at last it was with the determination to make a new attempt to purchase Texas from Mexico. On August 13th, 1829, Jackson sent a memorandum to his Secretary of State, Martin Van Buren, directing him to draft instructions to Poinsett authorizing him to offer five million dollars for an extension of the American boundary to the watershed between the Nueces River and the Rio Grande.

The occasion for this new move was the receipt of news at Washington that Spain was beginning a war against Mexico with the object of recovering the "rebellious province". An expedition of fifteen transports carrying three thousand men under command of Gen. Isidro Barradas, and convoyed by a fleet of five men-of-war, had sailed from Havana for the Mexican coast on July 6th. In view of this, it was reasoned at Washington that in such a war Mexico would need financial help and the friendship of the United States, and Jackson and his advisers concluded that the Mexican Government would be willing to relinquish Texas in order to preserve the independence of the country.

Unfortunately for this view, Spain's effort to reconquer Mexico proved to be a feeble and futile one and ended in complete disaster. General Baradas

landed his three thousand troops near Tampico on
July 27th and sent out copies of a proclamation calling upon the people of Mexico to rally to the support of their king. The people didn't rally, however,
and while the transports and their guardian fleet
sailed back to Cuba, General Baradas began a march
toward Tampico. This march of three weeks
through unfamiliar country was enough to defeat
Barradas. The extreme heat and the swarms of in-
sects were as effective against these invaders as an
army would have been, and when an epidemic of
fever broke out among his men Barradas almost gave
up in despair. Arriving at Tampico he found the
town completely deserted, the inhabitants having fled
at the first news of his approach. Meantime, Gen.
Antonio Lopez de Santa Anna, at that time Govern-
or of the State of Vera Cruz, had organized an expi-
detion and gone forth to meet the Spanish invader.
On September 11th, after some hide-and-seek ma-
neuvering by the two forces, Barradas surrendered
to Santa Anna, with the understanding that the remnant of his troops should be sent back to Cuba. And
so the Spanish "war" against Mexico ended within
less than two months after it had begun. Its chief
results were to make Santa Anna the national hero
of the moment and to get President Guerrero into
trouble through his exercise of dictatorial powers
which Congress had bestowed upon him in the first
frenzy of fright caused by the news of the invasion.

In the United States early in August, however, it
looked as if a formidable effort by Spain to reconquer Mexico was beginning and President Jackson
had prepared to take full advantage of the situation

this was expected to create. The suggestion that it
would afford an opportunity to negotiate the purchase
of Texas seems to have come from Anthony Butler of
Mississippi, a political hanger-on of the Jackson
camp who was among the army of job hunters that
had invaded the capital during the first months of
the new administration. Butler was ready to turn
his hand at anything that might prove profitable and
a special mission to Mexico to conduct a negotiation
involving the payment of five million dollars would
just about suit him. Poinsett also was a good Jackson
man, however, and while the President became convinced of the feasibility of the project, evidently he
decided to give Poinsett a chance at it first. Had he
consulted Poinsett about the matter before hand, he
might have been persuaded that it was impracticable.
For just about the time that Van Buren at Washington was preparing instructions on the proposed negotiation, Poinsett at Mexico City was writing an
official communication to the State Department in
which he expressed the conviction that the boundary
would never be changed without trouble. "I am still
convinced," wrote Poinsett, "that we never can expect to extend our boundary south of the river Sabine
without quarreling with these people and driving
them to court a more strict alliance with some European power."

As things turned out the whole negotiation was
entrusted to Butler. Poinsett's declaration that nothing could be done caused Jackson to have him return
to Washington on leave, while Butler went to Mexico City on this special mission. Before Butler left
the country, however, Poinsett reached the end of

his rope in Mexico. Sentiment against the American minister became so strong that Guerrero was finally compelled to yield to its pressure and he asked the American Government to recall him. The formal request that Poinsett be recalled was handed to the State Department by the Mexican minister at Washington on October 16th. Jackson changed the instructions to Poinsett accordingly, and then appointed Butler to succeed him as the American minister to Mexico.

The time was to come when Jackson would call Butler a scamp and a liar, and the record more than bears out "Old Hickory's" judgment in this respect. Butler's six years as American minister to Mexico constitute about the most disgraceful page in American diplomatic history, for his mere presence in the office for that length of time was a continuous and unmerited insult to the people of the country to which he was accredited. He was unfit for the mission entrusted to him in every imaginable particular. Aside from the fact that he was indeed both a scamp and a liar, immoral and corrupt, he had no talents calculated to qualify him for diplomacy. He was ignorant, ill-tempered, rude, and ill-mannered. His idea of the best way to acquire Texas was to use part of the purchase price in bribing Mexican officials and his general conduct in dealing with the Mexican Government fully justified every suspicion of American intention and good faith harbored by the most rabid haters of the United States in Mexico.

As chance would have it, at the moment of Butler's departure for Mexico, a new occasion of excitement arose in Texas. On October 16th, the very day that the Mexican minister at Washington was formally requesting the American Government to recall Poinsett, a letter was received at San Antonio by the Political Chief of Texas, Ramón Músquiz. It was from the Governor of the State, J. M. Viesca, and it notified him that President Guerrero, exercising the dictatorial powers bestowed upon him by Congress during the excitement of the Spanish invasion, had issued a decree absolutely abolishing slavery throughout Mexico! A copy of the decree was transmitted to Músquiz for publication in Texas and he was instructed to see that it was put into effect. There were about one thousand slaves in Texas at that time, recognized as property under the laws and the Constitution of the State of Coahuila and Texas, and their value was close to a million dollars. The effect of Guerrero's decree was to destroy all of this property by a stroke of the pen.

The real author of this decree was a certain José Maria Tornel, who was violently opposed to the policy of Anglo-American colonization in Texas and who for some time had been advocating the absolute prohibition of slavery as an effective measure to break up the Texas settlements and stop American immigration. On two occasions he had succeeded in getting a bill passed by the Mexican Senate embodying his ideas on this subject, but each time the Chamber of Deputies had defeated it. When Guerrero was invested with dictatorial powers, Tornel saw an opportunity to have his pet measure put into effect. Accordingly he prepared a decree abolishing slav-

ery absolutely and prohibiting it in the future and he
induced Guerrero to sign it.

The total effect of Tornel's slavery decree, however, was to demonstrate in striking fashion the attitude of the native leaders of Coahuila and Texas
toward the Anglo-American settlements. It happened that Austin was ill at the time and confined to
his bed. But without waiting to consult him about
it, Músquiz took upon himself the responsibility to
withhold publication of the decree and immediately
he prepared a strong representation to Governor
Viesca, to be transmitted by him to Mexico City, setting forth why Texas should be excepted from its
provisions. Músquiz made clear that the slaves in
Texas were there under the authority of the laws and
the Constitution of the State of Coahuila and Texas,
as well as under the Federal laws, that they constituted an immense amount of property which not only
was guaranteed by the laws, but was absolutely necessary to the carrying on of agriculture in Texas, and
finally that to put the decree into effect would ruin a
great number of peaceful and desirable citizens of
the State.

Governor Viesca in transmitting this representation to the President added one of his own, in which
he declared that he would have asked that the decree
be suspended as to Texas, even if the Political Chief
had not made the request. He paid a tribute to the
Anglo-American settlers as peaceful and law-abiding citizens, but expressed the opinion that if the
decree should be published in Texas it would be certain to cause violent resistance and "commotions", in-

timating that the settlers would be more than human if they should act otherwise. José Antonio Navarro, one of the Texas members of the Legislature, and several members of that body from Coahuila joined in writing strong letters to the Federal Government and appealing to influential friends in Mexico City to assist in having Texas excepted from the decree. It was a striking demonstration of the attitude of the native leaders of Coahuila and Texas toward the Anglo-American settlements.

News that such a decree had been issued leaked out at Nacogdoches and spread widely as a rumor, causing great anxiety and excitement. John Durst, a leading citizen of Nacogdoches, wrote Austin about it. "In the name of God," he wrote, "what shall we do? For God's sake advise me on the subject by the return of mail. We are ruined forever should this measure be adopted."

In replying to Durst, Austin made his own position clear. He held that the decree was plainly unconstitutional and declared that if Texas were not excepted from its provisions it should be resisted. "Mexico has not within its whole domain," he wrote, "a man who would defend its independence, the union of its territory, and all its constitutional rights sooner than I would, or be more ready and willing to discharge his duties as a Mexican citizen; one of the first and most sacred of those duties is to protect my constitutional rights, and I will do it so far as I am able. I am the owner of one slave only, an old decrepit woman, not worth much, but in this matter I should feel that my constitutional rights as a Mex-

ican were just as much infringed as they would be if
I had a thousand; it is the principle and not the
amount, the latter makes the violation more aggravated but not more illegal or unconstitutional."

In due course President Guerrero acted on the representations from the Governor and the Political
Chief. It happened that Augustín Viesca, brother
of the Governor, was the Secretary of Relations, and
he saw to it that the matter received prompt attention. Under date of December 2nd he wrote the Governor that the President had been pleased to accede
to the petitions and to "declare the department of
Texas excepted from the general disposition comprehended in said decree." "Therefore," he continued,
"his Excellency declares that no change must be made
as respects the slaves that legally exist in that part of
your State."

But it was in the midst of the anxiety and excitement caused by the news of the slavery decree that
Anthony Butler passed through Texas on his way to
assume his mission at Mexico City. His big secret was
too much for him to keep to himself. He told a few
persons "confidentially" that he was going to the capital to buy Texas for five million dollars, and very
naturally the news got around. It reached Mexico
City ahead of him, and by the time he arrived there
the newspapers had already fully apprised the public
at large of the object of his coming.

Meantime, there had begun to appear in newspapers in the United States inspired articles in which
the old grounds of the claim of the United States to
Texas were rehashed and the advantages that would
accrue to the United States from an extension of the

boundary beyond the Sabine were set forth. News of this was duly communicated to the Mexican Government by its minister at Washington. Guerrero, however, was having his own troubles at home, and Butler never got an opportunity to present the proposal to him. For a new revolt, headed by Vice President Bustamante, was now in progress, a revolt backed by the very men who most strongly suspected the intentions of the United States and who believed there existed a direct connection between those intentions and the Anglo-American colonization of Texas. Even Poinsett did not receive his passports from Guerrero, for when the time came for him to leave a new regime was already in charge. It was to this new regime that Butler was destined to propose the sale of Texas to the United States, a regime which prepared at once to take steps to stop Anglo-American immigration to Texas altogether and thus to defeat the "plot" of the Colossus of the North to dismember the Republic!

While all this was going forward, *The Genius of Universal Emancipation,* an obscure propaganda periodical edited by Benjamin Lundy and a certain William Lloyd Garrison, commented on the articles appearing in American newspapers advocating the purchase of Texas, branding them as unmistakable evidence of a scheme of the Southern "slave power" to add "five or six more slave-holding States to this Union." "A greater curse could scarcely befall our country," declared this oracular organ of abolition, "than the annexation of that immense territory to this republic, if the system of slavery should likewise be reestablished there."

And this, be it noted, was in 1829!

CHAPTER XV

MEXICO PUTS UP THE BARS

During the closing months of 1829 and the opening months of 1830 there was general apprehension among public men in Mexico over the intentions of the United States with respect of Texas. All kinds of rumors were current. The commander of the garrison at Nacogdoches, the Mexican outpost on the American frontier, reported to his superior, the Commandant of the Eastern Interior Provinces, which included Texas, that the United States was moving troops to the border. He reported also that an unusual number of Americans were arriving in Texas, not all of them to settle, that there was a story current that men were being recruited at New Orleans for a filibustering expedition into Texas with the object of revolutionizing it, and that the chief subject of conversation throughout the frontier country was the intention of President Jackson to take possession of Texas.

This communication was dated December 8th, 1829, which, it should be noted, was immediately after Anthony Butler, the new American minister to Mexico, had passed through Texas on his way to Mexico City. The Bustamante revolt against Guerrero had broken out only a few days before.

The Commandant of the Eastern Interior Provinces at this time was General Manuél de Miér y Terán. He was a well educated and enlightened man, intensely patriotic and public spirited, and, like many others of his caliber, was sincerely and genuinely concerned about the fate of Texas. As has already been recorded, he had visited Texas for the first time more than a year before this, as a commissioner to investigate ancient landmarks of the border, and his observations at that time, as reported to President Victoria, were of such a characer as to impel him to recommend strongly that Mexico must "occupy Texas or lose it". He noted that as one travelled east from San Antonio to the American border the dominance of Anglo-American influence became absolute, that the only Mexicans in the region were of the lowest and most ignorant class, that the American colonists maintained the closest relations with the United States, trading exclusively with that country, sending their children there to attend school, and maintaining only the most superficial relations with the rest of Mexico.

Incidentally, Terán met Austin during this visit, and the latter had urged upon him the importance of several economic reforms which would serve to promote the progress and prosperity of Texas and at the same time bind the Texans to Mexico. Chief among these were the creation of a port at the mouth of the Brazos, the suspension of all import duties for a period of years, and the establishment of a coastwide trade, so that Texas cotton might be exported to England by way of Vera Cruz, instead of going to the

United States. Terán had been impressed with the
importance of these measures, but he had also decided, on the basis of his observations, that Mexico
should maintain a stronger military force in Texas
and take steps to colonize the border and coast regions
with native Mexicans and immigrants from other
countries besides the United States. All this he had
come to believe as the result of his sojourn in Texas
in 1828. It is not to be doubted that he talked with
Bustamante on this subject, for in addition to the fact
that Bustamante was then the Commandant of the
Easern Interior Provinces, the two men were fast
friends. Terán had succeeded Bustamante as Commandant when the latter had resigned to become Vice
President, and now Bustamante, as the result of a
successful revolt, was about to become President. It
can be well imagined that the report from the commander of the Nacogdoches garrison served to con-
firm Terán in his belief that something should be
done to "save Texas" without delay, and it is not remarkable that he took the first opportunity after the
triumph of his friend, Bustamante, to submit detailed recommendations with respect to the matter.

Meantime, Anthony Butler arrived in Mexico
City. Poinsett lost no time in turning the affairs of
his office over to him and departed for home. It was
now to be Butler's task to undertake the delicate negotiation at which Poinsett had failed. At this distance the spectacle of the polite and suave Poinsett,
a man of undoubted diplomatic talents, being sup-
planted by such a man as Butler seems grotesque.

But President Jackson had absolute confidence in Butler.

"I have full confidence," wrote Jackson in a personal letter to Butler, "you will effect the purchase of Texas, so important for the perpetuation of that harmony and peace between us and the Republic of Mexico, so desirable to them and to us to be maintained forever, and if not obtained, is sure to bring us into conflict, owing to their jealousy and the dissatisfaction of those Americans now settling in Texas under the authority of Mexico—who will declare themselves independent of Mexico the moment they acquire sufficient numbers. This our own Government will be charged with fomenting, although all our constitutional powers will be exercised to prevent. You will keep this steadily in view, and their own safety, if it is considered, will induce them to yield now in the present reduced state of their finances."

This was Jackson's view. The Mexican view was voiced shortly after Butler's arrival in Mexico City by the newspaper *El Sol,* which expressed the opinion that the American minister had so far made no overtures on the subject of the purchase of Texas because "we presume that he does the new administration the justice to suppose it incapable of a transaction as prejudicial and degrading to the Republic as it would be disgraceful to the minister who would subscribe to it".

Within two weeks after Butler had taken charge, Terán's recommendations with respect to Texas were presented in a report to the war department by his

aide, Col. Constantino Tarnava. Terán's view of
Butler's mission may be summed up in his own words,
for he declared that "he who consents to, or does not
oppose the loss of Texas is an execrable traitor."

Terán's program was a combination of some of
the economic measures which Austin had urged upon
him and other measures of his own, born of his fear
of the United States. They were divided into military and political measures, the military measures
being as follows:

1. The removal to the Nueces of several companies
now on the Rio Grande.

2. The establishment of a strong and permanent
garrison at the main crossing of the Brazos River,
that there might be an intermediate force in the unsettled region separating Nacogdoches and San Antonio.

3. The reinforcement of the existing garrisons in
Texas by filling the quota of infantry properly belonging to them.

4. The occupation and fortification of some point
above Galveston Bay, and another at the Brazos, for
the purpose of controlling the Anglo-American settlements.

5. The establishment of communications by sea between other Mexican ports and Texas.

The political and economic measures recommended were as follows:

1. The transportation of Mexican convict soldiers
to Texas where they would settle after the expiration
of their terms.

2. The encouragement by all legitimate means of the migration of Mexican families to Texas.

3. The colonization of Texas with Swiss and German immigrants, whose language and customs, being different from those of the people of the United States, would make less dangerous the proximity of the latter to Texas.

4. The encouragement of coastwise trade as the only means of establishing close relations between Texas and the other parts of the Republic, to the end that the department of Texas, so North American in spirit, might be nationalized.

Terán had previously submitted to the Government an argument setting forth why such measures should be adopted to insure the safety of Texas against American encroachment. He cited the events of the previous thirty years, during which Louisiana and Florida had been acquired by the United States. He pictured the coming of Anglo-American settlers into a region as an inevitable forerunner of the diplomatic negotiations which ended always in the region passing under the American flag. He made out a convincing case, from the Mexican point of view, for the thesis that the stage had been reached in Texas where it was necessary for Mexico to occupy that region or lose it. In recommending Mexican colonization, he said he recognized that "Mexicans are little disposed to enterprises of this nature," but he added that "whatever obstacles may be encountered must be overcome, for these measures involve the safety of the nation and the integrity of our territory." It is significant, however, that Terán did not recommend that further American immigration be prohibited.

But this last proposal was added by Lucas Alamán, whom Bustamante had chosen as his Minister of Foreign and Domestic Relations, and whose duty it became to present the matter to Congress. Alamán, who subsequently became a distinguished Mexican historian, had been educated in Europe, and his whole attitude toward the United States was European. He was now thirty-one years old, well launched on a public career in his native country, and he palpably enjoyed the rôle assigned him of checkmating the ambitions of the United States. In presenting the matter to Congress, which he did on February 8th, 1830, he adopted Terán's arguments and even his language as his own, and added some special arguments prompted by his intense aversion to all things American and his perverted view of American history.

"The United States of the North," Alamán declared to the Mexican Congress, "has been going on successfully acquiring, without awakening public attention, all the territories adjoining theirs . . . . They begin by introducing themselves into the territory which they covet, upon pretense of commercial negotiations, or of the establishment of colonies, with or without the assent of the Government to which it belongs. These colonies grow, multiply, become the predominant party of the population; and as soon as a support is found in this manner, they begin to set up rights which it is impossible to sustain in a serious discussion, and to bring forward ridiculous pretentions, founded upon historical facts which are admitted by nobody . . . These extravagant opinions are for the first time presented by unknown writers; and the labor which is employed by others in offering proofs and reasonings is spent by them in repetitions and multiplied allegations, for the purpose of drawing the attention of their fellow-citizens, not upon the justice of the proposition but upon advantages and interests to be obtained or subserved by their admission."

This was a reference to the articles which had appeared in American newspapers during the previous few months in which a claim had been set up to Texas as a part of the Louisiana Purchase on the ground of La Salle's settlement.

"Their machinations in the country they wish to acquire," continued Alamán, "are then brought to light by the appearance of explorers, some of whom settle on the soil, alleging that their presence does not affect the question of sovereignty or possession of the land. These pioneers excite, by degrees, movements which disturb the political state of the country in dispute, and then follow discontent and dissatisfaction, calculated to tire the patience of the legitimate owner, and to diminish the usefulness of the administration and of the exercise of authority. When things have come to this pass, which is precisely the present state of things in Texas, the diplomatic intrigue begins. The inquietude they have excited in the territory in dispute, the interests of the colonists therein establshed, the insurrection of adventurers, and savages instigated by them, and the pertinacity with which the opinion is set up as to the right of their possession, become the subject of notes, full of expressions of justice and moderation, until, with the aid of other incidents, which are never wanting in the course of diplomatic relations, the desired end is attained of concluding an arrangement as onerous for one party as it is advantageous to the other.

"Sometimes more direct means are resorted to; and taking advantage of the enfeebled state, or domestic difficulties, of the possessor of the soil, they proceed upon the most extraordinary pretexts to make themselves masters of the country, as was the case in the Floridas; leaving the question to be decided afterwards as to the legality of the possession, which force alone could take from them. This conduct has given them the immense extent of country they occupy, and which they have acquired since their separation from England; and this is what they have set on foot with respect to Texas."

It is hardly necessary to say that this description of the expansion of the United States was entirely imaginary. The chief expansion which the United States had undergone was that into Louisiana, and it was Napoleon Bonaparte who took that territory from Spain, and who sold it to the United States for a cash consideration. Anglo-Americans who had become Spanish subjects in Louisiana had had nothing to do with the transfer of the territory to the United States. And there had been no Anglo-American colonization of Florida.

In any event, the description did not fit Texas at all, for the Anglo-American settlers had come at

Mexico's invitation and under the terms of Mexican colonization laws. Moreover, the Texans had nothing whatever to do with the efforts of the United States to acquire Texas; they had helped to put down the Fredonian disturbance, the only one that had occurred in Texas; and they were in no wise responsible for the fear of American encroachment which had taken hold of so many Mexican leaders with such violence.

Indeed, almost at the very time Alamán was presenting this argument to Congress, Stephen Austin was writing to his brother-in-law, urging his removal from Missouri to Texas, as follows: "I have never been so thoroughly convinced as I now am of the future rapid rise of this country. You have no idea of it, or you would be here before April, family and all. This is the most liberal and munificent Government on earth to emigrants—after being here one year you will oppose a change even to Uncle Sam." And a few weeks later he was to write him again as follows: "We have nothing to fear from this Government nor from any other quarter except from the United States of the North. If that Government should get hold of us and introduce its *land system,* etc., etc., thousands who are now on the move and who have not yet secured their titles, would be totally ruined. The greatest misfortune that could befall Texas at this moment would be a sudden change by which many of the emigrants would be thrown upon the liberality of the Congress of the United States of the North—*theirs would be a most forlorn hope.*"

Austin had seen Anglo-American settlers in Spanish territory ruined before by a sudden transfer of sovereignty—in Missouri at the time of the Louisiana Purchase—and he didn't want to see it repeated in Texas. But it is only fair to say that he wrote these letters in the first flush of rejoicing over the prompt revocation of Guerrero's edict abolishing slavery. However, that does not change the circumstance that he and his colonists were loyal to Mexico and had every expectation of remaining so.

But Alamán was convinced apparently that the situation was quite otherwise, and he went Terán one better. Not only did he recommend the enactment of the military and economic measures proposed by Terán, but he urged Congress to repeal the national colonization law so far as it applied to the State of Coahuila and Texas, suspending all existing colonization contracts and taking away from the State the power to make new contracts.

As these recommendations were made to Congress as measures involving the national safety and the integrity of the national territory, they were promptly enacted into law. Congress did not find it necessary to annul the State colonization law, however, but adopted another means toward the same end. The Federal colonization law provided that "foreigners of any particular nation might be excluded at any time," so in addition to the provisions covered in Terán's recommendations, Congress enacted the following provision:

"Article II. In accordance with the right reserved by the General Congress in the seventh article of the Law of August 18th, 1824, it is prohibited that emigrants from nations bordering on this Republic shall settle in the States and territories adjacent to their own nation. Consequently, all contracts not already completed and not in harmony with this law are suspended."

The intent of this provision was to prohibit Americans from settling in Texas, New Mexico, or California.

Because of the date on which it was signed and promulgated, the new law came to be known as the Law of April 6th, 1830. It was the fruit of the suspicion, distrust, and fear which had been planted in the hearts of Mexican leaders by the attitude of the United States toward the Treaty of 1819 during the administrations of John Quincy Adams and Andrew Jackson, and the efforts to have the boundary fixed by that treaty changed so as to include Texas within the borders of the United States. Its intent was to reverse completely the colonization policy adopted at the birth of the Mexican Republic, and its avowed object was to "save Texas from the imperialistic designs of the United States." And yet it was aimed at the very heart of Mexico's chief safeguard against such a danger—the safeguard, that is, which was afforded by the loyalty of her Anglo-American citizens in Texas.

CHAPTER XVI

WANTED: MEXICAN COLONISTS

THE object which the Law of April 6th, 1830, was designed to accomplish was that of occupying Texas and nationalizing or "Mexicanizing" it. Its intent was to stop American immigration altogether and to promote the settlement of Texas by Mexicans and colonists from European countries. The establishing of four new military posts and the strengthening of those already in existence had a double object. This measure was intended, first of all, to insure the territorial integrity of Texas against the designs of the United States and the suspected purpose of the Anglo-Americans in the country to separate it from Mexico. It was intended, secondly, that the new posts should form the beginnings of settlements of Mexicans. Soldiers were to be encouraged to settle in the country at their discharge, the Government paying the expenses of the transportation of their families to Texas, and the supply was to be replenished by sending convict soldiers to Texas, instead of to Vera Cruz and other penal forts. In addition to this, Mexican colonists were to be recruited in others parts of the Republic, settled in Texas under a generous system of Government aid, and everything done to make their settlements permanent and prosperous. In other words, the new law was intended to induce Mexicans to live in Texas, something which more than a century of previous effort had failed to accomplish.

There are no reliable figures with respect to the population of Texas in 1830, but the total was probably around 12,000. Ten years before the population had not been more than 3,000. The new population was almost entirely made up of Anglo-Americans. Nearly half of the total was in the region referred to roughly as "Austin's colony"—the settlements along the Colorado and Brazos rivers. The bulk of the Mexican population was west and south of this region, along San Antonio River, centering chiefly at San Antonio and Goliad. East of the Austin settlements, in the region around Nacogdoches and along the streams near the coast, the country was populated by immigrants from the United States, most of whom were without formal titles to the land they occupied, and by Spanish and Mexican creoles, some of whom were descendants of the earliest European settlers of Texas. A large majority of the population of Texas, therefore, exclusive of Indians and negro "servants", was composed of Anglo-Americans. The region between the San Antonio River and the Sabine was populated almost entirely by Anglo-Americans, and considerably more than half of them were in Austin's settlements. Indeed, if those of DeWitt's colony, which was situated between Austin's settlements and San Antonio, are included, it may be said that at least two-thirds of the Anglo-

Americans in Texas in 1830 were west of the Trinity River.

Practically all of these were landholders, introduced by the *empresarios* Austin and DeWitt, and had either already received formal titles to their land or would receive them in due course in accordance with well established governmental procedure. In the region to the east of these settlements, however, there was a considerable population of Anglo-Americans, most of whom had not been introduced by an *empresario* and very few of whom had valid titles to the land they occupied. Both the State and Federal Governments had formally recognized these settlers as entitled to their land under the colonization laws, and had promised that they would be given titles, but this promise had not been redeemed when the Law of April 6th, 1830, went into effect.

Aside from Austin and DeWitt, the various *empresarios* who had received contracts under the State law to introduce settlers had made little progress toward fulfilling them. Some of them had organized land and colonization companies in the United States through the sale of stock, and had inaugurated a practice of selling "land scrip". During the previous year one of these companies had inserted glowing advertisements in newspapers in the United States, inviting investors to purchase its stock, and representing that it owned an immense "grant" of land in Texas. The scrip issued by these companies also was supposed to represent a stated amount of land. Of course, none of these companies owned any land in Texas, for the *empresario* contracts did not carry with them the ownership of land. They provided merely for a bonus of land to be given for the introduction of every one hundred families, but even this bonus land could not be owned by non-residents of Mexico. Whether the representations made by these companies were the result of an honest misunderstanding of the law or not, in effect they were fraudulent, and purchasers of this stock and scrip alike were destined to lose their money. This would have been true if the Law of April 6th, 1830, had never been passed. But one effect of the law was to suspend and, in fact, cancel all such contracts.

General Terán, who, as Commandant of the Eastern Interior Provinces, would have had charge of the military measures in any event, was named commissioner to carry out the other features of the law also. It will be recalled that the stopping of American immigration had not been part of his recommendations to the Government, not because he favored American immigration, but because he believed it would be impracticable to attempt to stop it. When Austin insisted, therefore, that the new law did not apply to his colony, on the ground that it already was "established" and consequently exempt, Terán agreed with him, and in the course of a few months the official interpretation of the law was that immigration of Americans to Texas was prohibited, except in the case of those bound for Austin's or DeWitt's colony, and a regular procedure to insure the safe conduct of such immigrants across the frontier was established. So Alamán's pet provision of barring Americans from Texas altogether was circumvented and made a dead letter. But this was not accomplished without much plain-speaking by Austin, who wrote frank letters to Alamán, Terán and other State and Federal officials, and even to Bustamante himself, condemning the law.

The first effect of the law on the public mind in Texas was very disturbing, especially in East Texas where the settlers were without titles to their lands, but Austin, while criticising the law severely in his correspondence with Mexican officials, minimized its worst features and defended its better ones in dealing with the settlers. He inspired a series of editorials in the *Texas Gazette* in which it was pointed out that the law did not prohibit American imigration, as had been charged, that only the paper contracts which had not been fulfilled were cancelled, that the new garrisons provided protection for the frontier, relief from militia duty and a home market for Texas products, and finally that other features of the law were intended to promote trade between Texas and other Mexican ports and to encourage the development of domestic industry. He did everything to allay discontent among his own colonists, and he urged upon Terán the importance of having the East Texas settlers set at rest with respect to the titles to their lands. When Terán suggesed that Austin might fill his own contracts by inducing the East Texans to move into his colony, he pointed out emphatically that this would be unfair to those settlers who had improved their lands and established homes, and that instead of being compelled to move they ought to be given titles to their lands without delay, so as to reestablish their confidence in the Government.

It was during this period that Austin developed in his correspondence with Mexican officials the main outlines of the policy toward Texas which he continued to urge during the next five years as the proper one for Mexico to follow. Texas should be peopled as rapidly as possible with honest and industrious immigrants, irrespective of nationality, and be given local self-government by being made a State, separate from Coahuila. Military rule should not be attempted in Texas; the Anglo-Americans could not be ruled in this way; to attempt such rule was to court the loss of Texas through secession; the Anglo-Americans did not want to separate from Mexico, and especially they did not want to unite with the United States of the North; they could be trusted to remain loyal to Mexico if they were permitted to govern themselves; but the subjection of Texas to Coahuila was bad, and the establishing of military rule in Texas was worse; Texas should be made into a separate State, and troops should be withdrawn. This was the advice which Austin now began to urge upon those Mexican leaders with whom he corresponded. The policy embodied in the Law of April 6th, 1830, would condemn Texas to be permanently a wilderness, he declared, for Mexicans could not be induced to emigrate to Texas, and there was little hope of obtaining immigrants from Europe.

Austin made it clear to Terán that he was very much discouraged by the enactment of such a law,

and that he did not relish the prospect of passing
the remainder of his life as he had passed the years
since 1821.

"Better to adopt a system of free immigration to
Texas," he wrote Terán, "or condemn it at once to
the wilderness, the Indians, and the presidials. You
know the difficulty of populating this country with
Mexicans, and to do so with Europeans is the work
of a century. . . . I have had the idea that it was the
interest and the policy of Mexico to make Texas a
State in order to have a bulwark on its northern frontier; and I have had an ambition to assist in the advancement of this country to the extent of my ability.
But I confess that I am beginning to doubt whether
Texas will for a great many years be more than a depopulated waste."

Austin's object in writing in this strain to Terán,
Alamán, and other leaders was obviously to win them
away from the mistaken policy embodied in the Law
of April 6th, 1830, but meantime they were proceeding to put this law into effect. While the provision
barring Americans from the country was modified so
as to admit them into Austin's and DeWitt's colonies,
the most thickly settled sections of Texas, it was the
cause of much friction and not a little discontent.
This was especially true in East Texas, which did not
enjoy the privileges of this exemption, and where
Americans were forbidden to settle. For a time
there was danger of trouble in that section. Only a
few months before the passage of the law, the State
Government had sent a commissioner to that section
to put the settlers in legal possession of their lands

and issue them titles, but before he had well started this work the commissioner had been arrested in connection with a killing, and the settlers were compelled to face another delay. It had been in the midst of this disappointment that the East Texans had received the news of the provisions of the new law, which seemed to mean that they would never receive titles to their lands and that they might be in danger of being ordered to leave the country. Austin, in this situation, suggested that they petition the State Government to appoint a new commissioner, and it was decided to take his advice. This allayed the discontent for the time being, but it was likely to flare up again at any time.

Terán carried out the military provisions of the law as promptly as his resources permitted. The garrisons at Nacogdoches, San Antonio, and Goliad were strengthened, and new posts were established as provided for in his original plans. In accordance with the patriotic object of these new posts, which were expected to become Mexican settlements in due course, they were given Aztec names. Tenoxititlán was established on the Brazos, near the point where it was crossed by the San Antonio-Nacogdoches road; Anáhuac was planted on Galveston Bay; and Lipantitlán near the mouth of the Nueces. A small garrison was stationed on the Neches and named Terán, in honor of the Commandant, and another on the Lavaca simply took the name of that stream, which at least was Spanish. Later a garrison was established near the mouth of the Brazos at Velasco, and this name, too, was deemed suitable.

These posts were distributed in such a way that the Mexican settlements which were expected to grow up around them would be strategically placed in connection with the program to Mexicanize Texas.

The mere establishing of the new posts, however, constituted little progress in carrying out that ambitious program. It was necessary that Mexican colonists should be brought in from other parts of the Republic. In this connection, it soon developed that the State authorities of Coahuila and Texas were not enthusiastic about the new law. As a matter of fact most of the Mexican citizens of Texas and many of the leaders were absolutely opposed to the law because it was calculated to retard the development of the country. The State authorities insisted that Terán, though a Federal official, should comply with the State colonization law in every way, that the Mexican settlers should be introduced under contract, that the number it was intended to introduce should be stated, and so on. All of the obstacles which red tape could provide were put in the way. But these were hardly necessary, for the plain truth was that the Federal Government could not induce Mexican settlers to move to Texas. It was in vain that Alamán sent circulars to the various Governors suggesting that they make known to the poor of their respective States the advantages which the Government was offering to those who would move to Texas. These appeals simply brought no response. There were no Mexican colonists to be had. Terán admitted as much to Austin in due course. The plan of Mexicanizing Texas was a failure before it was well started.

Meantime great damage had been done to the policy of settling Texas with Anglo-Americans. The net result of the new policy had been to station garrisons all over Texas, to interfere with the flow of immigration to Texas, and to create widespread discontent among the Anglo-Americans, especially those in East Texas. This was not a gain for Mexico. On the contrary, the strain it placed upon the loyalty of the Anglo-American citizens in Texas was so great as to constitute a net loss to Mexico. It was a partial defeat of the very object the new policy was intended to serve: that of protecting the national territory from the "imperialistic designs of the United States". For it turned the thoughts of some of the Texans toward the United States as a source of relief. However, during the first year of the new policy nothing occurred in Texas against which the Government could complain as indicating disloyalty or even insubordination on the part of the Anglo-American citizens, a circumstance which surprised some of those who had been responsible for the policy. It was admitted that the law was a mistake, but nothing was done. Had all the new troops been withdrawn from Texas without delay and the policy reversed, the damage might have been repaired. But the troops remained, and in due course real occasions for friction arose, as was natural in such circumstances. And these occasions were of Mexico's own making.

CHAPTER XVII

A PAIR OF PETTY TYRANTS

It is a curious fact that when the Mexican Government embarked upon the task of "nationalizing" Texas, and thus saving it from the "imperialistic designs of the United States," it selected Americans as two of its most important agents.

George Fisher, a native of Serbia who had been naturalized as a citizen of the United States in 1822, was literally imported into Texas to assume the post of "administrator of the port of Galveston," and Col. John Davis Bradburn, a Kentuckian by birth, who had been an officer in the Mexican army for a number of years, was sent by Terán to Galveston Bay to establish and maintain the fort of Anáhuac near the mouth of the Trinity.

From all accounts, both men were unfitted for the tasks to which they were assigned, Fisher being described as an egotistical and windy sort of a person, whom the Texans suspected of double-dealing, and Bradburn being a pompous, irascible, and arbitrary man, utterly devoid of a sense of humor and apparently without imagination. In sending these two men to Texas, the Mexican Government contributed to the situation the very elements necessary to insure friction with the Anglo-Americans and to lead ultimately, though inevitably, to disturbances of a serious character.

Fisher at first made a good impression. He arrived in Texas early in May, 1830, and announced in the *Texas Gazette* that he would establish a custom house temporarily at the mouth of the Brazos, and would place a deputy at Galveston. No port had been officially established at the mouth of the Brazos, though this had been promised, but it had been the practice for several years for vessels to unload cargoes at Brazoria. Fisher's announcement that he would establish headquarters at the mouth of the Brazos, merely sending a deputy to Galveston, indicated that he proposed to adjust himself to the existing situation and cause as little friction as possible. However, before he had carried this plan into effect, Terán issued an order suspending establishment of custom houses in Texas for the time being, thus leaving Fisher without employment.

Having a knowledge of both English and Spanish, he did not remain unemployed very long, and in due course he was installed as temporary secretary of the *ayuntamiento* at San Felipe. That he had won the confidence of the leaders of Austin's colony is indicated by the circumstance that in August, 1830, he was named a member of a committee, with Austin and Samuel M. Williams, to make arrangements for a formal celebration of the anniversary of Mexican independence. But this condition did not last, for it was soon discovered that Fisher was doctoring his translations of the proceedings of the *ayuntamiento* and its communications to the State and Federal Governments in such a way as to misrepresent the sentiments of the Texans, and he was dismissed in disgrace. The *ayuntamiento* expressed the belief, in notifying Terán of this action, that Fisher was a spy, representing some interest unfriendly to the Government or interested in making trouble between the Government and the Texans. Thenceforth, the feelings existing between Fisher and the Texans were hardly to be described as cordial, a circumstance of no little importance in relation to subsequent events.

Meantime, in the fall of 1830, Bradburn arrived in Texas, in command of about 150 Mexican soldiers, to establish the fort of Anáhuac on Galveston Bay, near the mouth of the Trinity. Terán's instructions to Bradburn were detailed and specific. He was to use the utmost tact in dealing with the Texans and avoid occasions for friction. In building the barracks, for example, he was to employ carpenters and other workmen from among the settlers at Atascosito, and he was to impress upon them the advantage of having the fort so near to their settlement in that it would provide a profitable market for their products and contribute generally to their prosperity. These settlers, Terán informed Bradburn, had settled in Texas originally without proper authority, but both the State and Federal Governments had approved their settlement and had promised them titles to their lands. Bradburn must reassure them with respect to their titles and invite them to act through him in petitioning the Government. Terán instructed Bradburn further that he must notify all alcaldes in his district of his arrival, and must be careful not to interfere in any way in the administration of civil

affairs. Had Bradburn followed these instructions
faithfully, undoubtedly there would be a different
story to tell.

The settlement then known as Atascosito (later
called Liberty) was on the Trinity River, a short distance from the coast. It was one of five large settlements in East Texas composed of Anglo-Americans who had taken up land originally without authority, but whose settlement had been subsequently
approved by the Federal and State Governments.
Three of these settlements were along the Louisiana
border, being known as Ais, Tenaha, and Sabine, and
like the settlers at Atascosito they had been promised
titles to their lands. The fifth such settlement was
along the San Jacinto, nearer to Austin's colony than
the others, and in response to a petition which the
settlers there forwarded to the Government, the area
covered by Austin's colony had been extended so as
to include their lands within its boundaries.

All of these settlements had opposed the Fredonian
revolt during the winter of 1826-27, and in recognition of this President Guerrero, in 1828, had signed
formal orders approving and legalizing them, and
acknowledging the right of the settlers to their lands.
As has already been related, a commissioner was sent
to Texas in February, 1830, to survey and issue titles
to these lands, but before he had started work he had
been arrested in connection with a killing and nothing further had been done. This was the situation
when Bradburn established Anáhuac on Galveston
Bay.

The general character of these settlements may be
judged from a report made by a representative of

the Government in 1827, with respect to those along the Louisiana border. This report related that the settlers had introduced many improvements in the country, including roads, ferries, flour and meal mills, and five cotton gins, that their houses ranged in value from $200 to $800, that they owned herds of cattle and hogs, and that they had marketed two hundred bales of cotton in Louisiana in 1826. By 1830 the border settlements had grown considerably, and the settlement at Atascosito on the Trinity was of the same general character.

The State authorities of the State of Coahuila and Texas, it should be remarked, regarded these settlements as an important part of the material development of the State, and were friendly toward them, as they were toward Anglo-American colonization in general. It was their intention that valid land titles should be issued to these settlers and encouragement given to their progress and prosperity. About the time that Bradburn was being sent to Texas by Terán, therefore, the State Government appointed J. Francisco Madero as commissioner and José Mariá Carbajal as surveyor to put the East Texas settlers in legal possession of their lands. On January 14th, 1831, Madero announced by formal notice in the *Texas Gazette* that he would begin surveys at the settlement on the Trinity at once, and would proceed later to the border settlements. This announcement was greeted with rejoicing by the settlers affected, for it meant that their fears with respect to the Law of April 6th, 1830, had proved groundless. This feeling was shortly turned to indignation, however, when it became known that Bradburn took the position that Madero was without authority to issue any titles. Bradburn contended that the issuance of such titles would be a violation of the Law of April 6th, 1830, and notified Madero to that effect. Madero replied that Bradburn was mistaken, that the settlers' right to their lands had been recognized and approved by both the State and Federal Governments long before the Law of April 6th, 1830, had been enacted, and that he intended to issue titles only to settlers who had been in the country prior to the enactment of the law. Bradburn, however, insisted on his own interpretation of the law, and forbade Madero to proceed. Madero stood his ground, and in spite of Bradburn's threats he and his surveyor, Carbajal, began their work. Whereupon, Bradburn placed the two officials under arrest and imprisoned them in the fort at Anáhuac.

Thus intimidated by the military power, Madero agreed not to attempt to issue any titles, and he and his surveyor were released. The settlers at Atascosito were without any local government, however, and Madero proceeded, under State authority, to organize them into a municipality and to institute an *ayuntamiento* for their settlement. He gave the municipality the name of "the village of the Holy Trinity of Liberty," which was promptly shortened to "Liberty." He then returned to the State capital to report Bradburn's high-handed action.

But Bradburn was not through. He declared that Atascosito or Liberty was within the ten league coast reserve and beyond Madero's jurisdiction, and issued an order annulling the action creating the *ayuntamiento*. He then proceeded to institute an *ayunta-*

miento of his own at Anáhuac. This extraordinary
interpretation of the relative powers of the Federal
military and State civil authorities was upheld by
Terán and vehemently repudiated by the State Government. Thus the East Texas settlers found themselves betwixt the devil and the deep sea, and still
without titles to their lands and apparently in danger
of being banished from their homes.

Stephen Austin was in Saltillo when he heard of
this controversy between Bradburn and Madero, and
he wrote immediately to Samuel Williams, with
whom he had formed a partnership, to advise the
settlers to follow a policy of hands-off. "What the
people of the Trinity ought to say," wrote Austin,
"is that they can not and ought not to take any part
in any quarrel between any two officers or authorities, unless officially called on to do so by the competent superior authorities. If they take sides, they
will in the end be licked by both sides as a person
who intermeddles in a quarrel between man and
wife." This, to be sure, was sound advice, but it can
be well imagined that it was difficult for the settlers
to follow. The remarkable thing is that they did
follow it to a surprising degree. Bradburn's action,
which was calculated to rob them of the fruits of
years of labor and privation in the wilderness, was
nothing short of military usurpation, but the settlers
bore the situation patiently and without disturbance.
All of this occurred between the months of February and November, 1831, and yet it is a remarkable fact that on January 2nd, 1832, the Governor
of the State of Coahuila and Texas could write with
perfect truth in his annual message that "the public

tranquility has not been disturbed in any manner in any place in the State, even though Colonel Davis Bradburn assumed without the authority of the Government the power of arresting a commissioner of the Government itself for the distribution of lands."

A like statement could have been made truthfully by very few other Governors of Mexican States. During the two years since Bustamante had seized the Government, revolutionary activity had been widespread throughout the republic, and ruthless usurpation of the civil powers by the military had been common. Revolts had broken out in Michoacan and other parts of the southern region of the Republic, and in the State of Mexico, in San Luis Potosí, and in Puebla. All these had been put down ruthlessly, Governors had been ousted because they were of a different party from that of Butamante, the prisons had been filled with political suspects, and prominent leaders had been forced to flee the country to save their lives. On February 14th, 1831, while Madero was a prisoner at Anáhuac, former President Guerrero, who had been captured as the result of treachery, was executed for no better reason than that alive he was regarded as a menace to the existing regime. And finally, on January 2nd, 1832, the very day on which the Governor of Coahuila and Texas was calling attention to the tranquility of that State, the garrison at Vera Cruz revolted and called upon Santa Anna to take the leadership of their movement. Two days later Santa Anna assumed command and a new revolution was on. And yet in Texas, where so many Mexican leaders professed to believe the national domain was in danger, public tranquility remained unbroken.

This was not the fault of either Bradburn or George Fisher, however. For Bradburn's interference with Madero in the performance of his duty had not been the only provocation he had given the Texans for dissatisfaction, and George Fisher, who had finally assumed his duties as administrator of the port of Galveston, had contributed his full share toward creating public grievances. Bradburn was guilty of all manner of aggravating offenses against the Texans. He pressed their slaves into service, without compensation to their masters; he appropriated their products for his soldiers, and neglected to pay for them; and he was guilty of many acts of petty tyranny calculated to add to the resentment of the Texans. In September, 1831, Terán reappointed George Fisher as administrator of the port of Galveston, and directed him to establish a temporary custom house at Anáhuac, but as soon as possible to erect buildings at Point Bolivar and at the mouth of the Brazos. For the time being, he would appoint a deputy to act at Brazoria. Fisher proceeded to exercise his new authority in a manner that gave the Texans generally the impression that he was seizing the first opportunity to retaliate for the humiliation he had suffered at the hands of the *ayuntamiento* at San Felipe.

Fisher's first act was to issue an order that all vessels loading or unloading cargo at Brazoria must obtain clearance papers at his office at Anáhuac before sailing. This order was made public in a proclamation which was published by Fisher on November

24th, 1831. It caused great excitement, for the regulations it set forth, to quote Austin's characterization of them, "as to their views were utterly impracticable and their execution was impossible." Austin wrote this opinion frankly to Bradburn, and took upon himself the responsibility to advise the small detachment of soldiers at Brazoria not to attempt to enforce the regulations. The commanders of the vessels making Brazoria, all of whom operated under the American flag, decided to ignore them, and when the Mexican guard there sought to prevent them from sailing without complying with the regulations, shots were exchanged and a Mexican soldier was wounded. This occurred on December 15th, 1831, and the next day the citizens of Brazoria held a mass meeting and appointed a committee to call on Fisher and Bradburn and demand that the regulations be changed so as to permit vessels to be cleared at Brazoria. Meantime, Austin wrote a full account of the occurrence to Terán, and pointed out that Fisher's impossible regulations were the cause of all the trouble and strongly urged his dismissal. Terán was furious and he held Austin partly responsible for the trouble because of the attitude he had assumed. He required that any tonnage duties due from the vessels should be paid by the parties receiving the goods, and that if any of the vessels returned, they should be detained until the persons guilty of assaulting the guard and wounding the soldier were handed over for punishment. At the same time, Terán wrote Fisher that he had been unreasonable, and the obnoxious regulations were modified.

Austin bore himself firmly in connection with this incident, and insisted that the dismissal of Fisher was necessary to the restoration of confidence. He frankly expressed the fear that trivial friction might lead to more serious disturbances, in view of all the circumstances. "It would be a lamentable misfortune," he wrote, "if a man like George Fisher should destroy all that has been done in ten years to redeem this country from the wilderness. Every man who has anything to lose or who has three grains of common sense is opposed to separation from Mexico, and to all disorder, and I believe that it is very important to allow the momentary excitement to die of itself, as in effect it has already done; and if possible to remove Fisher, it would, in my mind, be conducive to the preservation of harmony." Fisher remained on, though the regulations were modified. In a few months, however, he asked to be relieved of his duties, and turned his office over to a deputy.

Meantime, Austin and every man in Texas "with three grains of common sense" realized that something must be done to cure the situation. The effect of the Law of April 6th, 1830, had been totally unfavorable from every standpoint and it had benefitted nobody. The attitude of Bradburn, supported by Terán, in withholding land titles from the East Texas settlers was not only unjust, but it threatened the continued tranquility of the country. And finally, the attempt to enforce at Texas ports tariff laws which had been drafted to apply to the rest of the country and which worked hardship on a frontier population like the Texans, was yielding no great revenue and was supplying many occasions for trouble. Austin was now a member of the State Legislature, and he proposed that the State Government should take cognizance of these matters and call them to the attention of the Federal Government. Accordingly, when he left for Saltillo to attend the session of the Legislature in the spring of 1832, he took with him a memorial from the *ayuntamiento* of San Felipe, indorsed by the *ayuntamiento* of San Antonio, praying for exemption from the tariff of 1827, for modification of the law of April 6th, 1830, and urging the granting of titles to the East Texas settlers. This memorial was approved by the State authorities and transmitted to Mexico City, and Austin had every reason to believe that in due course the reforms prayed for would be granted. If public tranquility could be continued unbroken in Texas, so as not to disturb the Mexican leaders anew with the bugaboo of secession, all would go well.

"If things can be kept quiet in the colony," he wrote Williams from Saltillo, "all will end right and prosperously, of this I have no doubt. What is needed is a dead calm. All reflecting men will become convinced that the true interest of Texas is never to separate from Mexico, and that it is the true interest of this nation to encourage the population of Texas and make a State of it. This being the case, the Government will remove the restrictions and the country will prosper."

The Bustamante Government, however, was getting in a precarious situation, and the movement of Santa Anna was spreading. Austin's view of this movement at this time is interesting. He had no

great admiration for Santa Anna, but he believed
that the democratic principles represented by the
party which now bore his name would ultimately
triumph in Mexico.

"I think," he wrote, "that the party that has risen
against the ministry is very badly named the party
of Santa Anna. As I understand the situation, it
ought to be called the democratic republican federal
party. It appears to have made use of Santa Anna
for lack of another leader and this has given his
name to the party, which seems to me to be a misfortune, because it gives it a personal character when
it ought to be named for principles. It appears that
this party is very strong and that sooner or later it
will embrace the great mass of the nation and triumph as it has done in the north and also in England
and France, with a difference of form and men; and
I do not doubt that in the end it will triumph over
all Europe and the Americas."

Austin's sympathies, of course, were with the party
of federal republicanism. But he was anxious that
the Texans should keep free of all party allegiance.
"Now is a critical time," he wrote Williams. "It is
said that a new and liberal party are getting up.
Pray try and keep the people there from any acts
that may be construed into opposition to the Government, for that would turn all parties against us."

This was more wise counsel. But while Austin was
writing it, an armed body of Texans had already
adopted a formal declaration in support of Santa
Anna's revolt. And Col. John Davis Bradburn had
been directly responsible for this also.

CHAPTER XVIII

TEXAS BACKS SANTA ANNA

SOMETIME in May, 1832, Bradburn imprisoned several Anglo-Americans in the fort at Anáhuac for alleged offenses, the character of which is not very clear today, though it is certain they were trivial. Among them were Patrick C. Jack, who was charged with illegally organizing a company of militia, and William Barrett Travis, whose offense seems to have been that he called on Bradburn in the capacity of attorney for a Louisiana planter and demanded the delivery of a fugitive slave who was being harbored in the fort. Jack's brother, William H. Jack, who had settled at San Felipe and opened a law office, went to Anáhuac and asked that the prisoners be turned over to the civil authorities to be tried under the laws of the State. Bradburn refused, and informed Jack that the prisoners were military prisoners and would be given military trials. He seems to have hinted that they might be sent to the interior of Mexico. In any event, such was the story Jack told on his return to San Felipe. He expressed the fear that unless the prisoners were rescued they would be sent to the interior of Mexico, and he proposed to certain leading men at San Felipe that a company be organized to rescue them.

This suggestion was taken up by such men as Wily Martin, William Pettus, Robert M. Williamson, Frank W. Johnson, John Austin, and others, all of them solid citizens, and soon runners were on the way to different settlements to recruit men to meet at a rendezvous near Liberty on the Trinity. On June 9th a considerable force of men gathered, elected Frank W. Johnson to be their captain, and proceeded toward Anáhuac. Encountering a small detachment of Bradburn's cavalry, they took the surprised Mexicans prisoners without ceremony, and then camped for the night.

Meantime, news of the "uprising" spread throughout Texas. John Austin, who had been sent from San Felipe to the lower Brazos to obtain recruits, laid the whole matter before Colonel Ugartechéa, the Mexican officer in command of the post at Velasco, and induced him to authorize a lieutenant to accompany him to Anáhuac with a request that Bradburn release the prisoners in order to avoid trouble. While consenting to this, Ugartchéa dispatched letters at once to the Political Chief, Ramón Músquiz, at San Antonio. About the same time, Samuel M. Williams, Austin's partner, and others at San Felipe also sent letters to Músquiz, informing him that the expedition was purely a personal one against Bradburn, and had no political significance. The *ayuntamiento* of San Felipe officially invited Músquiz to come to the Anglo-American settlements, assuring him that his presence would serve to restore confidence and preserve order.

The company of armed men on the Trinity, however, was in earnest, and on June 10th, a delegation, headed by its captain, Frank W. Johnson, and accompanied by the unrecognized alcalde of Liberty, called on Bradburn and demanded that the prisoners be turned over to the civil authorities. John Austin and Ugartechéa's lieutenant presented a written request from the Velasco commander to the same effect. Bradburn gave them evasive answers, and two days passed without any result. On June 12th, through the offices of a Colonel Subarán, who for some reason was visiting Anáhuac, an agreement was reached by which commissioners representing both sides should arrange an exchange of the prisoners held in the fort for the Mexican cavalrymen held by the Anglo-Americans. Terms of an exchange were arranged, by which the Anglo-Americans released the Mexican cavalrymen and withdrew to Turtle Bayou. Bradburn failed to keep his part of the agreement, however, and Travis and his companions remained imprisoned in the fort. Captain Johnson and his company then held a meeting to determine what to do, and it was decided to attack the fort.

Realizing the gravity of taking up arms against a Government post, they proceeded to make a formal declaration of the causes and objects of their action, and so it came about that a declaration in favor of Santa Anna and the "plan of Vera Cruz" was adopted. After enumerating their grievances against Bradburn and interpreting them as "arbitrary and unconstitutional measures of the administration of Bustamante," they declared their support of "those patriots under the highly talented and distinguished chieftain, Santa Anna" and resolved "that as freemen devoted to a correct interpretation and enforcement of the Constitution and laws, according to their true spirit, we pledge our lives and fortunes in support of the same, and of those distinguished leaders who are now so gallantly fighting in defense of civil liberty." They invited all the people of Texas to cooperate with them. Then, concluding that artillery would be needed to attack the fort, and recalling that two cannon had been left at Brazoria by a ship, which had unloaded them with other heavy ballast in order to clear the Brazos bar, they dispatched a party, headed by John Austin, to Brazoria to get them. They also sent out parties to recruit reinforcements from San Felipe and other settlements and posted guards to keep an eye on Anáhuac. They then settled down to await the arrival of the artillery.

In a few days, however, the pledge of their "lives and fortunes" to the support of Santa Anna was forgotten, and the members of the little army dispersed to their homes, when Colonel Piedras came down from Nacogdoches, obtained the release of the prisoners, induced Bradburn to resign, promised the reestablishment of the *ayuntamiento* at Liberty, and agreed that property confiscated by Bradburn would be paid for. Meantime, Músquiz, the Political Chief, accepted the invitation to come to San Felipe, and assured himself that the movement against Anáhuac was directed solely against Bradburn. He presided over a meeting of the *ayuntamiento* on June 30th, which condemned the proceedings at Anáhuac and called a mass convention of the Anglo-American citizens of Texas to be held at San Felipe on July 7th. Similar meetings were held at eight or ten other points throughout Texas, denouncing the attack on

Anáhuac and pledging support to the national and State Governments. Finally, on July 7th, the convention at San Felipe was attended by several hundred men and resolutions expressing allegiance to the Government were adopted. The overwhelming sentiment of the Anglo-American citizens of Texas undoubtedly was against the attack on Anáhuac and the declaration in support of Santa Anna.

The movement in favor of Santa Anna, however, was not to be so easily headed off. John Austin and the party sent after the cannon at Brazoria knew nothing of what was going on between Johnson and Piedras at Turtle Bayou, and they proceeded to carry out their mission. Arriving at Brazoria, they called a meeting and laid before the citizens of that place the declaration in favor of Santa Anna, which was promptly ratified. A delegation was then sent to Colonel Ugartechéa at Velasco, calling upon him to declare for Santa Anna and to permit the cannon to be taken by boat past Velasco to the sea and thence to Anáhuac. Ugartechéa refused both demands, and as a result a party from Brazoria, under command of John Austin, attacked him on the morning of June 26th. After several hours of fighting, in which a number of men were killed on both sides, Ugartechéa surrendered. On June 29th, the very day Piedras was agreeing to release the Anáhuac prisoners and the little army under Johnson at Turtle Bayou was laying down its arms, Ugartechéa signed a formal capitulation of the fort at Velasco in which he agreed "not to return to take up arms against the expressed plan ... formed under the orders of General Antonio Lopez de Santa Anna, and by the garrison of Vera

Cruz." He was permitted to march overland to
Matamoros. Then, on the night of July 11th, the
garrison at Anáhuac revolted and declared for Santa
Anna, and Bradburn and his officers escaped across
the border into Louisiana. And finally, on July 16th,
a squadron of five vessels, commanded by Col. José
Antonio Mexia, one of Santa Anna's chief officers,
and carrying four hundred soldiers, arrived at the
mouth of the Brazos, with Stephen F. Austin as a
passenger.

Mexia and Austin had met at Matamoros, the former having come to that place to take possession of
it in Santa Anna's name, and the latter being enroute
on a return journey to Saltillo from a visit to Terán,
who was encamped near Tampico. The news of the
move against Bradburn had reached Matamoros on
June 20th, and Austin with characteristic prompt-
ness and thoroughness had written letters to everybody he regarded as important, to Ugartechéa in
Texas, to Terán, to Williams at San Felipe, and others, all of them calculated to restore tranquility. The
burden of the letters to Ugartechéa and Terán was
that Bradburn undoubtedly was the cause of all the
trouble, and no political significance was to be attached to it. That Terán accepted this view, is evi-
denced by the fact that he wrote Ugartechéa on June
25th to relieve Bradburn of his command. Austin had not regarded the matter as serious
enough to necessitate his return to Texas, and had
prepared to continue his journey to Saltillo. Then
on June 28th Colonel Mexia arrived at Matamoros,
the town being evacuated before him by the Government garrison under command of Col. José M.

Guerra. Mexia had come north to cooperate in a campaign which was being carried on by Gen. Esteban Moctezuma, the commandant at Tampico who had pronounced for Santa Anna. Terán had made an unsuccessful attack on Moctezuma at Tampico, and was encamped near that city. It was Mexia's purpose to secure Matamoros for the rebel cause, and then proceed to cooperate with Moctezuma against Terán. Four days after Mexia's arrival at Matamoros, Terán, in a fit of despondency over personal matters, committed suicide, and about the same time alarming reports reached Matamoros of continued trouble in Texas. It was declared that the Anglo-Americans were in revolt, with the object of separating Texas from Mexico. In this situation, Mexia had a conference with Colonel Guerra, who had encamped at San Fernando, and an agreement was reached by which a truce was declared between them until Mexia could go to Texas and protect the country against dismemberment. This remarkable document was signed on July 6th. At the request of both Mexia and Guerra, Austin agreed to accompany the former to Texas. Austin assured Mexia that he would find that the Texans had no thought of separating from Mexico, that whatever else might be the nature of the trouble the national territory was in no danger. And so the Santa Anna squadron, with Mexia and Austin, arrived at the mouth of the Brazos on July 16th.

In this situation, there was nothing to do but to stick to the declaration in favor of Santa Anna, and when Austin learned the facts he fell in with this plan at once. The thing was admirably managed.

Mexia sent a formal communication to John Austin, as chairman of a committee of citizens of Brazoria, enclosing a copy of the armistice agreement he had made with Guerra as explanatory of his mission to Texas. However, if it were true, as he had been informed, that the movement in Texas was on account of the Texans having adhered to the plan of Vera Cruz, he wrote, "and I am officially informed of that fact in an unequivocal manner, you can in that case apprise the inhabitants that I will unite with them to accomplish their wishes, and that the forces under my command will protect their adhesion to said plan." To this John Austin made a formal reply, enclosing copies of the Turtle Bayou resolutions, the ratification resolution of the citizens of Brazoria, and the articles of capitulation signed by Ugartechéa, all of which made specific reference to Santa Anna and the plan of Vera Cruz. He then proceeded to refute the charge that the Texans were disloyal to the Republic and desired to separate from Mexico.

"The enemies of Texas," he wrote, "the enemies of the enterprising men who have devoted their time and labors to improve a country that was never before trod by civilized men, have taken pains and are continually doing it, to attribute to us a disposition to separate from the Mexican confederation. We have not entertained and have not any such intention or desire. We are Mexicans by adoption, we are the same in heart and will so remain. If the laws have granted to us the honorable title of citizens, we wish that title should be respected, and that the authorities established by the Constitution of the State shall govern us. We are farmers and not soldiers, and there-

fore desire that the military commandants shall not
interfere with us at all. Since 1830 we have been
pretty much governed militarily, and in so despotic
a manner that we were finally driven to arms, to re-
strain within their limits the military subalterns of
the General Government. We have not insulted the
flag of our adopted country, as has been falsely stated
by our enemies, but on the contrary we have defended and sustained its true dignity, and attacked
those who have outraged it by using it as a pretext
for their encroachments upon the Constitution and
sovereignty of the State of Coahuila and Texas, and
as a cover for their baseness and personal crimes . . . .
It is a matter of pride and congratulation to me that
you have come to this place to see, with your own
eyes, the rectitude of our sentiments, and that it has
afforded us the opportunity of presenting to you our
respects, and the assurances of our hearty cooperation
in the great and glorious cause which is so nobly
advocated by our distinguished commander-in-chief,
General Santa Anna."

Mexia accepted the invitation of the Texans to remain a few days as their guest, and a grand banquet
and a ball were given in his honor. Toasts were drunk
to the success of Santa Anna's cause and the future
of the Republic. And incidentally, one toast was
drunk to separate statehood for Texas!

Apparently satisfied as to the loyalty of the Texans,
Mexia sailed back to Matamoros to continue his
campaign in the interest of Santa Anna where he had
left off, and Austin remained in Texas to deal with
the delicate situation which had been precipitated.
The policy of aloofness from the family quarrels of

the Mexicans had been abandoned under the com-
pulsion of circumstances. The Texans must now
make the best of it. "We must all pull at the same
end of the rope," Austin wrote Williams, who had
been placed in a very embarrassing position by the
turn of events, "right or wrong, we must all pull together."

So, in spite of the previous action of the *ayuntamiento* of San Felipe, of the various local meetings,
and of the mass convention of July 7th, Austin now
proposed to make the adhesion to Santa Anna official
and general throughout Texas. Acting under Austin's direction, four days after Mexia had left Texas,
the *ayuntamiento* of San Felipe adopted a formal
declaration in support of Santa Anna, and took occasion to set forth certain declarations of its own which
were no part of the "plan of Vera Cruz." For one
thing, it made a formal declaration against the ex-
clusion clause of the Law of April 6th, 1830. "The
measures of the administration since 1830," it declared, "have been directed to embarrass and retard
immigration from foreign countries, rather than promote and encourage it; thus paralyzing the advancement of the nation, and preventing the settlement of
its uninhabited lands, to the evident injury of the
national prosperity." Then it adopted a ringing declaration against a large standing army and military
rule. "A large standing army," it declared, "is totally
unnecessary for national defense, in the present state
of friendly relations between Mexico and all foreign
powers except Spain, which latter, it is well known,
is too impotent to attack her; . . . such an army is a
burden to the people and consumes the revenue of the

nation without any benefit; . . . it endangers the national liberty and is continually disturbing the public tranquility by affording the means of committing and defending despotic acts and producing revolutions." The *ayuntamiento* further declared "that conciliatory measures ought to be adopted to put an end to the present civil war on a basis that will effectually gurantee the security and rights of all persons who have taken part on either side and prevent the recurrence of similar difficulties by adapting the laws and the administration of the Government to the genuine principles of the federal republican system."

These resolutions were forwarded to the Governor, through the Political Chief, and Austin wrote to Músquiz urging that the *ayuntamiento* at San Antonio should take similar action. A month later, after some hesitation, San Antonio declared adhesion to Santa Anna. Meantime, the *ayuntamiento* at Nacogdoches, in spite of the presence of a garrison under Piedras still loyal to the Bustamante Government, boldly declared for Santa Anna, and invited the inhabitants of Ayish Bayou to come over and help them get rid of the troops. "We do make a solemn pledge one to another and to you all," it declared, "that we will rally around the standard of Santa Anna as the champion of our freedom; and that we will risk our lives and properties in support of the Constitution and the laws, and of our rights and liberties." In response to this call, a force from Ayish Bayou, under John W. Bullock, attacked the garrison at Nacogdoches on August 2nd, and the next day Piedras evacuated the town and attempted to escape. Intercepted by a small force of Texans at the crossing of the Angelina River, and believing his retreat cut off, Piedras resigned his command to Major Francisco Medina. Medina, with the enthusiastic approval of his men, immediately declared for Santa Anna. They then proceeded to San Antonio. Two weeks later, the small garrison stationed at Tenoxtitlán also retired to San Antonio, and thus by the end of August, less than three months after the move against Anáhuac, all the Anglo-American settlements were free of Mexican soldiers. The military features of the Law of April 6th, 1830, were no longer in force.

As for the other features of the law, particularly the provision excluding Americans from Texas, there was nobody left to enforce them. The Bustamante regime was fighting for its life. Alamán had been forced out of the cabinet several months before; Terán was in a suicide's grave; and Bustamante had been compelled to take the field early in August.

Meantime, Gomez Farias, one of the most sincere republicans in Mexico, who had started a new revolt in the States of Zacatecas and Jalisco, formed a coalition with Santa Anna and the revolution thus became general throughout the Republic. But rumors that the Texans were plotting independence continued to spread over Mexico, and with the object of presenting a united front in some expression of their true position, the *ayuntamiento* of San Felipe, on August 22nd, issued a call for a consultation of delegates, representing all the settlements, to be held on October 1st. The revolution was still in progress when the delegates assembled for this consultation, the first of its kind ever held in Texas.

CHAPTER XIX

ENTER SAM HOUSTON

ANTHONY BUTLER had continued his intrigues at the Mexican capital during the year 1832. He started the year with a big idea. The boundary treaty, which accepted the line fixed in agreement with Spain in 1819, was then pending before the United States Senate, and Butler's big idea, which he communicated to President Jackson under date of January 2nd, was that ratification should be withheld, thus leaving the question open, until he could put through the purchase of Texas. He suggested that Jackson take steps to influence the Senate to delay action. But Jackson's respect for Butler's suggestions had waned considerably by this time, so he did nothing to interfere with the treaty's progress through the Senate. Besides, it was high time for the United States to prove its good faith in this matter. The treaty was approved by the Senate in due course, and ratifications were exchanged on April 5th, 1832. Thus the United States, in solemn fashion, again formally renounced all claim to Texas.

Meantime, news of the discontent of the Anglo-Americans in Texas with the measures of Bradburn and Fisher reached Washington, and it was reported that an armed outbreak was imminent. The American Secretary of State, Edward Livingston, wrote

Butler in February, 1832, calling his attention to this report, and cautioning him to make clear to the Mexican Government that the United States had nothing to do with the activities of the Texans.

"As the persons most active in these movements," wrote Livingston, "are said to be emigrants from the United States, suspicions may arise in the minds of those ignorant of the principles on which our Government is conducted, that it has fomented or connived at these discontents, should they break out into action. These it will be your duty, by every means in your power, to remove, declaring, should any such suggestions be made, that you are instructed to say that they are totally unfounded, and that your Government will consider them as the expression of an unfriendly doubt of good faith."

Butler was absent from the Mexican capital when this letter arrived, having gone on a trip north which extended into Texas. Though there is no record of the object of his visit to Texas, Ramón Músquiz, the Political Chief, afterwards interpreted it as having a connection with the disturbances of the summer of 1832, a circumstance which illustrates how Butler, far from allaying Mexican suspicions of the United States, contributed by his actions toward increasing those suspicions. On his return to Mexico City in June he reported to President Jackson that he had had a number of conferences with Alamán, and expressed confidence that if he could deal with that gentleman alone he could succeed in obtaining Texas. "I think," he wrote, "I hold the key to unlock his heart and the means of enlightening his understanding." Alamán was no longer a member of the cabinet when this letter was written, having resigned a month previous in an effort to check the spread of Santa Anna's movement, but Butler regarded him as still possessed of influence and evidently was proposing to bribe him into supporting the plan to cede Texas to the United States.

"Although that gentleman," Butler wrote to Jackson under date of July 18th, 1832, "has apparently withdrawn from the cabinet, he still directs the Department of Foreign Affairs *sub rosa* and is in fact as much the Minister as at any time heretofore . . . . The amount I am limited for the purchase by my instructions will very probably be in part applied to *facilitate the negotiation,* in which case we shall provide for that portion of the payment by a secret article."

Butler's correspondence shows him in so many other ways to have been careless of the truth, there is no real reason to believe that Alamán gave him any encouragement whatever or that he had indicated that he would accept a bribe. Nor is it to be thought that Jackson would have sanctioned the paying of one. But neither Alamán nor any other Mexican whom Butler approached had any reason to doubt that the American minister was acting strictly under instructions from Washington, and so suspicion of the United States Government was increased.

This suspicion might have increased further had it become known that on August 6th, 1832, three weeks after the above letter was written by Butler, and two weeks before the issuance of the call for the consultation of the Texans at San Felipe, the United States War Department, undoubtedly by direction of President Jackson, had handed instructions and passports to Sam Houston, a former Governor of Tennessee, for a trip into Texas "to confer with the Indians".

At the moment Sam Houston was the hero of Jackson men throughout the country, for he had just come triumphantly through a sensational affair in which he had bested the enemies of the President in Congress. For three years—ever since he had separated from his wife and had resigned from the office of Governor of Tennessee—Houston had been under a cloud. During most of that time he had been living among the Cherokee Indians on the Arkansas River, and he was regarded, as he has said himself, as "a man of broken fortune and blasted reputation".

In 1830 he had come from his retirement and had endeavored, through President Jackson's influence, to obtain a Government contract to supply the Indians, but Jackson's enemies had been able to prevent this. Some time after this Representative William Stanberry of Ohio, in the course of an attack on Jackson in Congress, referred to Houston and to Jackson's support of his application for a contract, and characterized him in insulting terms. A friend sent Houston a copy of a newspaper containing a report of the remarks, and he wrote to Stanberry demanding a retraction. He received no reply. In March, 1832, Houston was in Washington again, and while he was on the floor of the House, the privileges of which he enjoyed as a former member of that body, Stanberry again mentioned his name in a speech, referring to him as "one of Jackson's bullies". Houston sent a friend to him with a note demanding an explanation, to which Stanberry replied that he had no right to question him about remarks made in the course of debate. A few days later the two men met on the street and an encounter resulted, during which Houston beat Stanberry with a cane. For this Houston was haled before the bar of the House to answer to a charge of assaulting one of its members, and the trial, which lasted nearly a month, became the political sensation of the hour.

"I was dying out," said Houston afterwards, "and had they taken me before a justice of the peace and fined me ten dollars for assault and battery it would have killed me; but they gave me a national tribunal for a theatre, and that set me up again."

That was precisely what happened. Jackson's enemies made great capital of the assault, and distinguished counsel was retained by each side, but Houston himself behaved in such a manner as to turn the technical victory of Jackson's enemies into a moral defeat, and thus he became the hero of the hour among Jackson men everywhere. Great stress was laid upon the circumstance that Houston, a former member of Congress and an ex-Governor of an American State, had become an outcast from civilization, a renegade from his kind. In a speech in his own defense, Houston shamed his traducers for thus attacking him because of his misfortunes.

"Though it may have been alleged," he declared, in the high-flown oratory of the time, "that I am 'a man of broken fortune and blasted reputation', I never can forget that reputation, however limited, is the high boon of heaven. Perhaps the circumstances of adversity, by which I have been crushed,

have made me cling to the little remains of it which
I still possess, and to cherish them with the greater
fondness. Though the ploughshare of ruin has been
driven over me, and laid waste my brightest hopes,
yet I am proud to think that, under all circumstances,
I have endeavored to sustain the laws of my country,
and to support her institutions. Whatever may be
the opinions of gentlemen in relation to those matters, I am here to be tried for a substantive offense,
disconnected entirely with my former life or circumstances. I have only to say to those who rebuke me,
at the time when they see adversity sorely pressing
upon me, for myself

"I seek no sympathies nor need;
The thorns which I have reaped are of the tree
I planted; they have torn me and I bleed."

That speech won the sympathy of the public, and
though the House voted a reprimand, and a Washington court fined Houston $500, which Jackson
promptly remitted, the political victory was with
Houston and the party of Jackson. The whole country was talking about it and Houston was in the public eye, when he was commissioned to make a trip to
Texas to negotiate with certain Indians, formerly
resident in the United States.

The parley with the Indians was the ostensible
purpose of Houston's mission to Texas, but that his
own interest in such a trip was related to the possibility of the separation of Texas from Mexico there
can be little doubt. A letter written to him by John
Van Fossen of Livonia, N. Y., and dated August 3rd,
1832, three days before the date of his passports, is
proof today that he was concerned in some plan

which included the detaching of Texas from Mexico.

"I was informed by Colonel Shote, with whom I parted at Baltimore on my way home," Van Fossen wrote to Houston, "that there was reason to fear that your friends in New York would fail of their engagements to furnish the means of prosecuting your Texas enterprise. I hope it will not prove true, for I had indulged the expectation of hearing of, if I could not witness and participate in, the most splendid results from this undertaking. I do not believe that that portion of the country will long continue its allegiance to the Mexican Government, and I would rather see it detached through your agency, than to learn that the object had been effected by other means, or even to learn that it had become the property of the United States on the most favorable terms of purchase. I shall feel uneasy until I learn from you how the matter has resulted."

As this letter would indicate, the "Texas enterprise", whatever it was, had failed to obtain the necessary financial support, but the letter shows also that Houston's interest in Texas was not confined to his mission to confer with the Indians. It is probable that he expressed to Jackson a desire to go to Texas, and that the President had arranged to have the War Department send him. The mission, no doubt, was not a mere subterfuge, as some have supposed, but a legitimate one. Nor is there any reason to believe that the United States Government was in any way concerned in Houston's "Texas enterprise". The probability is that when Houston finally started to Texas he had no definite plans, except that he hoped that he would find opportunity to rehabilitate himself completely. He needed to make a new start in life, and as he probably believed, like many others, that sooner or later Texas would separate from Mexico, there was good ground for the hope that he would find greater opportunity to exercise his talents in such circumstances than in the United States. During the previous three years among the Cherokees on the Arkansas River, which was practically the Texas-American frontier, he must have kept himself fairly well-informed on conditions in Texas, and it was quite natural that he should see in those conditions the opportunity for the rehabilitation which he sought. In any event, there is no reason to believe that Houston went as a representative of Jackson or the United States Government to connive at separating Texas from Mexico. Aside from his mission to confer with the Indians, his objects were more than probably entirely related to his perfectly laudable ambition to make a new career and regain his former high position among men. He was within a few months of his fortieth birthday, and, if the heights from which he had been suddenly dashed more than three years before were ever to be attained again, he must soon make a new start.

It was while Houston was preparing to depart for Texas, that the first convention of the Texans, composed of fifty-eight delegates representing every Anglo-American community, met at San Felipe on October 1st, 1832, to consider their grievances. Mexico was still in a condition of revolution, with the fortunes of Santa Anna yet undecided, and the outlook for stability was not very bright.

CHAPTER XX

THE FIRST CONVENTION

THE objects for which the convention of the Texans was called were four in number. As enumerated by John Austin, in calling the delegates to order, these were (1) to declare their firm and unshaken adhesion to the Mexican Confederation and Constitution and their readiness to do their duty as Mexican citizens, (2) to memorialize the national Government to repeal the obnoxious features of the Law of April 6th, 1830, (3) to petition for the appointment of a commissioner to put the East Texans in legal possession of their lands, and (4) to petition the national Government to modify the tariff laws so as to permit the importation of necessities without the payment of duty.

"These four topics," said John Austin, "embrace all that the alcaldes had in view at the time of making the request for this convention. It is considered by us that it is the duty of the people of Texas to lay their situation before the General Government in order that such legislative aid may be afforded as the general good of the nation, and of Texas, may require; and to accompany it with a firm declaration of our unshaken allegiance to the Mexican Constitution and nation."

The first object, that of declaring firm and un-shaken adhesion to the Mexican Confederation and Constitution, was by no means the least important. Indeed, in its inception, the chief object of the convention was to allay the suspicions which had been aroused among Mexican leaders of the intentions of the Anglo-Texans, by making clear the character of the grievances under which they suffered and by repudiating in formal fashion any desire to separate from Mexico.

"The revolution which commenced at Vera Cruz, on the second of January last, under the command of General Santa Anna," said John Austin, in his opening address, "reached this remote section of the nation, and movements of a warlike character have taken place—the consequence of which has been that the military garrisons have been compelled to quit the country. These movements have been greatly mis-represented by the enemies of Texas, and have been attributed to objects entirely different from the true ones. It was, therefore, considered to be highly im-portant to the interests of Texas, and of the nation, to counteract these misrepresentations by a plain statement of facts; and that a decided declaration should be made by the people of Texas, convened in general convention, of our firm and unshaken adhe-sion to the Mexican Confederation and Constitution, and our readiness to do our duty as Mexican citi-zens."

Had the convention confined itself to these four ob-jects, it is altogether probable that the ultimate sup-port of the authorities of the State of Coahuila and Texas would have been obained and that in due

course the national Government would have granted
the petitions to repeal the obnoxious provisions of
the Law of April 6th, 1830, and to reform the tariff laws, and that the East Texans would have been
given legal titles to their lands. Before the convention completed its deliberations, however, an altogether new subject was introduced, and action was
taken on it which overshadowed everything else in
the eyes of all Mexicans. This action was the adoption of a memorial to the national Government asking that "that part of the Mexican Republic known
by the name of Texas shall become a separate State
of the Confederacy, to be placed on an equal footing
with any of the States of the Union." This was interpreted as a move in the direction of separating
Texas from Mexico, and the emphatic declarations
of the convention against such a course were lost sight
of entirely.

The convention was indeed emphatic in its expression of loyalty to Mexico. In a memorial, drafted by
William H. Wharton, it pointed out that if independence had been the object of the Texans it would
have been adopted at the time when they declared
for Santa Anna and expelled the Government
troops. "Would it not have been easy to have taken
advantage of the troubles in the interior, and to have
battled for independence?" it asked. "Was there ever
a time more opportune and inviting? Why did we
not then declare for independence? Because in the
honest sincerity of our hearts, we assure you, and
we call upon Almighty God to witness the truth of
the assertion, we did not then, and we do not now,
wish for independence. No, there is not an Anglo-

American in Texas whose heart does not beat high for the prosperity of the Mexican Republic; who does not cordially and devoutly wish that all parts of her territory may remain united to the end of time; that she may steadily and rapidly advance in arts, arms, agriculture, commerce, manufactures, and in learning, in virtue, freedom and all that can add to the splendor and happiness of a great nation."

The memorial repudiated the idea that the Anglo-Texans desired a "coalescence with the United States of the North." "A short time since," it declared, "it was rumored among us that the President of the United States of the North expressed a determination to make the Neches River, instead of the Sabine, the line between the two republics. This hitherto unheard of claim provoked the indignation of every inhabitant of Texas, and our constituents have with one voice called upon us to memorialize your honorable bodies on the subject of the injustice of such a demand."

Having thus reassured the Government on the score of the loyalty of the Anglo-Texans, the convention proceeded to petition for the repeal of the Law of April 6th, 1830, on the ground that American immigration was necessary to the development of Texas. "Can the resources of Texas be properly developed with this law hanging over it? We believe not. We believe under such circumstances it would remain the comparative wilderness it now is. Experience shows that native Mexicans will not settle it; but should they do so it would not augment the physical force of the nation, for it would only be taking population from one part of the Republic to place it

in another. Will Europeans settle it? We believe
Europeans of the right description to benefit the
country will not, for many reasons. Our hopes then
for the development of the resources of Texas are
naturally turned to the United States of the North
. . . . When all these things are considered, we can
but believe that the former characteristic justice and
liberality of your honorable body will return to our
aid, and bring about an immediate repeal of this, to
us, ever to be deprecated measure."

In petitioning that Texas be made a separate State,
the convention set forth that the differences between
Coahuila and Texas and the distances between the inhabited parts of each from those of the other were
so great as to make such separation desirable.
"Coahuila being so distant from the population of
Texas," said the petition, "and so widely variant from
it in interests, the rights and wants of the people of
Texas can not be properly protected and provided
for under the present organization, admitting the
several departments of the Government of the State
to be prompted by the utmost purity of intention, in
their efforts for the administration of justice.
Coahuila and Texas are dissimilar in soil, climate,
and productions, in common interest, and partly in
population—the representatives of the former are
numerous and those of the latter few, in consequence
of which any law passed peculiarly adapted for the
benefit of Texas has only to be the effect of a generous courtesy. Laws happily constructed for the benefit of Coahuila, and conducive to its best interests,
might be ruinous to Texas—such are the conflicting
interests of the two countries."

The convention, before adjourning, created a central committee of safety and correspondence, with local committees in the settlements throughout Texas, and then named William H. Wharton as envoy to present the memorials at the State and national capitals. The central committee was composed of Frank W. Johnson, chairman; J. B. Miller, Stephen F. Austin, L. L. Veeder, Robert Peebles, Wily Martin and William Pettus.

Stephen Austin had not favored the holding of the convention in the first place, but once it was called and assembled he consented to preside over it. He had not favored the petition for separate statehood, not because he did not desire separate statehood, but because he believed such a petition inopportune at a time when it was important to regain the confidence of the Mexican leaders and because he feared it would result in nothing but renewed suspicion. However, when his judgment was overruled by the majority, he adopted the convention's view as his own and defended it against all criticism. And there was criticism enough. First the alcalde of San Antonio, then the Political Chief, and finally the State Government pronounced the convention illegal and its proceedings revolutionary in character. Ángel Navarro, the alcalde at San Antonio, and Ramón Músquiz, the Political Chief, both agreed that the objects sought were desirable. But the method was objectionable. "All such meetings are prohibited by the supreme power and by existing laws," Navarro wrote to the *ayuntamiento* of San Felipe, and Músquiz, in a letter to the same body, a copy of which he sent to Austin personally, declared that in participating in the convention the Texans had exercised powers which belonged exclusively to the Government.

Austin wrote Músquiz frankly that in his opinion it would have been better not to have written his letter to the *ayunamiento*. "I tell you candidly," he wrote, "that in my opinion it would be very impolitic to translate and print your communication. I shall not do so. The *ayuntamiento* may do as they please. In times like the present, any measure is bad that tends to irritate and produce excitement; every measure is good that is calculated to soothe, bind up and bring about tranquility and good order .... There is little probability that we shall soon have a stable and peaceable order of public affairs, and I give it as my deliberate judgment that Texas is lost if she takes no measure of her own for her welfare. I incline to the opinion that it is your duty, as chief magistrate, to call a general convention to take into consideration the condition of the country. I do not know how the State or General Governments can presume to say that the people of Texas have violated the Constitution, when the acts of both Governments have long since killed the Constitution, and when the Confederation itself has hardly any life left. I can not approve the assertion that the people have not the right to assemble peaceably, and calmly and respectfully represent their wants. In short the condition of Texas is bad, but we may fear to see it worse."

Finally, the State Government, in formal fashion, declared the convention to have been held in violation of the law, pronounced the central committee and the local committees of correspondence to be illegal and revolutionary bodies, and ordered them to disband.

In this situation, Austin determined there was only one thing to do. The cooperation of the Mexican population of Texas, at San Antonio and Goliad, must be obtained in making representations to the State and national Governments. Goliad had sent delegates to the convention, but they had arrived at San Felipe after it had completed its work. However, they approved of everything that had been done, and one of their number, Rafaél Manchola, had been named by the central committee to accompany Wharton to the State and national capitals. The action of the State Government made it useless to carry out the insructions of the convention and present the petitions, but the central committee had been empowered to call another convention should this become adviseable. Austin now decided to win San Antonio and Goliad over to some program of action that would have the support of all of Texas, Anglo-Americans and Mexicans alike, and to this end he paid a visit to San Antonio and Goliad. The other members of the central committee were informed of the object of these visits, and Austin understood that they agreed not to call another convention during his absence.

Austin succeeded in obtaining the cooperation of the leaders at San Antonio to the extent of having the *ayuntamiento* to adopt the whole program of the convention, including a much stronger memorial for separate statehood than that which the convention had framed. But before he got back to San Felipe, the central committee, acting under presure from the

local committees of correspondence, called another
convention for April 1st, 1833, the delegates to be
elected at an election to be held throughout Texas on
March 1st. This destroyed all chance of close cooperation between the Mexican citizens of Texas and
the Anglo-Americans, for the former were determined to have nothing to do with an extra-legal
movement, which they believed to be prohibited by
law.

About three weeks before the second convention
was called, Sam Houston crossed Red River into
Texas. This was on December 10th, 1832. He went
immediately to Nacogdoches, then to San Felipe,
and finally to San Antonio. At San Antonio he conferred with some Comanche chiefs, and then returned to the American border. Everywhere he
talked with Anglo-American leaders, and, in view
of his recent prominence in the newspapers, everywhere his visit created great interest and he was received with consideration and respect. Two months
later he was in Natchitoches, Louisiana, from which
place he wrote an account of his observations to
President Jackson. His letter to Jackson was, in part,
as follows:

"Having been so far as Bexar, in the province of
Texas, where I had an interview with the Comanche
Indians, I am in possession of some information
which will doubtless be interesting to you, and may
be calculated to forward your views, if you should
entertain any, touching the acquisition of Texas by
the Government of the United States. That such a
measure is desired by nineteen-twentieths of the population of the province, I can not doubt. They are

now without laws to govern or protect them. Mexico is involved in civil war. The Federal Constitution has never been in operation. The Government is essentially despotic, and must be so for years to come. The rulers have not honesty, and the people have not intelligence. The people of Texas are determined to form a State Government, and separate from Coahuila, and, unless Mexico is soon restored to order, and the Constitution revised and re-enacted, the province of Texas will remain separate from the Confederacy of Mexico. She has already beaten and repelled all the troops of Mexico from her soil, nor will she permit them to return; she can defend herself against the whole power of Mexico, for really Mexico is powerless and penniless to all intents and purposes. Her want of money, taken in connection with the course which Texas *must and will adopt,* will render a transfer of Texas to some power inevitable, and if the United States does not press for it, England will, most assuredly, obtain it by some means.

"Now is a very important crisis for Texas. As relates to her future prosperity and safety, as well as the relations which it is to bear to the United States, it is now in the most favorable attitude, perhaps, that it can be, to obtain it on fair terms. England is pressing her suit for it, but its citizens will resist, if any transfer should be made of them to any power but the United States. I have travelled nearly five hundred miles across Texas, and am now enabled to judge pretty correctly of the soil and resources of the country, and I have no hesitancy in pronouncing it the finest country, for its extent, upon the globe; for the greater portion of it is richer and more healthy than West Tennessee. There can be no doubt that the country east of the River Grand of the North would sustain a population of ten millions of souls.

"My opinion is that Texas, by her members in convention, will, by the 1st of April, declare all that country as Texas proper, and form a State Constitution. I expect to be present at the convention, and will apprise you of the course adopted, as soon as its members have taken final action. It is probable that I may make Texas my abiding-place. In adopting this course I will never forget the country of my birth."

Having written this letter, Houston returned across the Sabine, and two weeks later he was elected a delegate to the convention to be held on April 1st, as a representative of Nacogdoches.

Meantime, Anthony Butler was continuing his intrigues in Mexico City. Three days before Houston wrote the above letter, President Jackson had received a letter from Butler in which he outlined an entirely new proposal. He proposed that the United States Government make a large loan to Mexico and take a mortgage on Texas as security. This, he believed, would lead inevitably to a transfer of Texas to the United States. Jackson, who already had heard of the calling of the second convention in Texas, sent the letter to the Secretary of State with the following notation:

"Instruct Colonel Butler to bring the negotiation to a close. The convention in Texas meets the 1st of next April to form a constitution for themselves. When this is done, Mexico can never annex it to her jurisdiction again, or control its Legislature or exercise any power over its Territory—it will be useless, after this act, to enter into a treaty of boundary with Mexico."

About the same time, the Political Chief, Ramón Músquiz, came to the conclusion that the movement for separate statehood had independence for its real goal. Under date of March 11th, three weeks before the convention was to meet, he wrote to the State Government that "the cabinet at Washington, actively but secretly, instigated those movements." The Texans themselves, he wrote, were well aware that they were not yet entitled to separate statehood, and consequently complete separation was their real object. "They can not be so ignorant as not to know that Texas has not within its limits a sufficient number of men suitably competent to take in their hands the reins of government; and what is not less important, they must be conscious of the fact that the sources of revenue within their province are too limited to support a State organization. In view of such knowledge of prematureness of action on their part, and its consequences, it must be concluded that the revolutionary attempts, for some time observed among the people, have not for their object the erection of Texas into a separate State."

Músquiz argued that the same considerations which made a separate State untenable would apply to a separate republic, so he concluded that the real object of the Texans was either annexation to the United States or to a new confederacy of Southern States, yet to be formed. He suspected Butler of being concerned in this, and cited the fact that the

American minister had been in Texas during the previous June. "Immediately after that visit," he concluded, "the revolutionary movements of the colonists began; and anterior to that event they had been exceptionally orderly."

Finally, Santa Anna, who at last had come to terms with Bustamante and had been elected President, wrote about this time to Pedraza, who was filling the Presidential office until Santa Anna should be inaugurated on April 1st, the same date that the convention would meet at San Felipe. The subject of Santa Anna's letter was the Anglo-Americans in Texas, and it contained the suggestion that troops under General Filisola should be sent to Texas without delay.

"I deem it my duty," wrote Santa Anna, "to call special attention of the President to the condition of Texas. Satisfied as I am that the foreigners who have introduced themselves in that province have a strong tendency to declare themselves independent of the republic, and that all their remonstrances and complaints are but disguised to that end, I think it to be of paramount importance that General Filisola should forthwith proceed to fulfill his mission, having been first well supplied with good officers and the greatest number of troops possible, with instructions both to secure the integrity of our territory and do justice to the colonists. The interest of the nation requires a kind policy toward these people, for they have not on all occasions been treated with justice and liberality. That they have grounds so to feel toward our Government is derogatory to the honor of the Republic, and is deeply felt by them. Moreover, it is possible for them to become so exasperated as to make it impracticable to restore order among them without much trouble."

How Pedraza's Government felt toward the Texans, may be judged from the fact that on March 2nd, 1833, one month before the meeting of the convention, the Mexican Minister of Relations sent a formal communication to Butler, the American minister, informing him that the Anglo-Americans in Texas were preparing to secede from Mexico and unite themselves to the United States, and complaining that they were being assisted in their plans by people of the neighboring States of the North American Union. He expressed the hope that the Government of the United States would take steps to stop these activities so far as they involved citizens of the United States, and added that the President of Mexico had already issued such orders as were deemed necessary to prevent any attempt to detach Texas from Mexico.

It was amid such a maze of confusion and misunderstanding of their purposes that the Texas delegates assembled for their second convention at San Felipe on April 1st, 1833.

CHAPTER XXI

THE SECOND CONVENTION

WHEN the second convention of the Texans met on April 1st, 1833, it was found that the matters to come before it were very much the same as those which had been acted upon at the previous convention in October, with one exception. There was now a strong sentiment in favor of drafting a State constitution. Who first proposed this course is not known. Sam Houston had written to President Jackson more than three months before the convention met that a constitution would be adopted, and the fact he was made chairman of the committee appointed to draft such a document gave rise to the tradition that he originated the idea. This, however, is pure conjecture. But Houston, who at this time was not familiar with Mexican procedure, supported the proposal warmly.

The Mexican procedure for the erection of a new State, under the Constitution of 1824, was quite different from that followed in the United States. For one thing it required an amendment to the Constitution and the consent of three-fourths of the State Legislatures. For another, the idea of such an extra-legal body as a convention drafting a constitution was entirely alien to Mexican thought. Such matters, from the Mexican point of view, were for regularly constituted governmental bodies to decide, and a State constitution could be drafted only by a State Legislature. Consequently it could not be done until after statehood had been granted and a Legislature elected.

Very few of the delegates, however, were familiar with the Mexican Constitution or with Mexican procedure, and Austin's argument against the drafting of a constitution, to the effect that it would serve to create suspicion among the Mexicans and that it would accomplish nothing, was overruled by the majority. Austin's idea was to get statehood first, and then it would be time enough to draft a constitution. But the "frontier republicans" of the convention would not listen to him.

The constitution adopted was an extremely democratic one, even for an American State. Among other features, it contained the usual bill of rights, beginning with the ringing declaration: "All power is inherent in the people, and all free governments are formed upon their authority, and established for their peace, safety and happiness. For the achievement of those ends, they have the inviolable right to alter, reform and abolish the government in such a manner as they may think. Government being instituted for the protection and common interest of all persons, the slavish doctrine of non-resistance against arrogant power and oppression is discarded, as destructive to the happiness of mankind, and as insulting to the rights, and subversive of the wants of the people."

That to Mexican ears this might sound suspiciously like a declaration that the Texans had a right to do as they pleased about governing Texas and that any interference from the national Government would be regarded as the exercise of "arrogant power and oppression", and that the idea of submission to authority was "slavish doctrine", should not be surprising. However, as it turned out, this document played little or no part in subsequent events, so that the debate over it was in the nature of much ado about nothing. One of the most heated clashes in the convention was over a clause in this constitution prohibiting banks. It was adopted, however, with acclaim by the triumphant majority.

Austin's chief interest in the convention, now that he had bowed to the majority view that statehood should be petitioned for, was to see that this request should be put in proper form, and that a legal basis be urged in support of Texas's right to separate statehood without an amendment to the Constitution. In an address presented at the opening of the convention in the name of the committee of safety and correspondence, he set forth ably the chief reasons why separate statehood was necessary to the welfare of Texas, and outlined the legal grounds on which it should be prayed for. The outstanding reason he cited was the need of a judiciary in Texas with power to settle finally both civil and criminal cases, so that the protection of life and property might be secured. The legal ground for the request he set forth in the following language:

"The law of the constituent Congress of the 7th of May, 1824, evidently contemplates that Texas should form a separate State. The 2nd article of the law is in the following words as translated: 'Coahuila

and Texas shall also form another State, but so soon
as the latter is in a situation to figure as a separate
State, it shall inform Congress thereof for its resolution.' The right which this law confers upon the
people of Texas to inform Congress when they are
in a situation to figure as a State, and to apply for admission into the Union, is certainly very clear and
unequivocal."

The drafting of the petition for statehood fell to a
committee headed by David G. Burnet, and this
clause was quoted and made the basis of Texas's right
to separate statehood. The petition also set forth a
strong argument to the effect that the setting up of a
separate State in Texas was the only way to insure
an orderly government capable of protecting life and
property and to draw the people of Texas closer to
the national Government. Evidently at Austin's instance a paragraph was inserted excusing the method
employed to bring the matter to the attention of the
Government, thus forestalling any criticism that the
regular constitutional procedure had not been followed. This paragraph read as follows:

"The General Congress may possibly consider the
mode of this communication as informal. To this
suggestion we would, with great deference, reply that
the events of the past year have not only violated the
established forms and etiquette of the Government,
but have suspended, at least, its vital functions; and
it would appear exceedingly rigorous to exact from
the inhabitants of Texas, living on a remote frontier
of the Republic, a minute conformity to unimportant
punctilios. The ardent desire of the people is made
known to the Congress through their select repre-

sentatives, the most direct and unequivocal medium by which they can possibly be conveyed; and surely the enlightened Congress will readily concur with us in the sentiment that the wishes and wants of the people form the best rule for legislative guidance. The people of Texas consider it not only an absolute right, but a most sacred and imperative duty to themselves and to the Mexican nation, to represent their wants in a respectful manner to the General Government, and to solicit the best remedy of which the nature of their grievances will admit. Should they utterly fail in this duty, and great and irremediable evils ensue, the people would have reason to reproach themselves alone; and the General Congress, in whom the remedial power resides, would also have reason to censure their supineness and want of fidelity to the nation. Under this view, we trust the Congress will not regard with excessive severity any slight departure which the good people of Texas may in this instance have made from the ordinary formalities of the Government."

The convention, which lasted two weeks, adopted also petitions for the repeal of the obnoxious features of the Law of April 6th, 1830, and for modification of the tariff, and it went on record as opposed to the African slave trade. Austin had presided over the previous convention and William H. Wharton had been named to present the petitions to the Government at Mexico City. This was reversed at the second convention, for Wharton presided, and Austin, along with J. B. Miller of San Felipe, was chosen to go to Mexico City.

At the time, some suspicion was expressed that Austin would not urge the proposal of separate statehood with sufficient zeal. But the attitude of a majority of the colonists, as expressed by their representatives in the convention, had convinced Austin that separate statehood was absolutely necessary to tranquility and orderly government in Texas, and henceforth he was to urge it upon Mexican leaders in season and out, not only as necessary to the welfare of the people of Texas, but as essential to maintain the integrity of the Republic's territory. Indeed, he had become convinced that if the Government refused to grant statehood, the people of Texas should set up a State Government of their own without the permission of Congress, while declaring their absolute adherence to the Mexican Republic. He came to regard this course as the only way to prevent the separation of Texas from Mexico.

Having arrived at this conviction, Austin determined to make another effort to obtain the support of the Mexican citizens of San Antonio to the petition. For some reason, Miller was unable to make the trip to Mexico City, so Austin endeavored to have Erasmo Seguin accompany him. He failed to obtain the cooperation of the people of San Antonio, however, for some of their leaders were now suspicious of the whole move, and the general opinion among them was that the people of Texas had no right under the law to present such a petition to the Congress. Austin was compelled to be content with the assurance that San Antonio would do nothing against the petition. Seguín could not accompany him to Mexico City, so he made the trip alone.

The revolution which had resulted in the overthrow of Bustamante had been fought by a coalition
between Santa Anna and the movement headed by
Gomez Farias, a sincere Federal Republican, whose
program was more definite than Santa Anna's. Santa
Anna, aiming only at power and seeking only an excuse for revolt, had based his opposition to Bustamante on alleged unconstitutional acts of the cabinet,
and his original demand had been only for the cabinet's resignation. But Farias had formulated a program more in keeping with what he conceived to be
his country's needs. He deplored the fact that the result of the election of 1828 had not been accepted,
that Pedraza, the duly elected President, had not
been seated, but that Guerrero had been made President by violence. He demanded, therefore, a restoration of "legitimacy" by the seating of Pedraza to
serve out the unexpired term. He wanted to see the
officials of the Federal Government chosen in peaceable elections. To this end he also demanded a reduction of the size of the army, and the abolition of
the civil privileges and powers of the clergy. In this
age-old struggle in Mexico, which has persisted
down to the present day, Farias was decidedly a liberal. He was a civilian, and not a soldier, but in the
sincere hope that by doing so he might establish
peaceful elections in Mexico, he had taken up arms.
Santa Anna, in order to obtain his cooperation, had
agreed to the program of "legitimacy" and to the
seating of Pedraza, pending the holding of a peaceful election. The election had resulted in the naming of Santa Anna, who was still regarded as a Fed-

eral Republican, as President, and Gomez Farias as Vice President.

At the same time a Federal Republican Congress was elected. Indeed, to a very great degree it was a radical Congress, and it is said that many of its most violent members were elected through the deliberate support of Centralists and anti-republicans, who reasoned that this was the best course to follow in order to assure quick reaction over the country. This Congress went into session during the closing weeks of Pedraza's short administration, and on April 1st, the same day the Texans held their convention, Santa Anna and Farias were inaugurated. The Congress had launched immediately upon a program of "reform", enacting sweeping laws against the privileges of the clergy, secularizing education, and radically reducing the army. Santa Anna, thinking only of power and with no interest to serve save that of his own ambition, had no intention of becoming identified with such a program, so he discreetly retired to the quiet of his hacienda in the State of Vera Cruz, on some pretext, immediately after the inauguration and left Farias in charge of the Government. The Congress continued on its career of "reform", and within six weeks after the inauguration leaders of the Centralists had issued a document, denouncing that body and its acts in the most unequivocal language. At this juncture, Santa Anna appeared at the capital and took charge of the Government, and on May 26th, ten days after Santa Anna's return, Colonel Ignacio Escalada, of the State of Michoacan, issued a proclamation pledging himself and his followers "to defend at all hazards

the religion of Christ and the rights and privileges
of the Church and of the army." At the same time
he called upon Santa Anna to assume the rôle of pro-
tector of those rights and privileges. Santa Anna immediately made a great show of taking the field
against these "rebels", turning the Government over
to Farias again, and on June 6th, he contrived to
have himself taken prisoner by his own troops and
proclaimed dictator. But he rackoned without the
patriot Farias. Left without loyal troops at the capital, the Vice President seemed helpless. But in a
few days he raised a volunteer force of six thousand
men, repulsed an attack on the Palace, and then announced that he was going to rescue the "captive"
President. Santa Anna, of course, then "escaped" and
returned to the capital.

Stephen Austin reached Mexico City on July 18th,
having been delayed at sea in a storm-tossed vessel for
a month. A week before this, Santa Anna had again
left the capital to "suppress" another revolution. The
leaders of this new revolt were two army officers,
Arista and Durán, who had issued a pronunciamento
calling upon Santa Anna to assume dictatorial powers and abolish the federal system of government.
It was to the Vice President, Gomez Farias, therefore, that Austin presented the petition of the Texans
for separate statehood. And at the moment of its
presentation a revolution was being launched with
the object of invalidating the statehood of all the
States of the Federation.

CHAPTER XXII

AUSTIN AT THE CAPITAL

IF the events in Mexico City having relation to the petition of the Texans should be recounted in the same manner that a resident of the city at the time might have learned of them from the newspapers between July 18th, 1833, when Stephen Austin arrived, and December 10th, when he departed for home, they would take something like the following order:

July 18th: Austin arrives in Mexico City to confer with the Government on a petition of the Texans praying for the repeal of the provision of the law of April 6th, 1830, prohibiting American immigration to Texas, for certain modification of the tariff laws, and for the setting up of Texas as a separate State in the Mexican Confederation.

July and August, various dates: Austin is received by Carlos García, Minister of Relations, and Ramos Arispe, Minister of Justice. He is assured that the petition of the Texans will be given cordial consideration, and submitted to the Congress with favorable recommendations with respect to the reforms asked. Doubt is expressed by the two ministers, however, that separate statehood can be granted under the Constitution without a vote of two-thirds of the State Legislatures. The ministers request Austin to

submit further argument on this latter point. Austin
submits further argument in writing, making a strong
plea for separate statehood as the best means of binding the Texans to the Mexican Confederation. He
contends that the law of May 7th, 1824, creating the
State of Coahuila and Texas, is sufficient legal
ground for action by the Congress, granting Texas
separate statehood, without the consent of the various
State Legislatures.

August 21st: The whole matter of the petition of
the Texans is referred to the Congress.

September: Congress is not in session, on account
of an epidemic of cholera.

October 22nd: The Chamber of Deputies, by almost a unanimous vote, passes a bill, containing three
articles, repealing the provisions of the Law of April
6th, 1830, applying to American immigration to
Texas. The new bill would open Texas again to un-
restricted American colonization. The Senate, after
some debate, passes the first two articles of the bill.
(A few days later the Senate passed the bill finally).

November 5th: President Santa Anna, who has returned to the capital, has Austin to appear before a
meeting of the cabinet to discuss the whole Texas
question. Austin is promised everything except
separate statehood. He is even assured that the Government will make representations to the State Legislature of the State of Coahuila and Texas recommending that certain reforms in the interest of the
Texans be instituted, including trial by jury.

December 7th: The final answer of the Government is delivered to Austin. American immigration
is restored, representations have been made to the

Legislature of Coahuila and Texas to enact laws
which the Texans require, the question of tariff relief has been referred to the Treasury Department,
and favorable action may be expected. Hope is held
out that in the future, when Texas has more population, and if order is maintained in the meantime, separate statehood may be granted.

December 10th: Austin departs for home, having
accomplished all the objects of his mission, except
separate statehood for Texas.

This is the manner in which the sequence of
events might have been recorded in the newspapers
down to December 10th, 1833. And the record would
have been correct in every particular. But then in a
few weeks, like a bolt from the blue, would come
the news that Austin had been arrested at Saltillo
on January 3rd, 1834, by order of the Federal Government! The Government, it seems, was in possession of information that Austin had sent recommendations to the Texans that if the petition for
statehood was refused by the Government, to proceed to organize a State Government anyhow, without the Federal Government's consent, and it was
believed that he was returning to Texas to carry
out this plan. And then it would have been learned
that Austin had been brought back to Mexico City,
thrown in a dungeon of the old Inquisition prison,
and held there *incomunicado*.

Now what really had happened? Austin undoubtedly was a loyal Mexican citizen, and undoubtedly also he was returning to Texas to urge the
Texans to be content with the concessions the Government had made, and to help to stimulate the de-

velopment and progress of Texas by encouraging a big immigration of Americans to colonize the country. Why, then, did the Government order his arrest?

The occasion of his arrest was a letter which he had written to the *ayuntamiento* of San Antonio, informing that body that it appeared that nothing would be done to relieve the situation in Texas, expressing the opinion that the Texans must move to help themselves, and suggesting that the *ayuntamiento* take steps at once, by communicating with the other *ayuntamientos* in Texas, and that a local State government be organized without waiting for the consent of the Federal Government. The *ayuntamiento* of San Antonio transmitted this letter, through the Political Chief and the Governor of the State, to the Federal Government. It had arrived at Mexico City after Austin's departure for home, and Gomez Farias, who was acting President during the latest absence of Santa Anna from the city, immediately took alarm and ordered Austin's arrest.

Austin's letter to the San Antonio *ayuntamiento* was dated October 2nd, practically three weeks before the Chamber of Deputies acted on the bill restoring American immigration. At that time Congress had reconvened, but had made no move with respect to Texas, and on the previous day Austin had had a violent interview with Gomez Farias, in which he had expressed the fear that if something was not done to provide Texas with a local government, the Texans would take matters in their own hands. The same day that he wrote the San Antonio letter, Austin also wrote to his brother-in-law, James F. Perry, as follows: "I am so much afflicted by accounts of the deaths by cholera in Texas that I can scarcely write anything . . . Whether it has taken you all off is uncertain. I am too wretched to write much on this subject or any other . . . I will try to get home as soon as I can. There has been no meeting of Congress since early in August until a few days since, so that nothing is done. I am tired of this Government. They are always in revolution and I believe always will be. I have had much more respect for them than they deserve. But I am done with all that." Among the deaths from cholera in Texas, of which he had just heard, was that of his little niece, Mary Perry. His feelings were wrought up, and he was naturally depressed by the absolute inaction of Congress. He had been waiting in Mexico City for two months and a half, and absolutely nothing had been done. He despaired of anything being done, and sincerely believing that in such a situation the Texans would be compelled to act for themselves or that chaos would result in Texas, he wrote to the San Antonio *ayuntamiento* suggesting that it take the initiative, precisely because its members were native Mexicans and would not be suspected of disloyalty to the Republic. That is the whole explanation of Austin's letter.

Three weeks after it was written Congress made its first move, and from that time things went forward more rapidly. The whole situation had changed when he left Mexico City, and he had no idea of doing anything else than to make the best of the situation and to advise his colonists and all others in Texas to do likewise. Unfortunately Gomez Farias took counsel from his fears, and so ordered Austin's arrest.

If Austin's plea for separate statehood had been considered in its true light, and if Farias had recognized Austin for the real patriot he was in urging it, much that happened subsequently might have been avoided. Austin sought in every way to bring the leaders of the Government to recognize that the best interests of Mexico demanded that Texas be separated from Coahuila and granted a separate State government of its own. He continued this effort even after his arrest, publishing a pamphlet in Spanish on the subject in January, 1835. Austin's argument, which he presented in writing to the Government in July, 1833, and which he reiterated and elaborated during a year and a half after that, may be said to be summed up in the following paragraphs from his original brief:

"Interest is the most powerful bond that operates upon the actions and desires of humanity. By the application of this fundamental principle to Texas, all erroneous ideas vanish in a moment, and also the false rumors that may have existed concerning the danger of the Mexican territory in that country.

"The interests of Texas are: to cement her union with Mexico, and to have a local government as a State of this Federation.

"These interests are the natural bonds that unite and always will unite Texas to the Mexican Federation. But the last is of so much importance, and so indispensably necessary to the 'welfare' and 'happiness' of that people, that it cannot be ommitted or delayed. Consequently, if there were no way of obtaining it without breaking the bonds of the union with Mexico, it would then be the interest of Texas to attempt her separation. . . .

"I cannot imagine anything more urgent for the exercise of extraordinary power than this, since by its exercise in this matter the integrity of the territory may be preserved, Texas and her inhabitants may be saved, and a new and strong column may be raised to sustain the great edifice of the Mexican Federation."

Thus it was that Austin pointed out to Mexican leaders the course by which Texas might be saved to Mexico. But instead of heeding his advice, the Mexican Government had him thrown into a dungeon as a seditious person.

CHAPTER XXIII

SANTA ANNA UNMASKS

AUSTIN was kept in solitary confinement in an Inquisition dungeon for three months—from February 13th until May 9th, 1834. Two short interviews with a priest who had lived in Texas and one or two visits from officials constituted all the communication he had with the outside world during that period. He was supplied with only three books of indifferent interest, and there was sufficient light in his dungeon to read by only about five hours a day.

"What a horrible punishment is solitary confinement," he wrote, "shut up in a dungeon with scarcely light enough to distinguish anything. If I were a criminal it would be another thing, but I am not one . . . I prefer bread and water with books, to the best of eating without them. In a dungeon, the mind and thoughts require aliment more than the body."

He was not informed as to the nature of the charges against him; he was not permitted to consult a lawyer; and until nearly four months after his arrest no move was made by anybody, in Texas or elsewhere, in his defense.

On April 28th, 1834, the *ayuntamiento* at San Felipe adopted a memorial to be sent to the Government in his behalf, and whether in response to this or not, on May 9th the rigid regime of his confine-

ment was relaxed to the extent of permitting him to
visit other parts of the prison during the day, to receive and write letters, and to receive visitors. On
May 17th a newly created *ayuntamiento* at Matagorda adopted a similar memorial, and like action
was taken by the *ayuntamiento* at Liberty on May
31st. That was all, and even of that Austin knew
nothing.

Meantime, the Texans had begun to enjoy the ben-
efits of the reforms Austin had obtained for them at
Mexico City. The lifting of the ban against American immigration was not the only benefit he had obtained for them, though it was the most apparent, for
a steady increase of new colonists was brightening the
outlook for Texas considerably. But the State Legislature, in line with the suggestion of the Federal
Government, had taken a new attitude toward Texas.
Up to this time Texas had been divided into two departments—Bexar and Nacogdoches—each under a
Mexican Political Chief. The settlements along the
Brazos and the Colorado rivers were attached to the
Department of Bexar. During the period that Austin was in solitary confinement, the State Legislature
created a new department, the Department of the
Brazos, comprising all of the region of Austin's
original colony, and Henry Smith, an Anglo-American, was appointed Political Chief. A judiciary system for Texas, with trial by jury in criminal cases,
was created, and the use of the English language in
all official documents was legalized. Texas was given
an additional member of the Legislature, and four
new municipalities—those of Matagorda, Mina, San
Augustin, and San Patricio—were instituted. A high

degree of local self-government was thus granted the Anglo-American citizens of Texas, and unquestionably all of this was the result of Austin's labors in Mexico City during the latter half of 1833.

Meanwhile, Austin was lying in a dungeon, more than a thousand miles away from Texas, seemingly forgotten. He was not forgotten, of course, but he had no way of knowing this. He had requested that no excitement over his arrest be permitted, and that nobody should worry over his situation. In fact, he had asked that nothing be done unless he should be "unjustly dealt with". However, he probably had not expected solitary confinement when he made this request, and it would be difficult to imagine what the phrase "unjustly dealt with" would include if not that. All kinds of rumors were current as to Austin's ultimate fate, one being that he was to be sent to a penal settlement in California for ten years, and there is documentary evidence that land speculators were intriguing to get him out of the way and that this move was blocked by no less a person than Santa Anna, who returned opportunely to the capital after one of his periodical absences from the Presidency. It is difficult to explain the fact that during a period of three months when not a word was received in Texas directly from Austin, nobody went to Mexico City to inquire into his fate.

On May 26th, 1834, the American Secretary of State wrote the American minister at Mexico City, Anthony Butler, to look into Austin's case and report on it. Butler, however, was the last man to expect to do anything for Austin. He took two months to reply and then he informed the Secretary of State bluntly

that Austin was receiving his just deserts. "He is unquestionably one of the bitterest foes of our Government and people that is to be found in Mexico," he
wrote, "and has done more to embarras our negotiations upon a certain subject than all the rest of the opposition together; and I am very sure that he was the
principal cause of my being defeated in the last effort to obtain a cession of Texas."

What the nature of Butler's "negotiations" were
may be inferred from a personal letter which he
wrote to President Jackson in October, 1833, while
Austin was attempting to convince the Mexican Government that Texas should be given separate statehood. In this letter he reported to President Jackson
that he had had a conversation with "one of the most
shrewd and intelligent men in the country," who held
high official position, and whose influence with Santa
Anna was very great, and that this dignitary had informed him that the cession of Texas could be obtained by the payment of two or three hundred thousand dollars to a certain man of importance, and
another three or four hundred thousand to other parties. President Jackson replied hotly that the United
States would have nothing to do with bribery. But
Butler was not discouraged by his chief's "squeam-
ishness" for in March, 1834, while Austin was in
solitary confinement, he wrote to President Jackson
suggesting that it was a good time to take forcible
possession of Texas, and proposed that he (Butler)
be commissioned to head such an expedition. It was
on the back of this letter that Jackson inscribed his
famous characterization of Butler: "A. Butler.
What a scamp!" And yet Butler remained as the

American diplomatic representative at Mexico City for nearly two years after Jackson had so characterized him.

On June 12th, 1834, Austin was moved to another prison, known as the Acordada, where he occupied a room on the second floor, with a window opening on a balcony facing the street. Besides being deprived of his liberty, his chief inconveniences were now bad diet and lack of exercise. The uncertainty of his fate, however, and the persistent rumor, which came to his ears, that he was to be banished to a penal settlement for ten years, caused him some degree of anxiety. Three different courts had declined jurisdiction over his case, and he had no way of knowing when he would even be given a hearing. Meantime, there was gossip in Mexico City that the Anglo-Americans in Texas were indifferent to his fate, and, fearing that this talk would injure him, Austin wrote to Oliver Jones, member of the Legislature from the Department of the Brazos, and to S. M. Williams, suggesting that the *ayuntamientos* of Texas make representations to the Federal Government in his behalf. As a result of this request, several of the municipalities adopted memorials setting forth that Austin's policy had always been in keeping with a strict loyalty to Mexico, and Peter Grayson and Spencer H. Jack were chosen to go to Mexico City as the representatives of the Texans to appear in Austin's behalf.

Grayson and Jack arrived in Mexico City on October 15th, 1834, and obtained counsel for Austin, and on December 25th, 1834, almost a year after his arrest, the prisoner was released on bond, his surety being Pascual Villar, a wealthy resident of Mexico City. Under the terms of his bond, however, he was not permitted to leave the limits of the city.

Grayson said afterwards that they were disposed to regard Austin's release on bond "in substance as an acquittal". This was a natural inference "in a country where mere rumor and suspicion stand in the place of legitimate evidence, and imprisonment for an indefinite period, at the pleasure of the Government, is the only means relied upon for securing the person of any one they expect to punish."

Indeed, Austin immediately resumed his activities among Mexican leaders with the object of convincing them that the surest way of binding Texas to the Mexican Federation permanently would be to grant it separate statehood. Within a month after his release he published a pamphlet, written in Spanish, which attracted wide and favorable attention in Mexico City, and which gained many powerful friends for the cause of Texas statehood.

Things were looking better for Texas. Indeed, better conditions had prevailed in Texas during almost the entire period of Austin's absence. Aside from the cholera epidemic in the summer of 1833, which affected business conditions everywhere in Mexico, no untoward happenings had occurred, and with the renewal of American immigration and the setting up of local self-government in the Department of the Brazos under the legislative reforms of the spring of 1834, the outlook for continued progress and prosperity in Texas became better than at any time since 1830. All controversial questions had been settled, except those of statehood, the tariff, and the charges against Austin. It was expected that the charges against Austin would be dropped in due course, that there would be an amicable adjustment of the tariff question, and that statehood would come naturally in the future, developing from the self-governing departments of the Brazos, Nacogdoches, and Bexar. Indeed, if the Anglo-American population continued to increase, in the course of a few years Texas would have such a large representation in the State Legislature that Coahuila would be quite as eager for separation as Texas. In any event, so far as these questions were concerned, there was now no danger that they would lead to a break between Texas and Mexico. It is important to appreciate this fully in order to understand the causes of the final break in the fall of 1835. It is not too much to say that even if the Law of April 6th, 1830, had never been passed, and the demand for statehood had never been made, it is more than probable that Texas and Mexico would have come to the parting of the ways before the close of 1835 just the same. For it was a new and greater grievance which brought about the Texas revolution, a grievance for which the Texans were in no way responsible.

The train of events which led inevitably to the Texas revolution was started while Austin was still in prison. On May 23rd, 1834, the leading Centralists of the State of Morelos met at Cuernavaca and promulgated a "plan" declaring themselves ready to defend "the religion of Christ and the rights and privileges of the church and the army". They called upon Santa Anna to dissolve the radical Congress, assume the powers of a dictator, and become the

leader of a movement toward centralism. Up until
this time, as has been seen, Santa Anna had made a
great show of being opposed to all such revolutionary movements toward centralism; but it is significant that every such movement started during 1833
and 1834 offered the leadership to Santa Anna. In
spite of his protestations of allegiance to the Constitution of 1824, the Centralists apparently knew their
man. That they were not mistaken in him was proved
abundantly within a week after the promulgation of
the "Plan of Cuernavaca", when Santa Anna responded to the call of the Centralists and violated his
oath of office by becoming the leader of their revolution. He dissolved the Congress, dismissed the members of the Farias cabinet, dissolved the State Legislatures, dismissed Governors of States who did not adhere promptly to the "Plan of Cuernavaca", and even
ejected municipal officers who refused to do his bidding. The army and the clergy rallied to his support
and in the space of a few weeks he was "ruling as
dictator, without congress, council, legislatures, or
ministers". It was thus, by a series of unconstitutional acts, that the predicate was laid for the absolute abrogation of the Constitution of 1824.

The Legislature of the State of Coahuila and
Texas had just adjourned the session at which the reforms favorable to the Texans had been enacted, and
the members had dispersed to their homes, when the
news of the extraordinary acts of Santa Anna was
received. Becoming alarmed, the acting Governor
and the Permanent Deputation immediately issued
a call for a special session of the Legislature to meet
at Monclova on August 9th to devise measures for

the safety of the Federation. The call set forth that the peace of the nation was threatened by "the collision of the supreme national authorities and by pronunciamentos which as a pretext invoke religion, which is really free from danger". Steps should be taken, it declared, to prevent any disturbance in the State which such events might occasion, and the Governor was authorized to arrest anyone who attempted to start such a movement within the State.

Had all sections of Coahuila supported this move, the matter might have been brought to a crisis at once. But for more than a year an internal controversy had been in progress over the location of the State capital, it having been moved temporarily from Saltillo to Monclova, and this division affected all public questions. When the State Government at Monclova, therefore, declared against the "Plan of Cuernavaca", the municipal authorities at Saltillo declared in favor of it, and the inhabitants of Southern Coahuila supported Saltillo's view. A rival State Government was set up at Saltillo, and although the Monclova Government sought to rescind its stand with respect to the "Plan", the two Governments continued to claim the sole right to rule the State.

When Oliver Jones, member of the Legislature from the Department of the Brazos, arrived at Monclova for the special session, he found a condition of chaos. Reporting to Henry Smith, the Political Chief, Jones wrote, under date of September 2nd, 1834, as follows:

"The political affairs of this section of the country are in a state of anarchy and confusion. The State

Government has fallen into pieces, without a foundation on which another can be constitutionally erected. On the 30th of last month an officer of the permanent army was proclaimed Governor of the State by fifteen officers of the army, two members of the *ayuntamiento* of this place, and three of the deputies of the Congress (Legislature), and the former Governor turned out of office. There is not, nor will there be, any Congress or Permanant Deputation in this place during the present year. At one time since my arrival in this city there were seven members present, two of whom were of the Saltillo party, and refused to serve, and immediately left for that place . . . . I shall, if permitted remain here a few weeks longer. The Government established in Saltillo still exists and is gaining ground. The towns of Rio Grande, Morales, San Juan de Mat, and Santa Rosa have declared in favor of Saltillo. There are about five hundred militia and permanent troops in this place, but up to the present time they have remained inactive. The Government of Saltillo appears to be on an equal footing with that of this place, and has an equal number of supporters in this part of the State. Is not Texas as much entitled to a government as the former? She is without one, in fact none exists in the nation of which she forms a part. I am of the opinion that this is a subject worthy of your deliberation at this critical moment."

So it was that Santa Anna's unconstitutional acts precipitated a condition of confusion and anarchy throughout Mexico.

CHAPTER XXIV

DOOM OF THE CONSTITUTION

To understand fully the events of the years 1834 and 1835 which led inevitably to the separation of Texas from Mexico it is important to see Santa Anna in his true character, not as the constitutional President of the United Mexican States, but as the leader of a violent revolution the object of which was to change the form of government completely. The circumstance that he was in fact the President of Mexico at the time he placed himself at the head of this revolution did not give any degree of legitimacy to his revolutionary course, but on the contrary rendered him guilty of treasonable violation of his oath of office.

When Santa Anna was inauguarated on April 1st, 1833, he took an oath to observe the Constitution. "I, Antonio Lopez de Santa Anna," he swore, "appointed President of the United Mexican States, swear before God and His holy evangelists, that I will faithfully discharge the office with which the United States have trusted me, and that I will observe, and cause to be observed, exactly the Constitution and general laws of the Confederation."

One of the provisions of the Constitution which he thus swore to observe and cause to be observed "exactly" was the final clause of that document, which read as follows:

"Those articles of this Constitution and of the Constitutive Act which establish the liberty and independence of the Mexican nation, its religion, *form of government,* liberty of the press, and the division of the supreme powers of the Union and *of the States,* can never be changed."

And the first article of Title II of the Constitution, which treated of the "form of government of the nation", provided as follows:

"The Mexican Nation adopts for the form of its government a popular representative and *federal* republic."

In other words, in the first quoted article above it was provided that no matter how the Constitution might be amended, in accordance with the provisions made for amendment, certain provisions could never be changed, and these included the article which provided that the form of government should be "a popular representative and *federal* republic."

Santa Anna, when inaugurated, swore to observe "exactly" these provisions of the Constitution. But thirteen months after he had taken that solemn oath, on May 31st, 1834, he placed himself at the head of a violent revolution, the object of which was to abolish the federal form of government, destroy the autonomy of the States, and establish a centralized government at Mexico City. And from that day until April 22nd, 1836, when he became a prisoner of the Texans at San Jacinto, he proceeded on his revolutionary course, and was not, during all that time, in any strict sense, the constitutional President of Mexico.

The provision with respect to the unchangable character of the form of government was not the only one which Santa Anna violated, to be sure. Having embarked upon an absolutely unconstitutional course, all provisions of the Constitution were completely disregarded. As has been seen, he proceeded without constitutional warrant to dissolve the Congress, dismiss the Governors of States, dissolve the State Legislatures, and even to remove from office local officials who refused to do his bidding. He accomplished all this by force, of course, with the army as his instrument, and he crushed all opposition ruthlessly. But when he called an election for a new Congress, with the object of obtaining one which would be pliant to his will, he found himself faced by a military-clerical coalition among the Centralists who proposed to set the pace themselves. The election proved to be a contest between Santa Anna's personal following and this coalition, and the coalition won, the Federal Republicans of the country being completely overawed by military force, and prevented from playing any part in the election. When the new Congress convened on January 4th, 1835, Santa Anna found that the net result of his unconstitutional course had been to place the country in the absolute control of an ultra-centralist party which proposed to give him orders, rather than to obey any proceeding from him. So he retired again to his hacienda in Vera Cruz to await developments, leaving General Miguel Barragán in charge of the President's office.

The new Congress, which had been named in this unconstitutional fashion, set about at once to prepare the way for the absolute destruction of the federal form of government. It went through the hocus-pocus of receiving deputations and reading memorials petitioning for a centralized government, but it ignored remonstrances against this course which came from all parts of the Republic. In order to forestall armed opposition from the States, it passed, on March 31st, 1835, an act reducing the militia in all the States to one militiaman to each five hundred inhabitants, and under the provisions of this act, it ordered that the people of the States be disarmed. Then on May 2nd, 1835, it adopted a solemn declaration that it had been vested "by the will of the nation" with full discretionary power to change the Constitution. Under this altogether questionable authority, the Congress took up the discussion of a new Constitution.

It is against the background of all this that the events in Texas in 1834 and 1835 must be seen if they are to be understood fully. During this period the whole of Mexico was in a condition of ferment over the course of political events. But in Texas, during 1834 and the early months of 1835, the great mass of the people were paying little attention to "politics". When Henry Smith received the letter from Oliver Jones, quoted in the previous chapter, he attempted to hold an election to set up a separate government for Texas, like the two already existing in Coahuila, but he found the sentiment of the people against him. They were too busy picking their cotton and selling it at a good price to concern themselves about such matters. Smith's proposal was voted down, wherever the local officials took the trouble to hold the election at all, and even when the *ayuntamiento* at San Antonio, acting upon the advice of the member of the Legislature from the Department of Bexar, also suggested a separate State government for Texas, the suggestion was ignored.

The people of Texas were prosperous and they wanted nothing from the State or Federal Government so much as to be let alone. Both Governments were in a bad way, to be sure, but the majority of the Texans were not worrying much about that for the moment. An observation made by Col. Juan N. Almonte in a report to the Federal Government applies with striking aptness to conditions during the fall of 1834 and the winter of 1834-35. "In Texas," he wrote, "with the exception of some disturbers, they only think of growing the sugar cane, cotton, corn, wheat, tobacco, the breeding of cattle, opening of roads, and rendering rivers navigable." Henry Smith described the same condition, from a different point of view, when he declared that the people of Texas "are indeed, as in the days of Noah, marrying and giving in marriage, eating and sleeping, and selling their cotton forsooth at a tolerable price, and this . . . is irrefragable proof that all is well."

This condition continued during the winter and into the spring. During January and February two thousand new immigrants from the United States landed at the mouth of the Brazos alone. Austin's partner, Williams, wrote to him very optimistic reports of the outlook, and Austin himself wrote that "it is really not so *very* important whether anything is done or not (by the Government for Texas) if a dead calm and union can be preserved in the country. Immigration—good crops—no party divisions—no excitements—no personalities—should be the political creed of everyone in Texas."

For the moment such was the political creed of the majority of the industrious farmers who made up the great bulk of the Anglo-American population of Texas. The assembling of Congress in January disturbed them not, and the fact that the rival governments in Coahuila left the State without any generally recognized head was of little consequence. However, Santa Anna, finally settled the dispute in Coahuila, by deciding in favor of Monclova and ordering an election for a new Legislature. This election was held in Texas on February 9th, and the session of this new body began at Monclova on March 1st. It will be noted that up until this time the reactionary Congress had made no definite move toward changing the form of government, and it was not until March 31st that it passed the militia bill. When the Legislature of Coahuila and Texas assembled on March 1st, the people of Texas were getting ready for a new crop season with little fear of the political future. And yet before another crop was harvested Texas was in a condition of revolution. Nothing could illustrate more strikingly than that contrast the truth that the revolution was forced upon the Texans by events in Mexico, events over which they had no control.

The State Legislature convened, canvassed the returns of the election and declared that Augustín Viesca had been elected Governor, and Ramón Músquiz of San Antonio, Lieutenant Governor. In the absence of both of these gentlemen, José M. Cantú was named to serve until the arrival of one of them. So a State Government was reestablished, but the Saltillo delegation and members friendly to that city, were far from satisfied. However, the outlook was not disturbing. What might have happened were it not for the fact that before the Legislature was in session many weeks a giant land scheme was put through, by which nearly two million acres of Texas lands were sold for a pittance to speculators, can only be conjectured. This action gave the friends of Saltillo an excuse to withdraw from the Legislature and declare the new State Government and the election at which it was named illegal. As shall be seen, it also aroused much indignation against the State Government in Texas, and gave the Centralist reactionaries, in control of the national Government, the material with which to attempt to cloud the issue.

The reactionaries expected that opposition to their centralization program would develop in Coahuila, and the Commandant of the Eastern Interior Provinces was watching the situation closely. This office was now held by General Martín Perfecto de Cos, Santa Anna's brother-in-law. He anticipated that Coahuila would resist the process of disarming the militia, in accordance with the law of March 31st, and this belief was well-based. A storm of protest against this measure had gone up from other States, and Zacatecas, which bordered Coahuila on the south, had decided to resist it. When news of this defiance was received at Mexico City, and transmitted to Santa Anna, he emerged from his retire-

ment again in order to achieve new glories on the
battlefield. On April 9th Congress granted him
special permission to take to the field, and he proceeded to Zacatecas to crush the resistance in an orgy
of slaughter that is remembered in that State to this
day. It was at this juncture that the governor-elect of
Coahuila and Texas, Augustín Viesca, arrived at
Monclova. He was inaugurated on April 15th, and
he issued immediately a call for militia to support
the State Government against the national military
under Cos. The Saltillo contingent had appealed to
Cos, and he had decided to make their appeal and
the sale of the Texas lands the excuses for placing
the State under military rule. It was this move that
Viesca resolved to resist, and he asked each of the
three departments of Texas to place one hundred
militiamen at his disposal.

On April 22nd the State Legislature of Coahuila
and Texas, in keeping with the attitude assumed by
the Governor, adopted a strong memorial to Congress, protesting against the law regulating the militia and declaring against any assumption by Congress
of the power to modify the Constitution of 1824. This
memorial challenged the authority of Congress to
amend the Constitution or to change the form of the
Government or to exercise any powers beyond those
fixed by certain articles of the Constitution, which it
cited.

"The State of Coahuila and Texas," it declared,
"lawfully represented by its Legislature, protests in
the most solemn manner that, having joined the Confederacy by virtue of the fundamental pact, and on
the basis therein established, it neither does, nor ever

will, recognize the acts and measures emanating from the General Congress, should they not conform to the plain meaning of the aforementioned articles. It will admit no other amendment of the Constitution than those effected conformably to the steps and requisites provided in the same."

Pointing out that part of the State was settled by Anglo-Americans, it declared that "the contemplated reforms would highly compromit not only the internal order and tranquility, but also the very integrity of the national territory." The memorial specifically condemned Santa Anna's campaign against the "patriotic State of Zacatecas", and protested against the course of General Cos, who, it declared, was interfering with the internal administration of the State in a most turbulent manner and attempting to bring the civil authorities under subjection to the military.

On the subject of the law of March 31st, reducing the militia to one militiaman to each five hundred inhabitants, the Legislature had the following to say:

"This body would fail in its duty were it to be indifferent to the serious evils that the fulfillment of that decree would cause to the entire nation and to the State it represents.

"Coahuila and Texas suffers a cruel and desolating Indian war. The garrisons destined to pursue and chastise the savages, besides being incapable of acting, from absolute neglect, are separated from the purpose for which they were established at the pleasure and caprice of the commandant generals, who withdraw them from the frontier when they choose, as is actually the case in this State, in which the Commandant, Don Martin Perfecto de Cos, has considered it more proper and beneficial to coerce the supreme authorities, and favor the disturbances of one town, than to pursue the savages, although they are destroying the lives and property of the citizens.

"In so perplexed and difficult a condition of affairs, can the Legislature of Coahuila and Texas be desired not to remonstrate on seeng the civic militia disappear, the sole support and defense—the only force that can apply itself to the preservation of order, and support of the laws? What would be its condition in such an event? The most deplorable and abject that could occur."

All of this, be it noted, was adopted by a Legislature composed almost entirely of native Mexicans, just as the Legislature of Zacatecas, which had adopted similar memorials, was composed completely of native Mexicans. The Anglo-Americans in Texas at that moment were engaged chiefly in "growing the sugar cane, cotton, corn, wheat, tobacco, the breeding of cattle, opening of roads, and rendering rivers navigable".

CHAPTER XXV

STATE GOVERNMENT WRECKED

THE Legislature of Coahuila and Texas adjourned on May 21st, 1835, after authorizing Governor Viesca to remove the seat of Government to some safer place than Monclova and to put the State in a condition of defense. The "safer place" meant Texas, and four days later Governor Viesca, with an escort of militia, left Monclova with the object of establishing a new capital at San Antonio, thus making that town the center of resistance to Santa Anna and the national Congress. Within a few days after leaving, however, he was captured by a detachment of Cos's troops, then rescued by the State militia, and thenceforth was a fugitive and his Government a nullity. Cos took charge and proceeded to set up a new State Government, and he sent dispatches to the Political Chiefs in Texas notifying them of this action, and instructing them to continue to require the laws to be observed and to make no innovations. At Cos's suggestion, the national Congress had passed a decree nullifying the acts of the Legislature by which immense tracts of Texas lands were aliened for a pittance, and as this "land speculation scandal" had made the Legislature unpopular in Texas it was not likely that Viesca's Government would find much sympathy among the Texans.

Those Texans who had been at Monclova during the sessions of the Legislature, however, knew that the real reason for the suppression of the State Government was its opposition to Santa Anna and the national Congress in the move to abolish the federal system, and they hastened to San Felipe with the object of arousing the Texans to a recognition of the situation and inducing them to send the militia to Viesca's relief. They found everybody denouncing the Legislature because of the "land steal" and the general opinion prevailing that Cos had served Viesca according to his deserts. It should be said that the object of the Legislature had been that of raising revenue, and while such wholesale disposal of public lands seemed to the Texans a bad method of getting funds, the Mexicans had no such view of the matter. On the other hand, the opposition to the national Congress was sincere, and the few Texans who recognized this began a movement to convince their fellow Texans. They recognized that the national Congress intended to abolish the federal system and make Texas wholly subservient to a centralized government at Mexico City, and they favored resistance. This group, which was a very small minority at first, came to be known as the "war party".

Meantime, a new source of local annoyance had arisen in Texas. For a year and a half after the expulsion of the troops from Texas in 1833, the national Government had made no move to reestablish the collection of the import and export duties. This was due chiefly to the circumstance that troops could not be spared to be sent to Texas, the revolutionary condition of the interior of Mexico requiring the services of every available man. The laws governing imports and exports, therefore, had been practically ignored during most of the years 1833 and 1834. In December, 1834, however, Colonel Domingo de Ugartechéa was sent to San Antonio to take charge of Federal affairs in Texas, and in January a small force under Captain Antonio Tenorio was sent to the fort at Anáhuac on Galveston Bay, which had been unoccupied since Bradburn had left in 1833. At the same time a collector of customs and two deputies arrived in Texas, the collector taking up his post first at Brazoria and later at Columbia. The deputies were stationed at Anáhuac.

The enforcement of the customs regulations would have been difficult under the best conditions. But from the beginning the conditions were bad. Tenorio's force was small, and in a few months there were desertions due to poor rations and irregularity of pay. There was no uniformity in the manner in which the regulations were applied at Brazoria and Columbia by the collector and at Anáhuac by the deputies. There was much discontent at Anáhuac over this, and it was pointed out that law-abiding citizens who paid the duties required by the Government were thus penalized and made laughing-stocks because so many others ignored the regulations and brought in and shipped out goods without paying anything. This situation led to much friction, and finally the *ayuntamiento* or town council of Liberty, the nearest civil authority to Anáhuac, adopted resolutions condemning those who were ignoring the regulations, and pointing out that if any injustice existed the remedy was to petition Congress. This was followed by a mass meeting, called with the object of drafting such a petition, but this meeting went further and resolved that until the petition was granted no duties of any kind would be paid. The collector and his deputies found themselves in such a difficult situation that they decided to abandon all attempt to enforce the regulations. Tenorio, however, received assurances about this time that he would soon be reinforced, and was provided with money to pay his men, so he decided to enforce the regulations at Anáhuac himself. As a result there was more friction, and finally in a quarrel over a box about to be loaded on a vessel, and which was later found to contain nothing but old rubbish, a young American named William Smith was shot and wounded by one of Tenorio's soldiers. This happened on June 12th, just about the time the Texans who had been at Monclova during the session of the Legislature arrived at San Felipe.

The incident created some excitement, but there was general recognition that the shooting was the result of the resistance to the paying of import and export duties, whatever the particulars might be, and there was no sympathy in the interior of Texas with this sort of thing. The disposition was to regard those who resisted the tariff regulations as "foreigners", with no stake in the country. But the incident, nevertheless, contributed to the general excited condition of the public mind.

On June 21st, Cos's courier, bearing a letter for the Political Chief, Dr. J. B. Miller, as well as letters for Tenorio at Anáhuac, arrived at San Felipe. The

letter to the Political Chief was the one to which
reference has already been made informing him of
the suppression of Viesca's Government. A few
members of the war party, however, decided that it
would be worth while to examine the courier's pack
in order to see what Cos and Ugartechéa might be
writing to Tenorio. They waylaid him and took possession of his dispatches, the contents of which, when
made public, created new excitement of a very serious character. For the general tenor was to the effect
that a large body of Mexican troops would soon arrive in Texas. Ugartechéa, for example, wrote to
Tenorio as follows: "In a very short time the affairs
of Texas will be definitely settled, for which purpose the Government has ordered a strong division,
composed of troops which were in Zacatecas, and
which is now in Saltillo, to take up the line of march.
. . . These revolutionists will be ground down, and
it appears to me, since the Government has taken
their matters in hand, we shall soon see each other."

When these letters were shown to Dr. Miller, the
Political Chief, he became alarmed, and immediately he issued a proclamation calling upon the people
to arm themselves. He proposed that an expedition
be sent to conduct Governor Viesca to Texas. He
concluded, what the group known as the "war party"
had been urging all along, that the troops were being
sent to compel the Texans to submit to any kind of a
government the reactionaries in the national Congress might decide upon.

"Are you prepared," asked the Political Chief in
his proclamation, "to receive such a Government as
it may please Commandant General Cos and his

masters to give you and again receive a military officer for your Governor; or will you support and
maintain the officer your own voluntary vote placed
in office and who now lies in prison on account of
the vote made in his favor? I think by the feelings
which I have that I can answer: you will never submit tamely to such a course. The object is to establish the Supreme Executive authority of the State of
Texas. This is highly important, and it behooves
every man to strain every nerve to accomplish such
a desired object, and in obedience to the orders we
have received, to turn out immediately, organize, and
march to his relief and bring him to a place of safety in this favored Texas. . . . You will march to this
place as soon as possible and wait for further orders."

This proclamation caused great excitement. As
shall be seen, however, nothing definite came of it,
but for the moment it looked as if the Texans would
go to Viesca's relief and thus join the constituted authorities of the State in resisting Santa Anna and the
national Congress.

CHAPTER XXVI

TEXANS FACE CRISIS

THE first effect of the Political Chief's proclamation was a meeting of the citizens of San Felipe and the surrounding region, to adopt a suitable declaration, with the object of sending it to Federalist leaders in Coahuila, thus encouraging them to continue resistance to Santa Anna and the reactionary Congress. This meeting was held on June 22nd, and it declared unequivocally for resistance of the move toward centralism and for support of Governor Viesca and the duly elected State authorities. It was presided over by R. M. Williamson, popularly known as "Three-legged Willie" because he was one-legged and used crutches, who was one of the best lawyers in Texas and possessed a clear understanding of the real purport of the course things were taking at Mexico City. He was one of the ablest leaders of the "war party" and wielded great influence in shaping events during the next few months.

Although the action of the San Felipe meeting was promptly discountenanced by conservative public opinion throughout Texas, the declaration which was adopted sets forth so clearly the situation that was developing that its provisions should be given here. It took the form of an "address to the people of the State of Coahuila and Texas" and began by

expressing regret on the part of the people of the
jurisdiction of San Felipe that the hopes of patriots
and the desires of a numerous people, so recently
freed from Spanish tyranny, were being frustrated
by the imposition of a new tyranny on them by the
reactionaries in control of the national Government.
It declared that the people of Texas had been convinced for a long time that the object of the Congress
was to destroy the federal system, but that they had
preferred to leave the matter of resistance to the naive citizens of Mexico, feeling reluctant to act in
such a matter because of the recent character of
their citizenship. Had not the usurpations of the
General Government reached their own doors, they
would not protest even now. They had always supported the Constitution, and expected to continue to
do so, but the General Government had violated the
Constitution grievously by invading the rights and
powers of the State.

"We consider," the address continued, "that the
General Government was created for objects wholly
exterior, and that the regulation of their internal affairs was left to the States. An invasion of the rights
of another by whatever power is uniformly dangerous, and uniformly to be resisted. Such invasion has
been committeed by the General Government against
the State of Coahuila and Texas: (1) In the persons
of the representatives of the national Congress, when
they were prevented by military force from discharging the duties of their office; (2) by the decree
of the President ordering a new election of officers
in opposition to a regular constitutional election previously held; (3) by the decree of the General Con-

gress disbanding the civil militia and requiring the
States to surrender their arms; (4) by the decree of
the General Congress prohibiting the State of
Coahuila and Texas from issuing letters of citizenship to its colonists; (5) by the arrest by regular
troops of Don Augustín Viesca, the constitutional
Governor of the State; (6) by the overthrow of the
State authorities by regular troops; (7) by the recent
resolution declaring that the General Congress has
the right to alter the Constitution and form of government at its pleasure, without pursuing the mode
pointed out by that sacred instrument; (8) by the
creation of a dictator with absolute power whose only rule of conduct is his own will and pleasure; and
(9) by numerous other acts, all manifesting a total
disregard for the rights of the States, and a determination of the present ruling authorities of the nation
to prostrate the republican federative principle."

The address concluded by declaring that against
all these usurpations the people of the jurisdiction of
San Felipe protested, and that they would maintain
the Federal and State Constitutions, as originally
adopted, and support the regularly elected State officials in the discharge of their duties. They pledged
their "lives, fortunes, and sacred honor" to this cause,
and they would not abandon it, the address declared,
until the last drop of blood of the last man in Texas
was spilled.

Brave words! And spoken in defense of a clearly
defined and undoubtedly just cause. But when an attempt was made to hold a similar meeting at Columbia the next day, Henry Austin succeeded in getting
a postponement of action until the following Sun-

day, which was June 28th. Meantime, while both sides busied themselves to arouse sentiment, reaction set in definitely, and when the Columbia meeting was held it adopted much more conservative resolutions. But this meeting did resolve that the militia be strengthened and mobilized immediately for protection of the frontier against the Indians, and that all the jurisdictions of Texas be invited to send three deputies each to meet the Political Chiefs of the different departments in public council, with full powers to organize a provisional government, based on the principles of the Constitution, to serve during the reign of anarchy in the State.

The meeting adopted also the following significant resolution: "That the Political Chief be requested to address the Executive of the Federal Government of Mexico, representing to him the peaceable and loyal disposition of the citizens of Texas, and their great desire to remain attached to the Federal Government; that the Political Chief be requested to address the citizens of this department, commanding them to adhere strictly to the laws and Constitution of the land; and that we will support the Political Chief in the discharge of all constitutional duties."

The significant features of this declaration were that it provided for placing Texas in a condition of defense; that it provided for a consultation of representatives of all the people with the object of establishing an orderly local government; and finally that it expressed no revolutionary opposition to the Central Government, but on the contrary expressed a loyal disposition toward it. The men who domi-

nated the Columbia meeting were determined that
no precipitate action should plunge the people into
revolution, and that they should espouse no quarrel
of anybody else in Mexico, except the people of
Texas themselves, not even the quarrel of the State
officials of the State of Coahuila and Texas. However, they were determined also to be prepared to
meet any emergency that might arise in connection
with the welfare of the people of Texas, and to that
end they created a committee of vigilance, correspondence, and safety. On this committee were
placed W. D. C. Hall, J. A. Wharton, W. H. Jack,
J. G. McNeil, and G. B. McKinstry.

Having set in motion a movement toward conservative action, the meeting adjourned. But within twenty-four hours action of a most revolutionary character was taken in another part of the State.
On the night of Monday, June 29th, a party of
twenty-five men, under command of William Barrett
Travis, captured the fort at Anáhuac!

This was a direct result of the meeting at San
Felipe on June 22nd. Travis and some of the others
of the party were participants in that meeting, and
having resolved on resistance and support of the
fugitive State authorities, the opinion seemed general that Anáhuac should be taken without delay.
Immediately after the adjournment of the meeting, another gathering was held at which the question of measures was discussed. Inasmuch as Cos's
dispatches had revealed that reinforcements were
to be sent to Anáhuac, it was immediately proposed
that the fort there should be taken at once. Volunteers were called for, and a number signed to take

part in an expedition against the fort. Travis was one of these. Being a natural leader of men, though a young man, he was elected to command the party, and in due course he carried out the object for which the expedition was organized. Tenorio made little show of resistance, and on the morning of June 30th he signed articles of complete surrender, he and his men being guaranteed a safe conduct out of Texas. Both parties embarked together on a sloop for Harrisburg, where they arrived just in time to participate in a Fourth of July barbecue, Tenorio and his men being entertained as guests.

When the news of the taking of Anáhuac spread over Texas, however, there was a general condemnation of this "rash action", and Travis soon found himself and his companions being criticized severely for thus "endangering the country". This irked him to such a degree that for several weeks he published a card in the *Texas Republican* in which he requested that the people suspend judgment until he could prepare and publish an explanation and defense. Travis drafted such a defense, but it was never published. It consisted of a short statement of the facts, accompanied by supporting documents. They are still preserved. The statement, which is dated September 1st, 1835, reads as follows:

"To the Public:

"The undersigned published a card some time since, stating that he would give the public his motives in engaging in the expedition to Anáhauc which resulted in the capture of the garrison and that place on the 29th of June last. Circumstances beyond my control have hitherto prevented me from redeeming the pledge therein given. I will now do so in a few words.

"I refer the public to the following documents to show what were my motives in that affair. At the time I started for Anáhuac, it seemed to the unanimous opinion of the people here (San Felipe) that that place should be reduced. The citizens about Galveston Bay, who had formed a volunteer company for the purpose, sent to this place for aid. The Political Chief approved the plan and presided at the meeting of about two hundred persons who adopted the resolution which appears below.

"Being highly excited by the circumstances then stated, I volunteered in that expedition, with no further motives than of patriotism and a wish to aid my suffering countrymen in the embarrassing strait to which they were likely to be reduced by military tyranny. I was casually elected the commander of the expedition, without soliciting the appointment. I discharged what I conceived to be my duty to my country to the best of my ability. Time alone will show whether the step was correct or not. And time will show that when the country is in danger I will show myself as patriotic and ready to serve her as those who, to save themselves, have disavowed my act and denounced me to the usurping military.

"W. BARRETT TRAVIS."

Six months later, Travis more than made good this boast when he and his companions in the Alamo, by a vicarious sacrifice, aroused "all Americans in the world". But for the moment he was a fugitive and widely regarded as a trouble maker.

CHAPTER XXVII

A MOVE TO MAINTAIN PEACE

THE counter move started at the Columbia meeting on June 28th had the effect of driving the "war party" to cover and sentiment for a conservative course spread throughout the settlements during the next five or six weeks. But R. M. Williamson, who had presided at the San Felipe meeting of June 22nd, which had declared unequivocally for resistance, was not to be overawed by the arguments of the Columbia resolutions, and on July 4th he issued an appeal to the people in which he set forth in detail the situation they were facing.

"Your republican form of government is broken down," Williamson declared, "your State authorities have by the military been driven from the exercise of their constitutional duties and they detain in custody the Governor of your State and of your choice. Not only in Coahuila has this arbitrary and despotic course been pursued, but other States of the Federation mourn the loss of their Constitutions and their liberties, and at this moment the proud and republican State of Zacatecas mourns the loss of two thousand citizens, slain in battle by the troops of General Santa Anna, and the survivors now endure the galling chains of military rule . . . . All the States have succumbed to the military, and as Texas is the only

241

spot unconquered, Santa Anna is marching his troops here to compel a submission to the new Government. And the people have to determine whether they also will yield to the power of the Dictator, give up their arms, suffer their country to be garrisoned with strong military posts, and live under the rule and sway of the military. They must do this or they must prepare for war; they must submit to the military Government or they must defend their province and their rights with the sword and the bayonet; and they must do this without delay, for the enemy is fast approaching our country."

This description of the condition of the country and of the choice before the Texans was not exaggerated. But for the moment conservative counsels prevailed. One thing which Williamson pointed out was universally recognized, however, and that was that the republican form of government had broken down. The suppression of the State Government of Coahuila and Texas by General Cos had left the Political Chiefs of the three Departments of Texas with no civil authority whatever over them. It had been the sense of the Columbia meeting that the immediate need was a provisional State Government to preserve order and to prevent any minority from committing Texas to a revolutionary course. The attack on Anáhuac, which was generally regarded as a direct consequence of the hasty proclamation of Dr. J. B. Miller, Political Chief of the Department of the Brazos, served to emphasize the need of a central authority, and the leaders at Columbia and at San Felipe proceeded to take steps toward providing something of the kind.

Accordingly, on July 11th the *ayuntamiento* of
Columbia named five members of a proposed central
committee and directed them to proceed to San
Felipe to meet with members from the *ayuntamiento*
of that place on July 14th. The Columbia committeemen were instructed to open correspondence with
the authorities, either civil or military, of the Federal Government, and with the Political Chiefs of the
three Departments of Texas and to do whatever they
might think best calculated to promote the welfare of
Texas, "always bearing in mind that we *earnestly desire peace*." They were also instructed to endeavor
earnestly to bring about a consultation of delegates
of all the people of Texas "with the utmost expedition."

Meantime, local meetings were being held
throughout Texas. On July 4th such meetings were
held at Lavaca and at Mina, both of which endorsed
the program of the Columbia meeting. A meeting at
Gonzales on July 7th adopted resolutions even more
conservative than the Columbia program, expressing "full confidence in the favorable disposition of
His Excellency, the President, and of the General
Congress towards Texas" and citing the failure of the
Texans to respond to Governor Viesca's call for a
contingent of militia as "conclusive proof of the loyalty of the inhabitants of Texas toward the nation"
and of their unwillingness to become embroiled "in
the quarrels of the Republic". Three meetings on
July 14th—at Alfred, Caney Creek, and Harrisburg
—adopted resolutions of much different tone. The
one at Alfred emphasized the need of "union, organization, and moderation", while that at Caney

Creek declared that, though desiring peace if it could be had on favorable terms, "if not, we are willing to defend our rights and liberties." And at Harrisburg it was set forth that the Constitution was being violated and that it was the duty of all Texans to sustain its principles. This meeting went on record as favoring confiscation of the property of all persons who left Texas to avoid participating in "her struggle" and an award of one thousand acres of land to every foreigner who came to Texas to help in that struggle. On July 17th the settlers along the Navidad and Lavaca rivers met at William Millican's cotton gin and after declaring their conviction "that Santa Anna is hostile to State sovereignty and the State Constitution" and announcing that they "would oppose any force that might be introduced into Texas for any other than constitutional purposes", resolved in favor of "a general consultation of delegates from all the municipalities of Texas." At Nacogdoches a meeting was held on July 19th and a resolution was unanimously adopted asking the Political Chief of that Department to call a meeting for the purpose of adopting measures for acting in unison with the other parts of Texas.

A notable meeting was held by the settlers along the San Jacinto on August 8th. It was notable because of the conservative resolution, drafted by David G. Burnet, which was adopted. It declared in favor of a consultation of all Texas, but resolved that the delegates should be enjoined "to preserve by all possible means, compatible with the character of a free people, the peace of Texas and the unity of the Mexican nation." Among other things, the San Jacinto meeting resolved: "That we consider *names* as the mere signification of *things;* and that we are not so obstinately prejudiced in favor of the term 'Federal Republic' as peremptorily and without inquiry to reject another government purely because it has assumed a different external sign or denomination. That there are certain essential, sacred and imprescriptible rights which must be guaranteed to every citizen under any form of government that can or ought to be tolerated by an intelligent people who know how to estimate the dignity of their nature. That we believe those rights may be as well secured under a consolidated as under a federative government, provided that government is wisely and liberally organized . . . . That although the citizens of Texas may have the *political* right to reject the new Government of Mexico, and to adopt one more consonant to their habits and feelings, we do seriously question the policy of doing so, unless constrained by imperious circumstances, such as, we trust, do not and will not exist. That as *adopted* citizens we ought to exercise even our absolute rights with some diffidence, and with a peculiar regard for the moral obligations that may rest upon us."

At the same time, the San Jacinto resolution set forth that "we are ready now and at all times to declare our utter abhorrence of any government that is purely military in its character; and are now and at all times ready to resist the imposition of such a government with all the means and all the energies that Providence has conferred upon us." And it added the declaration "that we consider even the turbulence of a distracted republic incomparably preferable, to the sickly quietude of a military despotism."

These meetings, while reflecting a condition of disorganization and confusion, also revealed a great degree of unity of attitude on certain important points. It was clear, for one thing, that most of the people wanted peace and the restoration of order, and that there was a general fear that unauthorized revolutionary action by small minorities of irresponsible radicals might bring disaster to all of the people. There were probably about thirty thousand people in Texas in the summer of 1835, of which about five thousand were native Mexicans and about fifteen hundred were negro slaves. The great bulk of these people were farmers, whose chief commercial products were cotton and cattle. Colonel Almonte estimated that in 1832 more than 7,000 bales of cotton and more than 150,000 hides and skins of various kinds were exported from Texas and that there were more than 100,000 head of cattle in the region. The population had grown since 1832 and it is more than probable that agricultural production had increased also. In any event, it is certain that most of the Texas people in July, 1835, were more concerned about bringing a good cotton crop to maturity than they were about "politics", and were looking forward to harvesting and ginning this cotton during the next three months rather than to an armed conflict with the Mexican military. They wanted peace and the restoration of order, because to most of them war would mean ruin. Consequently many of them favored a general consultation of delegates representing all the people, to decide the future course to

be followed, as the only means of forestalling rash
and ill-advised minority action. Most of these also
wanted regular Mexican troops kept out of Texas,
pending the holding of such a consultation and the
making of such a decision.

It was with the object of bringing a central authority of some kind into being that the *ayuntamiento* of
Columbia sent five committeemen to San Felipe to
meet with similar committeemen from the *ayuntamiento* of that place on July 14th. The Columbia
members were John A. Wharton, Sterling McNeel,
James F. Perry, Josiah H. Bell, and James Knight,
all of them landholders and some of them among
the original settlers of the region. And the *ayuntamiento* of San Felipe named a similar delegation,
which included Wily Martin, John R. Jones, Alexander Somervell, C. B. Stewart, and Jesse Bartlett.
On July 16th these two delegations were joined by
D. C. Barrett as the representative of the municipality of Mina, and these eleven men, acting as a joint
committee, began a serious effort to reassure the Mexican military authorities and to insure peace. And
the first task they had to tackle was that of explaining away the action of the Political Chief, Dr. Miller, practically calling the Texans to arms, and the
attack on Anáhuac which followed. They induced
Dr. Miller to issue a new proclamation to the people, completely reversing his former position, and
calling upon them, "in the name of the Constitution
and laws of the land which we have sworn to support, to remain quiet and tranquil." Then they prevailed upon him to retire from the position of Political Chief for the time being, giving ill health as

the reason, and Wily Martin, who had been made President of the central committee, agreed to serve in his place. The central committee also issued a statement to the people of the Department of the Brazos, assuring them that the rumors with respect to the coming of Federal troops to Texas had exaggerated the truth. The committee said in this statement that its members took great pleasure in informing their fellow citizens that "there is no just cause for immediate alarm" and in assuring them that they had "the most sanguine hopes that the present commotion will be quieted and good order restored without any collision with the Federal troops." The committe then took up the task of convincing the Mexican military leaders that if Federal troops were kept out of Texas all would be well.

CHAPTER XXVIII

PEACE PARTY IN THE SADDLE

COLONEL Ugartechéa, who had been in command at Velasco during the trouble of 1833 and was now the commandant at San Antonio, had written Dr. Miller on July 5th assuring him that the Texans had nothing to fear from the troops which had been ordered to Texas. They were coming, he said, for no hostile purpose, but merely to garrison the ports and to provide protection against the Indians. He had previously written to General Cos, who was at Matamoros, that it would be advisable for him to issue a proclamation to the same effect. And Cos acted on this advice by writing a long circular letter on the subject to the three Political Chiefs in Texas. This letter was dated July 12th, and it was not printed in Texas until August 22nd, but it illustrates the attitude of the Mexican military authorities at the moment that the central committee at San Felipe was undertaking to convince them that troops should be kept out of Texas.

"The entire want of police for some time past in Texas," wrote Cos, "has necessarily contributed to the introduction of many men without country, morality, or any employment to gain a subsistence, who, having nothing to venture on a revolution, are continually occupied in fanning the flame of discord and endeavoring to persuade the honest people of Texas that the Supreme National Government entertains views and intentions hostile and fatally prejudicial to their interests. As this unheard-of falsehood might precipitate good citizens to confound themselves with the bad, I believe it to be my duty to save them by appealing to their good judgment for the rejection of those vile suggestions, and entreating them to think only of the augmenting of their property, respecting always the laws of the land, in which case they will always have the support of the General Government and every kind of guarantee which the General Government can give.

"I have been informed that seditious persons, in order to gain their ends, endeavor to make the entrance of troops thither from the President of the Republic to be looked upon as the commencement of military subjection. If this extravagant idea has blinded the incautious, the sound part of the people must surely have rejected it as it deserved, because it is not credible that assent can be given to an imputation so unjust."

Cos then proceeded to argue that if it be necessary for the Government to station troops in Texas in order to "establish the Custom House", this should in no wise alarm the people, because it really would add to their security rather than operate against it. He insisted that certainly the Government had a right to send troops to Texas, quite as much as to any other part of the Republic, and declared that it would be insulting to the Mexicans "for the new inhabitants of Texas to contemplate the national army in the same way as the Egyptians looked upon the

Mamelukes, their continual depredators." He directed the Political Chiefs to give the honest residents of their respective Departments to understand that so long as they remained attached to the Government and the laws they had nothing to fear. "For," he added "an armed force is sent to no part of the Republic with any other object than to maintain the peace and security of the citizens."

This last assurance was not one calculated to inspire confidence, for many Texans were well aware of the fact that the armed forces of the Government had been sent to many parts of the Republic, including Zacatecas and Coahuila, for quite other purposes than that of maintaining the peace and security of the citizens. Moreover, they knew that the letters from Cos and Ugartechéa to Tenorio at Anáhuac had revealed that troops were coming to Texas for other purposes than to "establish the Custom House". In any event, the members of the central committee, who wished to maintain peace, were convinced that the sending of Mexican troops to Texas in the existing circumstances, and considering the excited condition of the public mind, would only have the effect of precipitating trouble instead of preventing it. So they undertook at once to convince Ugartechéa and Cos of this.

But first of all it was necessary to make some expression to them with respect to the waylaying of the Government courier at San Felipe and the attack on Anáhuac. With this object in view, the central committee drafted a letter to Ugartechéa on July 17th, assuring him that these acts were not approved by the mass of the people and requesting him to transmit this assurance both to General Cos and Santa Anna.

"We whose names are undersigned," the committee wrote, "are chosen by the people of the jurisdictions we severally represent to investigate the truth of certain rumors and recent occurrences which tend to place the citizens of Texas in an attitude of hostility to the General Government. Time will not now admit of a detailed account of the *alleged* reasons for the acknowledged insult upon the Government agents and officers at this place (San Felipe) and at Anáhuac. Hereafter, and as soon as a full and free expression of the people of Texas can be obtained, every explanation will be given which justice and the honor and dignity of all concerned may require. The people at large, *we know,* have not participated either in the feeling which prompted the aggressions or in any acts opposed to the legal authorities of the Mexican Republic, and do and ever will disavow the course pursued by a few impetuous and misguided citizens, whose conduct, unexplained, might implicate the whole community."

The committee directed Ugartechéa's attention to the report of Captain Tenorio, who had been in command at Anáhuac at the time of the attack, and while disclaiming any knowledge of its contents or of Captain Tenorio's sentiments, expressed the belief that "he cannot but feel sensible of the general confidence of Texas citizens in the purity and justice of *our* Constitution and laws and respect for the Government which the Mexican States have chosen."

"You are respectfully requested," the letter continued, "to transmit this communication, or a copy of

it, to General Cos and the President of the United
States of Mexico, with a concluding assurance from
us that the citizens of Texas generally have become
adopted citizens of the Mexican Republic from
choice, after a full knowledge of the Constitution
and laws; that they entertain a grateful sense of the
liberality of the Government towards her colonies,
in the distribution of lands to settlers and other advantages tending to their convenience and prosperity in agriculture and manufacture; that they will be
prepared on every constitutional call to do their duty
as Mexican citizens, in the enforcement of the laws
and promotion of order, and respect for the Government and its agents; that they will cherish those principles which most clearly demonstrate their love of
peace, respect for their Mexican fellow citizens, and
attachment to the free liberal institutions of their
adopted country."

Having drafted this letter to Ugartechéa, the central committee then proceeded to consider what further steps ought to be taken. John A. Wharton, one
of the members from Columbia, mindful of the instructions of the *ayuntamiento* of that place that the
committee should endeavor earnestly to bring about
a consultation of delegates of all the people of Texas
"with the utmost expedition", suggested that a call
be issued for such a consultation. This proposal was
voted down and it was proposed instead that a general statement of facts with respect to the recent disturbances be made. A committee of five was appointed to draft such a statement, but it developed at
once that there was sharp disagreement among them
as to what it should contain and the idea had to be

abandoned. Then it was decided to send a delegation to wait upon General Cos in person, to explain
the disturbances and to urge that no troops be sent
to Texas.

The idea of waiting upon Cos seems to have been
suggested by Edward Gritten, an Englishman, who
had arrived at San Felipe from San Antonio about
the time the central committee was organized. He
had undertaken for Ugartechéa to ascertain the sentiment of the people and had visited the municipalities of Mina and Gonzales on his way to San Felipe.
He had already reported to Ugartechéa that the disposition of the people generally was for peace and
was favorable to the Government, but that there was
strong sentiment against the introduction of troops.
He expressed the opinion that while the great mass
of the people were loyal to Mexico, an advance of
troops into Texas would mean war, and he strongly
advised that a conciliatory policy be followed. Gritten reported all this to the central committee and apparently it was at his suggestion that it was decided
to send a delegation to wait upon Cos. Gritten and
D. C. Barrett were chosen for this mission, and as
they prepared to depart for San Antonio, with the
object of enlisting Ugartechéa's cooperation with the
plan, the central committee adjourned to meet again
on August 1st. It was hoped that by that time representatives from other municipalities would join the
committee.

When the Columbia members of the committee
returned home and reported that they had deferred
the calling of a consultation in the hope that the
Mexican military authorities might be induced to

abandon the plan of sending troops to Texas, some
dissatisfaction was expressed among the more aggressive leaders at that place and a new move for a
consultation was started at once. A committee,
headed by William H. Wharton, was formed, the
other members being W. H. Bynum, W. D. C. Hall,
A. Calvit, S. Whiting, P. Bertrand, W. T. Austin,
and W. G. Hill, and a call was issued for a public
meeting of citizens of Columbia, to be held on July
30th, with the object of expressing their sentiments
"in regard to the importance of having a convention
of all of Texas, through her representatives, for the
purpose of restoring peace and confidence." It soon
became apparent, however, that public sentiment was
overwhelmingly in favor of awaiting the outcome of
the visit of Gritten and Barrett to General Cos before making any further move, and when the meeting assembled at Columbia on July 30th it was a foregone conclusion that it would vote down any resolution favoring a consultation. F. W. Johnson, one of
the leaders of the "war party", anticipating such action, induced Josiah H. Bell to propose a postponement of the meeting until some later date as soon as
it was called to order. Accordingly, the only action
taken by the meeting was to adjourn until August
15th, by which time it was expected some report
from Gritten and Barrett would be received.

Immediately after adjournment of the meeting, a
conference of leaders of the so-called "war party"
was held, and it was decided to send representatives
to East Texas to confer privately with leaders of
the Department of Nacogdoches and endeavor to
bring about unity of action with respect to the whole

situation. F. W. Johnson and Mosely Baker were entrusted with this mission.

The "war party", be it said, consisted of those who recognized that sooner or later the Texans would be compelled to make a definite and unequivocal choice between two courses. Either they would have to accept without question a central military government at Mexico City or they would have to resist the move of the Centralists to abolish the Constitution of 1824. The members of this "party" held that the State Government, which already had been suppressed by Cos, would never be set up again unless the Texans established a local government themselves. And they favored a consultation in order that the facts of the situation might be laid squarely before the representatives of the people and a unified program decided upon. They had little faith in such negotiation with the Mexican military officers as had been undertaken by Gritten and Barrett, for they were convinced that troops were to be sent to Texas to compel the Texans to submit to a centralized military despotism.

This conviction was not mere speculation. All information coming from the interior of Mexico during the months of June and July supported this view. This information came chiefly in the form of personal letters to individuals, but these letters were passed around and in some instances they were published. A letter from James Bowie to Dr. Miller, for example, which was written from Hatch's Plantation on the Lavaca on June 22nd, said: "I left Matamoros on the 12th of the present month. All the vessels in the port were embargoed for the purpose of transporting troops to the coast of Texas. . . . Three thou-

sand troops had reached Saltillo on the way to
Texas." J. M. Carbajal, a Federal Republican leader
and a member of the State Legislature which had
been suppressed by Cos, and who had escaped to
Texas, wrote to Philip Smith, under date of July
4th: "Things in the interior are in great confusion.
The Governor and a part if not all of the Permanent
Deputation are prisoners because they tried to come
to Texas and to be free from the military intervention of the supreme authorities . . . Our only hope as
well as that of the whole nation depends on the in-
trepidity of the free and enlightened and noble resolution of the people of Texas." And on July 5th,
Ben Milam, who had been arrested with Governo
Viesca and his party, wrote from prison at Lampasas,
Coahuila, to F. W. Johnson as follows:

"The whole of this part of the State has and will
support the Central Government. The interior, from
the last information we have, has fallen to the central
system. Santa Anna is Dictator. The Constitution is
thrown away, and ridiculed by those who used to call
themselves Federal Republicans. The plan for the
dissolution and destruction is laid, and every preparation is making for its execution. In the last ten days
two hundred troops have left this quarter for San
Antonio, and from the best information I can collect
two thousand more will be on the march in a few
weeks. Their intention is to gain the friendship of
the different tribes of Indians, and if possible to get
the slaves to revolt. These plans of barbarity and injustice will make a wilderness of Texas and beggars
of its inhabitants if they do not unite and act with
promptitude and decision. If the federal system is

lost in Texas, what will be our situation? Worse
than that of the most degraded slaves. The hopes of
the Republican party here are all on Texas. I trust
that they will not be deceived. The people of Texas
will never submit to a Dictator."

Such letters as these were the basis of the conviction of the leaders of the "war party" that troops
were being sent to Texas to compel submission to a
centralized military despotism. And shown about
with discretion, they became the source of much of
the talk which conservatives characterized as "rumors". At first these "rumors" were not given much
weight, which explains the apparent indifference of
the mass of the people to the imminent danger of invasion. This indifference did not mean that Milam
was mistaken when he wrote that "the people of
Texas will never submit to a Dictator". The attitude
of most of the people during the month of July was
more than probably very much the same as that of the
members of the *ayuntamiento* of Gonzales. On July
19th this body issued a manifesto explaining that its
almost servile resolution of July 7th was based on a
firm belief in "the good faith of the General Government toward Texas, and its strict observance of the
laws and Constitution of the United Mexican States."
But, it added, "if it be discovered that the numerous
reports are correct, and the Government contemplates
a formidable invasion of the rights and properties of
the citizens of Texas", then the people of Gonzales
"hereby declared for themselves resistance to such
measures a virtue."

CHAPTER XXIX

PEACE MOVE A STALEMATE

THE manifesto of the *ayuntamiento* of Gonzales no doubt expressed the true attitude of most of the people of that place, but not of all, for there was at least one servile submissionist among them. He was Dr. James H. C. Miller, who had acted as secretary of the Gonzales meeting of July 7th, and who described himself as "one who will never forget his true allegiance to the supreme authorities of the nation." And it was a "bright idea" originated by this gentleman that doomed the mission of Barrett and Gritten to failure at its outset and introduced an entirely new complication into the situation. For on July 25th, in a letter to a friend at San Antonio, this Dr. Miller (who must not be confused with the former Political Chief of the Department of the Brazos) proposed, as the most effective method of putting a sudden end to all the trouble in Texas, the immediate arrest of the leaders of the "war party".

Dr. Miller's letter was written from San Felipe and was addressed to John W. Smith, a resident of San Antonio. Miller had been in San Felipe during the sessions of the central committee, and evidently he had obtained the impression that the people there were for peace at any price, even to the extent of having the leaders of the "war party" taken into custody and turned over to the Mexican military authorities. He wrote Smith as follows:

"All here is in a train for peace. The war and speculating parties are entirely put down and are preparing to leave the country. They should now be *demanded* of their respective chiefs—a few at a time. First Johnson, Williamson, and Williams; and perhaps that is enough . . . . The moment is auspicious. The people are up. Say so, and oblige one who will never forget his true allegiance to the supreme authorities of the nation, and who knows that until they are dealt with Texas will never be quiet. Travis is in a peck of trouble. Dr. J. B. Miller disclaims his act in taking Anáhuac and he feels the breach. Don Lorenzo de Zavala is now in Columbia, attempting to arouse the people. Have him called for, and he also will be delivered up. Williams, Baker, and Johnson are now on a visit to him and no doubt conspiring against the Government."

Smith showed this letter to Ugartechéa at once, as no doubt Miller had intended he should. Ugartechéa had just received an order from General Cos to take a detachment of cavalry and go to the Department of the Brazos and arrest De Zavala, a commission he did not altogether relish. De Zavala had arrived in Texas about July 1st, having resigned as minister to France when Santa Anna embarked on his unconstitutional course. He had been one of the original leaders of the Federal Republican party and had presided over the Congress that drafted the Constitution of 1824. As soon as word reached Mexico City that he was in Texas, Tornel, who was now Minister of War, issued an order directing Cos to ar-

rest him and Cos had passed this order on to Ugartechéa. Ugartechéa did not enjoy the prospect of riding into the Anglo-Texan settlements with a detachment of cavalry just at that time. So when Smith directed his attention to Miller's "bright idea" of requiring the Anglo-Texans to arrest both De Zavala
and the leaders of the "war party" he jumped at it.
Accordingly, on August 1st Ugartechéa issued orders
for the arrest of De Zavala and of F. W. Johnson,
R. W. Williamson, William Barrett Travis, Samuel
M. Williams, Mosely Baker, and John H. Moore.
Later he added the names of J. M. Carbajal and
Juan Zambrano, two Federal Republican leaders
who had escaped to Texas.

Gritten and Barrett, on their way to San Antonio,
met Ugartechéa's courier at Gonzales bearing an
order to the Political Chief of the Department of the
Brazos, directing him to arrest the proscribed men.
When they learned the contents of this order, they
prevailed upon the courier to wait at Gonzales until
they could go to San Antonio and have it countermanded. They did not share Dr. Miller's view that
this was the way to put an end to trouble in Texas
On the contrary, they were sure that it would start
new trouble. And they felt that they could convince
Ugartechéa of this.

When they arrived at San Antonio, however, they
soon discovered that they were mistaken. The San
Antonio commandant had become thoroughly convinced that the proscribed men would be arrested
and delivered, if the demand for them was made and
insisted upon. Moreover, Ugartechéa informed
Gritten and Barrett that it would be useless for them

to go to see Cos until these men had been arrested, and he showed them a letter from Cos which convinced them that this was true. So they had to content themselves with writing to Cos that they would call on him later, fully prepared to prove to him that the Anglo-Texans were loyal to the Government, and meantime Gritten returned to San Felipe to inform Wily Martin, the acting Political Chief, of the turn events had taken. What he had to tell Martin amounted to an ultimatum from Ugartechéa, backed up by Cos.

Writing Cos a full account of all this, and informing him that he was adding the names of Carbajal and Zambrano to the proscribed list, Ugartechéa expressed confidence that the men would be delivered. "I do not doubt," he wrote, "that in accordance with the necessity which they are under of showing the good intentions of the colonists they will make the arrest, not only of these individuals, but of the others already mentioned as well. I am the more of this opinion because their greatest desire is to avoid the introduction of troops into the colonies."

When Gritten reached San Felipe he found that the central committee which had authorized his negotiations had been disbanded, and while Martin agreed to issue warrants for the arrest of the proscribed men, he informed Gritten that these men had left the country and probably not one of them could be found. This was not strictly true, of course. Johnson and Baker, to be sure, had gone to the Department of Nacogdoches to confer with East Texas leaders, but the others were still within Martin's jurisdiction, though they stayed under cover for awhile when they learned of the warrants for their arrest. Ugartechéa readily accepted the explanation that the men had departed, when Gritten later reported the result of his interview with Martin, for this relieved him of the responsibility of going to the Anglo-Texan settlements with his cavalry to arrest them himself. Gritten also reported that while the proscribed men had disappeared, other leaders of the "war party" were still carrying on a continuous agitation for a convention of all Texas.

And so the Gritten-Barrett mission ended in a stalemate. Its chief result was to provide a new issue for the "war party", the leaders of which now demanded to know whether the Texans would permit six of their fellow citizens, some of whom were among the first settlers and not one of whom was guilty of any crime, to be delivered over to the tender mercies of the military authorities. Only the most servile Tory could answer a question like that in the affirmative. And so sentiment for resistance was given a new impetus.

This sentiment, however, was far from dominant. Johnson and Baker, for example, found a discouraging situation in East Texas. At the home of J. K. Allen at Nacogdoches they conferred with Sam Houston and Thomas J. Rusk, and were told that the time was not auspicious for their visit. Houston reported that the people of that section, with few exceptions, were submissionists. He said that a few days before he had left San Augustine where a public meeting had been held to consider the state of the country, that he had attempted to address the meeting and had been literally hissed down. The people

of Nacogdoches and of the jurisdiction generally, he
added, entertained a like feeling and were submissionists.

Nevertheless, Johnson induced the Political Chief
of the Department of Nacogdoches, Henry Rueg, to
call a public meeting, and when it was held on
August 15th a resolution was adopted declaring that
the Federal Constitution had been destroyed by numerous abuses and that the Texans must take measures
to preserve themselves from anarchy. This meeting
also adopted a motion, offered by Sam Houston, requesting the *ayuntamiento* of San Felipe to issue a
call for a convention of all Texas. Johnson and
Baker then moved on to San Augustine, nearer the
American border, and managed to get up a meeting
there which approved the Nacogdoches resolution.
A few days later, however, the *ayuntamiento* of
Nacogdoches enacted an ordinance prohibiting the
holding of any election to choose delegates to any
convention or consultation. And meantime, the
ayuntamiento of San Felipe, which the Nacogdoches
and San Augustine meetings had requested to call a
convention, was veering to an extreme "peace" attitude, absolutely opposed to the holding of such a
convention.

But the movement for a consultation or convention made progress nevertheless. As has been seen, a
meeting of the San Jacinto community on August
8th, while adopting a very conservative resolution,
went on record for a consultation of all Texas. On
the same day a meeting held at the near-by settlement of Lynch's endorsed a recommendation in a
written address by De Zavala that a consultation be

called to meet on October 15th. And then the adjourned meeting of the people of Columbia was reconvened on August 15th.

This meeting, it will be recalled, had been postponed in order to await the result of the Gritten-
Barrett mission, and in the meantime the news had
been received that Ugartechéa and Cos had demanded the arrest of six Texan leaders and three distinguished Mexican Federal Republicans. This news
had caused a marked reaction, and the meeting on
August 15th not only went on record for a consultation and created a committee of safety and correspondence to bring one about, but it also adopted a resolution declaring "we will not give up any individual
to the military authorities!"

The Columbia meeting, by creating a committee
of safety and correspondence, really provided for an
organized campaign to bring about a consultation of
all Texas and to insure that the people would be
equipped with accurate information upon which to
formulate a program for the future. For this committee was empowered and instructed to "communicate with all Texas in the most prompt manner by
sending confidential agents to each jurisdiction" and
to "keep the people correctly advised of all political
intelligence of general interest." The committee went
to work at once, and on August 20th it issued an address to the people in which it proposed that a similar committee be created in every local jurisdiction
in Texas, that these committees hold an election for
delegates on October 5th, and that a consultation be
held at Washington-on-the-Brazos on October 15th.

So it was that by the end of August, 1835, an organized movement was under way to bring about a consultation of all Texas. There was still much opposition to such a move, and while the trend of public opinion favored it, the people were still divided in factional groups, and they seemed likely to remain so, whether a consultation was held or not. There was no commanding leadership, recognized in all sections of Texas, and there were still powerful voices raised in defense of a policy of non-resistance.

On August 22nd, for example, which was two days after the issuance by the Columbia committee of the call for a consultation, a translation of General Cos's circular letter to the Political Chiefs was published in *The Texas Republican*. In this letter, it will be recalled, Cos declared that "it is not credible that assent can be given an imputation so unjust" as the charge that troops were being sent to Texas to compel the submission of the Texans to a central military authority. He also directed the Political Chiefs to make "the honest residents" of their respective Departments understand "that so long as they remain attached to the Government and the laws they have nothing to fear, as an armed force is sent to no part of the Republic with any other object than to maintain the peace and security of the citizens." There were still many people in Texas at the end of August, 1835, who accepted these assurances of Cos in good faith, and who regarded the members of the Columbia committee as alarmists and disturbers.

And yet, on August 31st, only nine days after the publishing of the Cos letter in Texas, there was sent to the military Governors and all local authorities throughout Mexico a communication from the Minister of Relations, Manuel Diez de Bonilla, which directly contradicted Cos's assurances. Here is what Bonilla said in that communication:

"The colonists established in Texas have recently given the most unequivocal evidence of the extremity to which perfidy, ingratitude and the restless spirit that animates them can go, since—forgetting what they owe to the Supreme Government of the nation which so generously admitted them to its bosom, gave them fertile lands to cultivate, and allowed them all the means to live in comfort and abundance—they have risen against that same Government, taking up arms against it under the pretense of sustaining a system which an immense majority of the Mexicans have asked to have changed, thus concealing their criminal purpose of dismembering the territory of the Republic. His Excellency the President *ad interim,* justly irritated by a conduct so perfidious, has fixed his entire attention upon this subject; and in order to suppress and punish this band of ungrateful foreigners, has directed that the most active measures be taken, measures required by what is in reality a crime against the whole nation. The troops destined to sustain the honor of the country and the Government will perform their duty and will cover themselves with glory."

In the face of such an impendng menace, the people of Texas were still badly divided as the month of August came to a close. Then on the first day of September there came news that electrified all Texas. Stephen F. Austin, returning home from enforced exile and imprisonment, had landed at Velasco!

CHAPTER XXX

AUSTIN UNITES THE TEXANS

AUSTIN'S return was hailed throughout Texas with warm manifestations of what may be adequately described only as public rejoicing. Gail Borden wrote afterwards that the people generally "looked upon the event as one which would settle all their doubts as to what should be done" and that even Austin's enemies "were constrained to greet him as the only physician that could correct the disorganized system and restore a healthy action to the body corporate." F. W. Johnson wrote to him at once ("with feelings inexpressable", he said) that his coming had been long wished for, and was not expected at that time, "but the God of Nature seems to have arranged all things better than even man could have desired." "Your coming would always have been hailed by the people as the coming of a father," Johnson wrote, "but your coming at this time is doubly dear to the people of all Texas."

The charges against Austin had finally been disposed of by a decision of the Government that his case came under the terms of a general amnesty act, passed by Congress the previous May, and he had finally been permitted to leave Mexico City. He had returned to Texas by way of Vera Cruz and New Orleans, and he had been given a striking demonstra-

tion of the chaotic condition of the country even before he landed, for as the American schooner *San
Felipe,* on which he was a passenger, approached
the mouth of the Brazos, it was fired on by the
Correo de Mexico, a Mexican revenue cutter, commanded by Capt. Thomas M. Thompson, an Englishman, and a running fight, in which the American
schooner was the victor, ensued. Guy M. Bryan has
written that he was told by eye-witnesses "that Austin walked the beach all night, his mind oppressed
with the gravity of the situation, forecasting the
troubles ahead of Texas".

The news of his arrival spread rapidly, and during
the next week delegations from all the surrounding
country called on him at the home of his sister at
Peach Point, about ten miles up the river from Velasco. The question that became uppermost in the
public mind was what his attitude toward the whole
situation was likely to be. And in order to provide a
suitable occasion for a public expression of his views,
as well as to celebrate his safe return, a "grand din-
ner and ball" was arranged at Brazoria, the nearest
town, for the evening of September 8th.

This affair was held at a tavern kept by Mrs. Jane
H. Long, widow of the famous Dr. James Long,
and from all accounts it was a memorable one.
Henry Austin, Stephen's cousin, in writing a description of it to his sister, said that it was gotten up "on
two days' notice in a manner very creditable to the
committee and port." "The only thing I did not
like," he wrote, "was $7 a head for ball and supper
and $30 more for a decent suit of clothes which I
had not and could have done without. There were

sixty covers and, despite the short notice, the table was three times filled by men alone. In the evening the long room was filled to a jam. At least sixty or eighty ladies who danced the sun up, and the Oyster Creek girls would not have quit then had not the room been wanted for breakfast. You never saw such enthusiasm."

It was a memorable affair in quite another sense, however, for in response to the rather glowing toasts that were offered in his honor, Stephen Austin made an address which clearly outlined the situation facing the country and the course which he thought should be followed with respect to it. He spoke less than fifteen minutes, but his speech had the effect of uniting all Texas on a common platform. And because of its importance in relation to the subsequent course of events in Texas, it is given here in full.

"I cannot refrain from returning my unfeigned thanks," said Austin, "for the flattering sentiments with which I have just been honored, nor have I words to express my satisfaction on returning to this my more than native country, and meeting so many of my friends and companions in its settlement.

"I left Texas in April, 1833, as the public servant of the people, for the purpose of applying for the admission of this country into the Mexican Confederation as a State separate from Coahuila. This application was based upon the constitutional and vested rights of Texas, and was sustained by me in the city of Mexico to the utmost of my abilities. No honorable means were spared to effect the objects of my mission and to oppose the forming of Texas into a territory, which was attempted. I rigidly adhered to the instructions and wishes of my constituents, so far as they were communicated to me. My efforts to serve Texas involved me in the labyrinth of Mexican politics. I was arrested, and have suffered a long persecution and imprisonment. I consider it my duty to give an account of these events to my constituents, and will therefore at this time merely observe that I have never, in any manner, agreed to anything, or admitted anything, that would compromise the constitutional or vested rights of Texas. These rights belong to the people, and can only be surrendered by them.

"I fully hoped to have found Texas at peace and in tranquility, but regret to find it in commotion; all disorganized, all in anarchy, and threatened with immediate hostilities. This state of things is deeply to be lamented; it is a great misfortune, but it is one which has not been produced by any acts of the people of this country: on the contrary, it is the natural and inevitable consequence of the revolution that has spread all over Mexico, and of the imprudent and impolitic measures of both the General and State Governments, with respect to Texas. The people here are not to blame, and cannot be justly censured. They are farmers, cultivators of the soil, and are pacific from interest, from occupation, and from inclination. They have uniformly endeavored to sustain the Constitution and the public peace by pacific means, and have never deviated from their duty as Mexican citizens. If any acts of imprudence have been committed by individuals, they evidently resulted from the revolutionary state of the whole nation, the imprudent and censurable conduct of the

State authorities, and the total want of local government in Texas. It is, indeed, a source of surprise and creditable congratulation that so few acts of this description have occurred under the peculiar circumstances of the times. It is, however, to be remembered that acts of this nature were not the acts of the people, nor is Texas responsible for them. They were, as I before observed, the natural consequences of the revolutionary state of the Mexican nation; and Texas certainly did not originate the revolution, neither have the people, as a people, participated in it. The consciences and hands of the Texans are free from censure, and clean.

"The revolution in Mexico is drawing to a close. The object is to change the form of government, destroy the Federal Constitution of 1824, and establish a central or consolidated government. The states are to be converted into provinces.

"Whether the people of Texas ought or ought not to agree to this change, and relinquish all or a part of their constitutional and vested rights under the Constitution of 1824, is a question of the most vital importance; one that calls for the deliberate consideration of the people, and can only be decided by them, fairly convened for the purpose. As a citizen of Texas I have a right to an opinion on so important a matter. I have no other right and pretend to no other. In the report which I consder it my duty to make to my constituents, I intend to give my views on the present situation of the country, and especally as to the constitutional and natural rights of Texas, and will, therefore, at this time, merely touch this subject.

"Under the Spanish Government Texas was a separate and distinct province; as such it had a separate and distinct local organization. It was one of the unities that composed the general mass of the nation, and as such participated in the war of the revolution, and was represented in the constituent Congress of Mexico that formed the Constitution of 1824. This constituent Congress, so far from destroying this unity, expressly recognized and confirmed it by the law of May 7th, 1824, which united Texas with Coahuila *provisionally* under the especial guarantee of being made a State of the Mexican Confederation as soon as it possessed the necessary elements. That law and the Federal Constitution gave to Texas a specific existence, and vested in its inhabitants special and defined rights, which can only be relinquished by the people of Texas, acting for themselves as a unity, and not as a part of Coahuila, for the reason that the union with Coahuila was *limited,* and only gave power to the State of Coahuila and Texas to govern Texas for the time being, but *always subject to the vested rights of Texas.* The State, therefore, cannot relinquish those vested rights, by agreeing to the change of government, or by any other act, unless expressly authorized by the people of Texas to do so; neither can the General Government of Mexico legally deprive Texas of them without the consent of this people. These are my opinions.

"An important question now presents itself to the people of this country. The Federal Constitution of 1824 is about to be destroyed, the system of government changed, and a central or consolidated one established. Will this act annihilate all the rights of

Texas, and subject this country to the uncontrolled and unlimited dictation of the new Government?

"This is a subject of the most vital importance. I have no doubt the Federal Constitution will be destroyed and a central government established, and that the people here will soon be called upon to say whether they agree to this change or not. This matter requires the most calm discussion, the most mature deliberation, and the most perfect union. How is this to be had? I see but one way, and that is by a general consultation of the people by means of delegates elected for that purpose, with full powers to give such an answer, in the name of Texas, to this question as they may deem best, and to adopt such measures as the tranquility and salvation of the country may require.

"It is my duty to state that General Santa Anna verbally and expressly authorized me to say to the people of Texas that he was their friend, that he wished for their prosperity, and would do all he could to promote it; and that, in the new Constitution, he would use his influence to give the people of Texas a special organization, suited to their education, habits, and situation. Several of the most intelligent and influential men in Mexico, and especially the Ministers of Relations and War, expressed themselves in the same manner. These declarations afford another and more urgent necessity for a general consultation of all Texas, in order to inform the General Government, and especially General Santa Anna, what kind of organization will suit the education, habits, and situation of this people.

"It is also proper for me to state that, in all my conversation with the President and ministers and men of influence, I advised that no troops should be sent to Texas, and no cruisers along the coast. I gave it as my decided opinion that the inevitable consequence of sending an armed force to this country would be war. I stated that there was a sound and correct moral principle in the people of Texas that was abundantly sufficient to put down all turbulent or seditious movements, but that this moral principle could not, and would not, unite with any armed force sent against this country; on the contrary it would resist and repel it, and ought to do so. This point presents another strong reason why the people of Texas should meet in general consultation. This country is now in anarchy, threatened with hostilities; armed vessels are capturing everything they can catch on the coast, and acts of piracy are said to be committed under cover of the Mexican flag. Can this state of things exist without precipitating the country into war? I think it cannot, and therefore believe that it is our bounden and solemn duty as Mexicans, and as Texans, to represent the evils that are likely to result from this mistaken and most impolitic policy in the military movement.

"My friends, I can truly say that no one has been, or now is, more anxious than myself to keep trouble away from this country. No one has been, or now is more faithful to his duty as a Mexican citizen, and no one has personally sacrificed or suffered more in the discharge of this duty. I have uniformly been opposed to having anything to do with the family political quarrels of the Mexicans. Texas needs peace and a local government; its inhabitants are farmers, and they need a calm and quiet life. But how can I, or anyone, remain indifferent, when our rights, our all, appear to be in jeopardy, and when it is our duty, as well as our obligation as good Mexican citizens, to express our opinions on the present state of things, and to represent our situation to the Government? It is impossible. The crisis is such as to bring it home to the judgment of every man that something must be done, and that without delay. The question will perhaps be asked, what are we to do? I have already indicated my opinion. Let all personalities, or divisions, or excitements, or passion, or violence be banished from among us. Let a general consultation of the people of Texas be convened as speedily as possible, to be composed of the best, and most calm, and intelligent, and firm men in the country, and let them decide what representations ought to be made to the General Government, and what ought to be done in the future.

"With these explanatory remarks I will give a toast: *The constitutional rights and security and peace of Texas—they ought to be maintained; and jeopardized as they now are, they demand a general consultation of the people.*"

In this speech Austin summed up the program that united all Texas. "Now we meet on middle grounds." Henry Austin wrote his sister. "Strict republican principles. That is, to stand upon our constitutional and vested rights—reject the Centralismo Plan if offered us, and if they send force to fight us, to repel force with force . . . . Stephen left last night to be at San Felipe on the 12th when all the upper world is to be there."

A committee from San Felipe, headed by Wily Martin, had called on Austin at Peach Point on September 5th to inform him that the people of that place were "prepared to receive him with open arms and acclamations of joy." A big meeting at San Felipe on September 12th was the result. It endorsed the Austin program with enthusiasm and it named a "committee of correspondence and vigilance". This committee was headed by Austin, and the other members were Wily Martin, Randall Jones, William Pettus, and Gail Borden, Jr. But from that moment Austin was the supreme leader, acknowledged by common consent.

CHAPTER XXXI

THE TEXANS TAKE UP ARMS

THE men associated with Austin on the San Felipe committee of correspondence and vigilance were all "old timers" in Texas. Martin, Jones, and Pettus had been among Austin's original colonists—the "Old Three Hundred", as they were called—and while Gail Borden, who was later to achieve world renown as the inventor of condensed milk, did not come to Texas until 1829, his brother, Thomas H. Borden, had also settled under Austin's first contract. They were certainly not the kind of men Cos had described in his circular letter as "men without country, morality, or any employment to gain a subsistence", who had "nothing to venture in a revolution". On the contrary, they were men with a big stake in the country who would venture everything they owned in the event of a revolution. And yet it was this group of men that called the Texans to arms.

The committee had immediately issued an address soliciting the cooperation of the other municipalities of Texas in support of the resolution of the San Felipe meeting in favor of a consultation. It suggested the same date as that fixed by the Columbia committee, October 15th, but expressed a preference for San Felipe over Washington-on-the-Brazos as the meeting place, and urged other local committees to

278

report the wishes of the people of their respective
communities on this point. The tone of this address
indicated that the committee intended to proceed
with deliberation to carry out a plan of systematic
oganization to insure an adequate expression of the
will of the people of Texas as a whole. But it soon
changed this tone. For within a week, when news
was received that Cos was expected at San Antonio
and that he would insist upon the arrest of the proscribed men and complete submission by the Anglo-
Texans, the committe called upon the people to prepare for war. In a circular, which was sent broadcast over Texas, it declared:

"This committee deems it to be their duty to say
that, in its opinion, all kinds of conciliatory measures with General Cos and the military at Bexar are
hopeless, and that nothing but the *ruin* of Texas can
be expected from any such measures. They have already and very properly been resorted to without effect. War is our only resource. There is no other
remedy but to defend our rights, our selves, and our
country by force of arms."

Even then the conscientious Austin caused the
committee to say that "until some compact authority
is established to *direct,* all that can be done is to recommend this subject to the people". But three days
later, when positive information was received that
Cos had landed with an army at Copano and that a
movement had been started to organize a force to
intercept him on his way to San Antonio, Austin and
the committee assumed even the responsibility of
"directing" the Texans, for they issued a call for volunteers for this expedition.

"An expedition is forming in the lower country to take the field at once," the committee declared. "They are called upon to rendezvous at League's old place on the Colorado on the 28th of this month. Every man in Texas is called upon to take up arms in defense of his country and his rights. Those who can join the expedition on the 28th are requested to do so! Or they can join it at James Kerr's on the Lavaca, which will be the principal rendezvous."

It was thus that the Texas "revolution" got under way. But before the plan to attack Cos could be carried out, news came that Ugartechéa was preparing to move against Gonzales, without waiting for Cos, and the volunteers turned about and marched to that place instead. And even before they arrived there, the first shot of the war had been fired at Gonzales and the cry of the volunteers became, "On to San Antonio!"

Austin accepted the turn of events without qualm. He summed up the situation in a letter to his friend, Peter Grayson. "The final answer of General Cos," he wrote, "is positive that the persons who have been demanded shall be given up and that the people of Texas must submit to any reforms that Congress chooses to make in the Constitution. I give you the substance, which is that we have no rights except what the Government thinks proper to grant us as a favor. Can or will the people submit to this? According to the position already taken by them they cannot. War then is *inevitable*. It is impossible to avoid it." And in another communication, written on September 21st, he declared: "I go into the war cheerfully, and with very different feelings from what I had in any of our past difficulties; we are now right; our basis is sound and just, and will be so declared by an impartial world; we are defending our constitutional rights against military usurpation."

It was in this spirit that Austin set about organizing all the local jurisdictions of Texas for resistance. "Frank Johnson starts tomorrow for Nacogdoches," he wrote, also on September 21st; "I have requested them in that country to raise all the men they can and march on without delay. There must be no half-way measures. War in full! The sword is drawn and the scabbard must be put on one side until the military are all driven out of Texas."

The people of the Department of Nacogdoches responded to Austin's appeal promptly. Mosely Baker again accompanied Johnson into that district, and while they reported later that they found "much division" among the people when they arrived, they added that "the letters of Colonel Austin and the actual invasion of the country had the happy effect of producing unanimity of sentiment and instant unison of action." Companies of armed men were started almost at once from Nacogdoches and San Augustin, and only the scarcity of arms, ammunition and other equipment prevented many more from going. Most important of all, however, was the fact that the committees at Nacogdoches and San Augustin jointly elected Sam Houston as commander-in-chief of the forces of the Department of Nacogdoches, vesting him with "full powers to raise troops, organize the forces and do all other things appertaining to such office." And acting under the authority bestowed upon him by this resolution, Houston promptly issued a call for volunteers. "Liberal bounties of land," he announced, "will be given to all who will join our ranks with a good rifle and one hundred rounds of ammunition. The troops of the Department will forthwith organize, under the direction of the Committee of Vigilance and Safety, with companies of fifty men each, who will elect their officers; and when organized they will report to the headquarters of the army, unless special orders are given for their destination."

Houston issued this call on October 8th. The "headquarters of the army" to whch he referred was Gonzales, more than two hundred miles away, where volunteers from all over Texas had been gathering during the previous week and where about three hundred armed men had already organized themselves into "the Volunteer Army of Texas". Gonzales had become the rallying point for the reason that a detachment of the Mexican army already had made an appearance at that place and the first shot of the war had been fired there on the morning of October 2nd.

Gonzales, which was the center of Green DeWitt's colony, was only about seventy miles from San Antonio, being nearer to that town than any of the other Anglo-Texan settlements. The settlers there had had much trouble with the Indians, and about three years before the military authorities at San Antonio had provided them with a brass cannon—an unmounted six-pounder—for their defense. As soon as Ugartechéa had received positive information that Cos had landed and was on his way to San Antonio, he sent a non-commissioned officer and four cavalrymen to Gonzales to get this cannon. The officer presented to the alcalde of Gonzales, Andrew Ponton, a formal order from the Political Chief of the Department of Bexar for the delivery of the cannon, and Ponton, after consulting with the leading men of the town, addressed a written reply to the Political Chief to the effect that he did not feel authorized to comply with the order without the permission of the Political Chief of the Department of the Brazos. This latter official was at San Felipe, of course, and under pretense of sending to that place for instructions, Ponton dispatched runners to Bastrop, the nearest settlement, and to other Anglo-Texan settlements for help. There were only eighteen men capable of bearing arms at Gonzales at the time, and Ponton feared that when Ugartechéa received his evasive reply he would send a larger force for the cannon. Meantime, the Mexican officer returned to San Antonio with Ponton's communication, leaving his four men encamped on the opposite side of the river from the town. The men of Gonzales were resolved not to give up the cannon, so they buried it in a safe place, and had the ferry and all other boats moved to their side of the river, and then proceeded to take the four cavalrymen into custody. One of the cavalrymen escaped, however, and rode off in the direction of San Antonio. All of this occurred during the last week of September. As was expected, on October 1st a force of about one hundred cavalrymen, under Capt. Francisco Casteñeda, arrived on the opposite side of the river and demanded that the ferry be sent over for them. This was refused and Castañeda was compelled to have one of his men swim the river to present the written order for the cannon.

Albert Martin acted as spokesman for the men of Gonzales, and in order to gain as much time as possible he pretended that Ponton, to whom the order was addressed, was absent from the town and would not return until evening. Castañeda then withdrew his company about a half-mile away, while the Texans prepared for a fight. Between eighty and a hundred men had responded to the appeal for help, and these were organized into a company and officers were elected. The cannon was dug up and improvised cannon balls were manufactured from old scrap at the town's blacksmith shop. A flag was provided by painting a picture of the cannon on a spread of cotton cloth, with the challenge, "Come and take it!" lettered underneath. While all these preparations were going forward, detachments of Mexican cavalry patrolled the opposite side of the river, and then about sundown Castañeda moved his men still further up the stream and camped for the night.

The Texans spent the night in making preparations to attack the Mexicans early the next morning. They crossed the river during the night and about four o'clock in the morning began moving toward Castañeda's camp. There was a heavy fog and just before daybreak the pickets of the enemy became aware of their presence and aroused the Mexicans. The Texans halted and decided to wait for daylight. As soon as the fog had cleared sufficiently, the Texans advanced and opened fire on the Mexicans with the disputed cannon. At the first shot, the Mexicans retired without returning fire, and Castañeda proposed a parley. John H. Moore, who was in command of the Texans, went forward and in response to

Castañeda's question as to why they were being attacked, Moore told him that the cannon had been given the Texans for the defense of themselves and of the Constitution and laws of the country, and that in demanding the cannon Castañeda was acting under the orders of the tyrant Santa Anna who had destroyed the Constitution. The Texans, Moore informed Castañeda, were prepared to fight for their rights and the Constitution, and they did not propose to deliver the cannon. Castañeda replied that he was himself a republican and that two-thirds of the people of Mexico were also republicans, but that as an officer of the army he would obey orders and that the people of Texas also were bound to submit to the Government. He said he did not want to fight the Texans, and that his orders directed him, in the event they refused to deliver the cannon, to encamp near Gonzales and await further orders. Moore then proposed to Castañeda that if such were his sentiments he should surrender and join the Texans in defense of the Constitution, assuring him that he would be received with open arms, but Castañeda replied that he would obey orders.

Moore then ordered an immediate attack, and advancing in double-quick time, the Texans opened fire again. Without attempting to make a stand, Castañeda ordered a retreat and the Mexicans galloped off in the direction of San Antonio, leaving one dead cavalryman on the field. Thus it was that Gonzales became "the Lexington of Texas" and the rallying point for volunteers from all the other settlements.

Meantime, Cos had proceeded to San Antonio, arriving at that place on October 9th. He left a quantity of arms, ammunition, and supplies at Goliad, guarded by thirty men under Colonel Sandoval. On the night of October 9th, a party of Texans, headed by Capt. George Collingsworth and including Ben Milam, who had escaped from a Mexican prison and just returned to Texas, made a successful attack on Goliad and captured the whole Mexican force, together with 200 muskets, two pieces of artillery and a quantity of ammunition. This not only provided the Texans with much needed arms, but it also cut Cos off from the most direct communication with the sea.

Austin arrived at Gonzales on October 11th and he was promptly elected commander-in-chief of the "Volunteer Army of Texas" by a unanimous vote of the various companies assembled at that place. And two days later he gave the order for the army to begin the march to San Antonio.

CHAPTER XXXII

REVOLUTION: FIRST PHASE

AUSTIN had been elected commander-in-chief of the Texan army in order to preserve unity and not because of any special qualifications he possessed. He was without military training or experience and he was in very poor health besides. But the question of who should be elected to supreme command was threatening to destroy discipline entirely and to divide the volunteers into a half-dozen or more warring groups at the time Austin arrived at Gonzales, and his name was proposed with the object of preventing a condition of chaos and confusion. W. T. Austin, who acted as his aide-de-camp, tells us that it was because "he plainly saw the unhappy state of affairs in the army" that he consented to serve, and that this was sufficient to "unite all parties and completely put an end to excitement and opposition". There was much "politics" among the "frontier republicans" who made up the Texan army and they were likely to divide easily into factional groups in support of various "leaders". At no time during the seven months of the Texas revolution was this condition entirely overcome, and this circumstance provides the key to an understanding of much that happened during that period.

A week after leaving Gonzales the Texan army arrived at Salado Creek, about five miles from San Antonio. And here the army was visited by a number of delegates of the Consultation, which had been adjourned until November 1st on account of the lack of a quorum, and a sort of mass meeting was held, with speeches by the visitors. Notably, Sam Houston delivered an address to the army. W. T. Austin, in reporting this address, says that Houston "did not favor active operations, but advised delay for drill and preparations". "He said that our troops were hastily assembled, composed of citizens, untrained, and that the Mexicans were regular soldiers and in a fortified town, and that we were not prepared for an active campaign and the reduction of San Antonio; he advised falling back to the east side of the Guadalupe until the army was reinforced, disciplined, and provided with artillery."

The lack of preparation was evident by that time to practically all the volunteers, for they had been short of bread and other necessary provisions for several days, although it had been less than two weeks since they left their original base at Gonzales. Austin, however, was of the opinion that the volunteers could overcome Cos's army and capture San Antonio, in spite of such handicaps, and he was determined to begin active operations against the town with as little delay as would be necessary. So, as soon as the Consultation delegates left for San Felipe, he moved the army to the San Antonio River and at the same time sent Col. James Bowie and Capt. J. W. Fannin, Jr., with a detachment of ninety-two men, to select a site for a camp as near to San Antonio as possible.

This expedition led to the first direct clash with the enemy, for, after selecting a site near the old Mission Concepcion, Bowie and Fannin decided to camp there for the night, and the next morning they awoke to find themselves surrounded by a good part of Cos's army. They were outnumbered at least four to one, and yet in the battle that ensued they completely bested the Mexicans, compelling them to retreat to the town, after leaving twenty or thirty dead on the field, with only one Texan killed. The advance guard of Austin's main army, a mounted company under Lieut. William B. Travis, caught sight of the fleeing Mexicans and followed them to the edge of the town. In his report of the affair to Austin, Bowie expressed the opinion that had it been possible to communicate with him and to have brought up the main force of Texans earlier "the victory would have been decisive, and Bexar would have been ours before twelve o'clock."

The "battle of Concepcion" took place on the morning of October 28th, at which time the whole Texan force amounted to about four hundred effective men. Next day about two hundred men from East Texas arrived, bringing the total to some six hundred. Word had been received that a company of volunteers from Louisiana was on its way to join the army at San Antonio, and that a piece of artillery, a twelve-pounder, was also being brought up. Austin decided to await these, and whatever other volunteers from the settlements that might arrive in the meantime, before attempting an attack on the town. And so, after an unsuccessful attempt to ob-

tain a parley with Cos, Austin and the Volunteer
Army of Texas settled down to a siege.

Meantime, the delegates to the Consultation were
gathering at San Felipe and on November 3rd a
quorum was obtained. With Dr. Branch T. Archer
as its presiding officer, this body, consisting of a full
membership of 81 delegates, representing twelve local constituencies, remained in session until November 14th. It adopted a "declaration" of reasons for
taking up arms and it set up a provisional State Government, with Henry Smith as Governor, James W.
Robinson as Lieutenant Governor, and a "General
Council", consisting of one representative from each
municipality. Moreover, it elected Sam Houston
"Major General of the armies of Texas" and provided that this officer should be "commander-in-
chief of *all* the forces called into public service during the war". And finally it decided to send three
commissioners to the United States to obtain financial and other support for the new Texas Government, and it named Stephen F. Austin, William H.
Wharton, and Dr. Branch T. Archer as the commissioners.

There was a considerable minority sentiment in
the Consultation for an immediate declaration of independence, William H. Wharton being the leading advocate of this course. A direct vote on this
question, taken on November 6th, showed fifteen
in favor of such a declaration and thirty-three opposed to it, a ratio of more than two to one against.
The vote in favor of "a provisional government, upon
the principles of the Constitution of 1824" showed
about the same division, thirty-three ayes and four-

teen nays. The "declaration" finally adopted set forth
that the Texans had taken up arms in defense of "the
republican principles" of the Constitution of 1824,
the word "republican" having been inserted as an
amendment to a committee draft from the floor.

This "declaration", which was adopted by the Consultation on November 7th, was as follows:

"DECLARATION OF THE PEOPLE OF TEXAS IN GENERAL
CONVENTION ASSEMBLED:

"Whereas, General Antonio Lopez de Santa Anna,
and other military chieftains, have, by force of arms,
overthrown the Federal institutions of Mexico, and
dissolved the social compact which existed between
Texas and the other members of the Mexican Confederacy; now, the good people of Texas, availing
themselves of their natural rights, SOLEMNLY DE-
CLARE,

"1st. That they have taken up arms in defense of
their rights and liberties, which were threatened by
the encroachments of military despots, and in defense
of the republican principles of the Federal Constitution of Mexico, of eighteen and twenty-four.

"2nd. That Texas is no longer morally or civilly
bound by the compact of union; yet, stimulated by
the generosity and sympathy common to a free people, they offer their support and assistance to such
of the members of the Mexican Confederacy as will
take up arms against military despotism.

"3rd. That they do not acknowledge that the present authorities of the nominal Mexican Republic
have the right to govern within the limits of Texas.

"4th. That they will not cease to carry on war against the said authorities while their troops are within the limits of Texas.

"5th. That they hold it to be their right during the disorganization of the Federal system, and the reign of despotism, to withdraw from the union, to establish an independent government, or to adopt such measures as they may deem best calculated to protect their rights and liberties, but that they will continue faithful to the Mexican Government so long as that nation is governed by the Constitution and laws that were formed for the government of the political association.

"6th. That Texas is responsible for the expense of her armies now in the field.

"7th. That the public faith of Texas is pledged for any debts contracted by her agents.

"8th. That she will reward, by donations of lands, all who volunteer their services in her present struggle, and receive them as citizens.

"These declarations we solemnly avow to the world, and call God to witness their truth and sincerity, and invoke defeat and disgrace upon our heads, should we prove guilty of duplicity."

In setting up the provisional State Government, the Consultation adopted a document known as "the plan and powers of the provisional Government of Texas", and the machinery it provided could hardly have been better designed to promote friction and confusion, for the powers of the Governor and those of the General Council overlapped in so many important particulars as to insure a maximum of occasions for disagreement. And as if to make disagreement and friction doubly sure, the Consultation placed the powers and duties of the office of Governor in the hands of Henry Smith, one of the most cantankerous and least suitable men in all Texas. Smith received the votes of thirty-one delegates for this office, while twenty-two voted for Austin. A change of five votes would have reversed this result, a circumstance which provides one of the "what-might-have-beens" of the Texas story. With Austin as Governor and Houston as commander-in-chief, a governmental authority might have been established which would have commanded respect and enforced discipline.

On November 14th, just before adjournment, A. E. C. Johnson, one of the delegates from San Augustine, introduced a resolution providing that "the Consultation of all Texas, in general convention assembled, recommend to the army of the people to abandon the proposed siege of San Antonio, and that they fall back upon La Bahiá and Gonzales, and place themselves in a condition of safety, by leaving a sufficient number of men, and the balance of the army be furloughed to their homes, to join the army by the first of March, or as soon as the emergencies of the country may require."

This resolution was promptly ruled out of order, for the very good reason that such details of conducting the war were not proper subjects to be passed upon by the Consultation. But the view which it embodied evidently had come to be widely held. As shall be seen, it had permeated the volunteer army which was besieging San Antonio.

The Consultation adjourned on November 14th "to meet on the first day of March next, unless sooner called by the Governor and Council", and it was resolved that "all the members of this body who can, repair to San Antonio to assist our fellow citizens in the field."

The siege of San Antonio had been continued in the meantime without any notable change. On November 18th, not knowing that the Consultation had adjourned, Austin wrote that body that as soon as the Louisiana volunteers, known as the New Orleans Grays, reached him, and a contingent under Col. Edward Burleson, which was absent, returned to camp, he intended to storm San Antonio. The same day Austin received a communication from the Provisional Government, informing him that he had been named a commissioner to the United States and directing him to report at San Felipe. Austin replied to this communication at once. "I can only say," he wrote, "that I am ready at all times to serve Texas in any station where it is considered I can be useful. Some prudence will be necessary to keep this army together should I leave at once. I therefore cannot at this time say when I can be at San Felipe, but will give you the earliest possible information on this subject."

Word came on the morning of November 21st that the cannon for which Austin had been waiting would be in camp in a few hours and that the New Orleans Grays would arrive before night. Austin therefore issued a general order directing the organization of the army into divisions for the purpose of storming San Antonio the following morning. He then proceeded to make all arrangements for beginning the attack at three o'clock on the morning of November 22nd. At one o'clock in the morning, however, just two hours before the attack was to begin, Lieut. Col. Philip Sublett of San Augustine, who was in direct command of the second division of the army, called upon Austin and presented the following note:

"To Stephen F. Austin, Commander-in-Chief:

"On receipt of your general order of this date announcing that an attack on the fortifications of Bexar would be made by storm tomorrow morning, I have ascertained the disposition of the officers and men of my division and believe it to be my duty to report that a majority of them are opposed to the measure and are unwilling to attempt it, and I concur in opinion with them.

"PHILIP A. SUBLETT
"Lieutenant Colonel"

Another note, identical with this one with the exception that the phrase "I concur in opinion with them" was omitted, was presented by Colonel Burleson. Austin was dumbfounded. He immediately ordered an investigation and soon found the situation to be as reported. Not more than one hundred men, with the exception of the New Orleans Grays, were willing to undertake the attack. Accordingly, Austin countermanded his general order.

Three days later Austin ordered a parade of the army and addressed the men in person. He told them he had decided to accept the commission to go to the United States and urged upon them the importance of continuing the siege. He announced that a call would be made for volunteers to remain under officers of their own choosing. Four hundred and five men responded to this call, and Col. Edward Burleson was elected commander-inchief of the Volunteer Army. Austin then took his leave of the army and departed for San Felipe on November 25th.

The army had a little excitement the day following Austin's departure, when a party of Mexican foragers, which Cos had sent out to obtain hay for his famished horses, was engaged in a running fight and compelled to retire without attaining its objective. But within a few days the monotony of the routine of the siege settled down upon the men, and there was so much evidence of restlessness that several of the officers proposed to Burleson that the siege should be raised. A council of Burleson's staff and all the field officers was held on December 3rd and it was decided to break camp the next day and retire to Gonzales. Accordingly, on the morning of December 4th the army was paraded and the order to prepare to break camp and march to Gonzales was communicated to the men. The persistent propaganda in opposition to the campaign against San Antonio had finally won out completely.

In the midst of the preparations for the march to Gonzales, however, a deserter from San Antonio, a Mexican lieutenant, suddenly appeared in camp and asked to be taken to the commanding officer. He was conducted to Burleson's quarters at once, while men crowded around in excitement, and in a few words he reported that the defenses of San Antonio were weak, that Cos's men were discouraged and discontented, and that the town could be easily taken. Col. F. W. Johnson, overhearing this and noting the ex-

citement among the men, remarked to Col. Ben
Milam that it would be a good time to call for volunteers to storm the town. Milam acted on the suggestion instantly. Turning to the men crowding
around Burleson's quarters, he called out, "Who will
go with old Ben Milam into San Antonio?" A
chorus responded, "I will!" "Then fall in line,"
commanded Milam, and more than two hundred
men stepped forward and formed in line. There
were hurried conferences, the upshot of which was
that Burleson agreed to permit Milam and Johnson
to lead an attack with such men as would volunteer,
and to hold the rest of his force in readiness to render whatever support might become necessary. The
march to Gonzales was forgotten.

Accordingly, at five o'clock in the morning, on
December 5th, while Burleson's artillery diverted
Cos's attention by beginning a bombardment of the
old mission at one end of the town which was known
as the Alamo, two parties of Texans, under Milam
and Johnson, quietly entered the town from the other
side and began a house to house fight toward the
plaza, where Cos's main battery and breastworks were
located. The two parties together numbered three
hundred and one men and they were going against an
entrenched enemy that outnumbered them more
than three to one. For four days they battled stub-
bornly, fighting almost inch by inch, from house to
house, each day bringing them nearer to the Mexican
position. On the afternoon of the third day, December 7th, the intrepid Milam was killed and Johnson
took over full command. On the fourth day the
Texans fought almost constantly for nearly twenty

hours, occupying the last building commanding the plaza about midnight, and at half-past six o'clock in the morning on December 9th the Mexicans raised a flag of truce and Cos and his entire army surrendered.

At no time during the four days of fighting did the Texans number more than three hundred and fifty men, including reinforcements sent into the town by Burleson, and they had accomplished what Sublett and the other officers of the volunteers had refused to undertake with practically twice as many men scarcely two weeks before. Indeed, they had accomplished more, for Cos had been reinforced by the arrival of about six hundred men during the course of the fighting. Cos's force was never less than one thousand men and at its highest strength it must have reached sixteen hundred. The victory was a complete demonstration of the fighting efficiency of the Texas volunteers when led by competent officers.

Under the terms of Cos's capitulation, he agreed to withdraw beyond the Rio Grande with his entire force and promised that they would not "in any way oppose the reestablishment of the Federal Constitution of 1824." Cos began his march to the Rio Grande on December 15th, and by Christmas there was not a Mexican soldier under arms in all Texas.

During the months that these events had been going forward in Texas, the Centralist Congress in Mexico City had been continuing its work of destroying the Constitution of 1824 and abolishing the Federal system. The actual abolition of the last vestige of the Federation was accomplished as the result of a decree, promulgated by the Central Government on October 3rd, which dissolved all the State Governments and all the State Legislatures and made all local officials absolutely subject to the will of the Supreme Government at Mexico City. Centralism was thus completely established.

When Austin obtained a copy of the decree of October 3rd, he immediately translated it for the information of the Provisional Government of Texas. He submitted a copy of it to the General Council at San Felipe on November 30th, at the same time pointing out that this decree changed the whole situation fundamentally for Texas and that in consequence a new election for delegates to a convention of all Texas should be ordered without delay.

"The character of the struggle in which Texas is engaged," said Austin, "is now clearly developed; it evidently is one of life or death, 'to be or not to be'. It is no longer a mere question about forms of political institutions; it is one of self-preservation. Texas is menaced with a war of extermination; the Government of Mexico has so proclaimed it. The people now understand their situation, and consequently are much better prepared to elect public agents to provide against such a danger than they were at the time of the last election. At that time the form of government was not changed by any act which had the influence and the character of law; it now is by the decree of the 3rd of October last. At that time the State Governments existed; at this, no such thing as a State exists, not even in name."

The General Council acted on this suggestion and called an election to be held on February 1st to name delegates to another convention to assemble on

March 1st. Governor Smith, who already was at loggerheads with the Council, vetoed this measure, but the Council promptly passed it over his veto. And so provision was made to enable the people of Texas to decide their future destiny.

When Cos reached the Rio Grande he was met by an army of fifteen hundred men under Gen. Ramírez y Sesma, which was on its way from Zacatecas to San Antonio to reinforce him, and this force was halted to await orders from Santa Anna. Santa Anna had then reached San Luis Potosí on his way to Texas, but learning that San Antonio had fallen to the Texans, he ordered Cos to continue his retreat to Monclova and directed Ramírez y Sesma to take up a position at San Juan Bautista on the Rio Grande, about eighty miles fom Laredo. And Santa Anna began immediately to plan a new invasion of Texas.

Two days after Christmas the commissioners to the United States, Austin, Wharton, and Dr. Archer, sailed from Quintana for New Orleans. At the moment of their departure a communication from the American State Department to Anthony Butler, the minister to Mexico, was on its way to Mexico City. It informed him, among other things, that the Mexican Government had requested his recall and that the nomination of his successor had been sent to the Senate. Butler had come to the end of his rope, but even at that late day his activities continued to create confusion and suspicion of the United States in relation to Texas. Butler had been in Washington during the summer of 1835 and he had returned to Mexico City by way of Texas just about the time the Texans were taking up arms. This circumstance was enough to prove to the Mexican officials that there was a direct relation between the American minister and the revolt in Texas. On October 21st, 1835, the Minister of Relations directed the Mexican *chargé d'affairs* in Washington to call the attention of the Government of the United States to the fact that public opinion in Mexico was very unfavorable to Butler, "to whom are imputed intrigues unbecoming a diplomatic agent which imputation is strengthened by the present occurrences in Texas, the revolt there having commenced whilst that gentleman was in those parts!" In consequence of this, the Government of the United States was requested to recall Mr. Butler and thus relieve the Mexican Government from the unpleasant necessity of tendering him his passports.

CHAPTER XXXIII

REVOLUTION: SECOND PHASE

DURING the first two months of 1836 the people of Texas were almost entirely without competent and effective leadership. Austin was away in the United States, though even his influence had begun to wane before he left, and the leadership of Sam Houston, which was finally to save Texas, was not yet widely felt. Austin seems to have realized that a different type of leadership from his own would be needed during the critical period the Texans were just entering and to have recognized that Houston was capable of providing this. The relations between these two men had not been very intimate, but Austin was not among those who underrated Houston's abilities. In any event, when Austin became convinced, shortly after his arrival at New Orleans, that an independent Texas could be successfully financed in the United States, he immediately wrote Houston a full statement of his views. This letter, which was dated January 7th, 1836, was at once a vindication of the kind of leadership Austin had given the Texans in the past and a recognition that the time had arrived when it would serve no longer.

"In all our Texas affairs, as you are well apprised," Austin wrote Houston, "I have felt it to be my duty to be very cautious in involving the pioneers

and actual settlers of that country by any act of mine
until I was fully and clearly convinced of its necessity, and of the capabilities of our resources to sustain it. Hence it is that I have been censured for
being over-cautious. When the whole fate of a people is in question, it is difficult to be over-cautious or
to be too prudent. Besides these general considerations, there are others which ought to have weight
with me individually. I have been, either directly
or indirectly, the cause of drawing many families to
Texas; also the situation and circumstances in which
I have been placed have given considerable weight
to my opinions. This has thrown a heavy responsibility on me—so much so that I have considered it
my duty to be prudent, and even to control my own
impulses and feelings; these have long been impatient under the state of things which has existed in
Texas, and in favor of radical change. But I have
never approved of the course of forestalling public
opinion by party or partial meetings or by manage-
ment of any kind."

Austin then proceeded to say that at the time he left
Texas he was of the opinion that a declaration of independence would be premature. This was contrary
to his own impulses, he said, for he wanted to see
the Texans free from the trammels of religious in-
tolerance and other anti-republican restrictions
which the Mexican Government imposed upon them.
But as long as there was hope of obtaining the help
of the Federal party of Mexico, he had felt that
anything that might tend to unite all Mexican parties against the Texans and make the war a purely
national war should be avoided. As an individual,

he was always ready, he said, to risk everything he had to obtain independence, but he could not feel justified in precipitating the question and involving others until he was fully satisfied that they would be sustained.

"Since my arrival here," he wrote, "I have received information which has satisfied me on this subject. I have no doubt we can obtain all and even much more aid than we need. I think the time has come for Texas to assert her natural rights, and were I in the convention I would urge an immediate declaration of independence."

Austin added that Santa Anna was at San Luis Potosí, according to the last accounts, preparing to march against Texas with a large force. "We must be united and firm," he declared, "and look well to the month of March and be *ready!*"

Houston, of course, agreed with this view entirely. But at the moment the prospect of uniting Texas did not seem very bright and there was little assurance that the Texans would be "ready" by the month of March. The Provisional Government, created by the Consultation, had turned out to be worse than no government at all, for while it collapsed in the middle of January and then ceased to have any real existence, it had managed to set afoot more mischief than would have been believed possible. While the Council was composed entirely of members of the Consultation, which had elected both Henry Smith and Sam Houston as Governor and commander-in-chief respectively, it consistently opposed the plans of these two officials from the first and finally worked openly against them. Smith, it must be said, was as much responsible for the situation as anybody, but aside from all question of blame, the total effect was to leave Texas entirely leaderless and adrift. It was a fortunate circumstance that the Council, at Austin's insistence and over Smith's veto, had provided for an election on February 1st of delegates to another convention on March 1st, for it was through this means that new leaders finally took charge. It is significant, in this connection, that very few of the members of the Council, or even of the Consultation, were elected to the new convention, and that its net result was to make Sam Houston's leadership effective and finally dominant. But this result was not brought about until the Texans had undergone a series of disasters which came perilously near to destroying the Anglo-American settlements in Texas altogether.

The most mischievous policy which the Council followed was that of assuming that Houston had no authority over the volunteers and that it was his business, without any great measure of support from the Council itself, to create a "regular" army to command. The document known as "The Plan and Powers of the Provisional Government of Texas", which was the "fundamental law" under which the Council was supposed to operate, provided that the "major general", which was the title of Houston's office, should be "commander-in-chief of all the forces called into public service during the war". Now, the only forces that were in the public service were "volunteers", but the Council from the first acted on the assumption that Houston had no authority over these "volunteers" and finally went to the extreme of commissioning "regular" officers, who plainly were subordinate to Houston's authority, to undertake expeditions quite independently of him and without even consulting him. At this distance it all appears as part of a systematic effort to eliminate Houston, and, in any event, it certainly had that effect.

After the capitulation of Cos at San Antonio, Burleson had left F. W. Johnson at that place with about four hundred men, and as the result of an election held by them Johnson had assumed the title of "commander-in-chief of the volunteers". As "the hero of San Antonio", Johnson's influence for the moment was very great. About two hundred volunteers from Georgia had arrived at Velasco in December, and Houston had placed J. W. Fannin, Jr., who was a native of Georgia and who had been commissioned as "Colonel of the artillery" of the "regular" army, in command of them. In addition to this there were about seventy men under arms at Washington-on-the-Brazos and about eighty at Goliad. And finally there were several small companies of volunteers in process of forming and there was the certain prospect of the early arrival of other volunteers from the United States. At the beginning of January, therefore, there were about seven hundred and fifty men under arms in Texas, all of them "volunteers", and under the assumption of the Council they were only nominally subject to Houston's authority.

As to the volunteers from the United States, it should be said that early in November, 1835, the American Secretary of State had sent a circular to all United States district attorneys notifying them of the fixed determination of the President to prevent American citizens from interfering in the domestic affairs of Mexico and instructing them to give prompt attention to all contemplated or attempted movements hostile to Mexico and to prosecute vigorously all violations of the neutrality laws. At the same time, Santa Anna caused advertisements to be inserted in American newspapers notifying all whom it might concern that foreigners found under arms on Mexican soil would be treated as freebooters and shot. However, there was strong public sympathy for the Texans among the American people and "Texas committees" were organized in many cities in the United States. One of the first things Austin had done after deciding in September that the Texans had to fight was to send an appeal to the American public for help to be printed in the newspapers in the United States, and this had brought almost instant response. Moreover, early in December absolute documentary evidence had been obtained that it was Santa Anna's purpose to wage a war of extermination against the Anglo-American settlements in Texas, treating the Texans as "foreigners", and in view of this the Texans proposed to accept help from any quarter in which it might be obtained. One of the duties of the commissioners to the United States, Austin, Wharton, and Dr. Archer, was to appoint agents to organize and equip companies of volunteers and send them to Texas. The prospect of more volunteers from the United States, therefore, was certain, in spite of all the American Government might do to prevent this. But the practical effect of the attitude of the Council was to destroy Houston's authority over such volunteers and finally it went to the extreme of authorizing subordinate officers to take command of them and to direct their movements without consulting Houston.

All of this developed out of a proposed expedition against Matamoros. Such an expedition was proposed immediately after Cos's capitulation at San Antonio, and Houston had sent an order to James Bowie directing him to undertake it. Bowie did not receive the order for several weeks, however, and nothing ever came of this. But with four hundred men under his command and nothing to do but garrison San Antonio, Johnson conceived the idea of undertaking such an expedition, and the Council adopted a resolution authorizing him to do so. When Smith vetoed this resolution, however, Johnson declined the commission, although, acting under his orders, a certain Dr. James Grant, a citizen of Coahuila, whom Johnson had appointed his aide-de-camp, had already started from San Antonio with a large portion of the volunteers who had been garrisoning that place. This was the situation when, on January 7th, the same day that Austin was writing to Houston from New Orleans, the Council appointed Fannin as a "special agent" of the Provisional Government of Texas to undertake such an expedition.

The resolution naming Fannin as "special agent", considering all the circumstances, is one of the most remarkable documents in the annals of organized government. For it provided that Fannin "is hereby appointed and empowered, as an agent for and on behalf of the Provisional Government of Texas, to raise, collect, and concentrate at, or as near the port of Copano as convenience and safety will admit, all volunteer troops willing to enter into an expedition against Matamoros, wherever they may be found—at the mouth of the Brazos, city of Bexar, or elsewhere, whether in Texas or arriving in Texas—and, when thus collected and concentrated, to report either to the commanding general or to the Governor and Council, *as he may prefer.*" It also authorized Fannin to call upon the general agent of the commissary department or any other public agent or supplying officer of the Government for the necessary munitions and provisions, and provided that Fannin's receipt for such things would be respected by the Government. And finally, it authorized Fannin to make a descent on Matamoros "if he deems it practicable to take such place, or *such other point or place as the said agent may deem proper,*" and empowered him to appoint such special agent or agents under him "as he may deem necessary to carry into effect the object of these resolutions."

In other words, the Council, without consulting Houston and entirely without his knowledge, gave to Fannin full authority to prosecute a privately managed and personally conducted war on Mexico and to use the armed forces of Texas and the munitions and supplies of Texas in prosecuting such a war!

Fannin was fully determined to act under this extraordinary authority, regardless of the attitude of Governor Smith or of Houston, and when Johnson learned of this he promptly decided to do the same. Whereupon the Council authorized Johnson to proceed to undertake an expedition against Matamoros, provided that he did not interfere with the "agency" bestowed upon Fannin. On January 8th, Fannin published a call for volunteers from San Antonio, Goliad, Velasco, and elsewhere, directing them to rendezvous at San Patricio between January 24th and 27th. And two days later, Johnson published a similar call, fixing the place of rendezvous the same as Fannin's and the dates as between January 25th and 30th. The result of this was that in a few days most of the armed forces of Texas were on the move in answer to these two calls, and without orders of any kind from the commander-in-chief.

It was at this stage of the proceedings that Governor Smith received a letter from Lieut. Col. J. C. Neill, who was now in command at San Antonio, describing the condition in which he and his little force had been left by the departure of Johnson and Grant. "We have one hundred and four men," wrote Colonel Neill, "and two distinct fortresses to garrison, and about twenty-four pieces of artillery. You, doubtless, have learned that we have no provisions or clothing since Johnson and Grant left. If there has ever been a dollar here, I have no knowledge of it. The clothing sent here by the aid and patriotic exertions of the honorable Council was taken from us by the arbitrary measures of Johnson and Grant, taken from men who endured all the hardships of winter, and who were not even sufficiently clad for summer, many of them having but one blanket and one shirt, and what was intended for them given away to men, some of whom had not been in the army more than four days, and many not exceeding two weeks. If a divide had been made of them, the most needy of my men could have been made comfortable by the stock of clothing and provisions taken from here. About two hundred of the men who had volunteered to garrison this town for four months left my command contrary to my orders and thereby vitiated the policy of their enlistments." Colonel Neill informed Governor Smith that he needed three hundred men at San Antonio.

Governor Smith had already reached the breaking point with the Council when he received this letter, so he made it the occasion to bring their relations to a crisis. He transmitted the letter to the Council, accompanied by a message in which he gave its members until noon the next day (this was on January 14th) to issue a public disavowal of the Matamoros expedition under penalty of having the Council dissolved until March 1st, when the convention would meet. The message fairly sizzled with denunciatory language. "You have acted in bad faith," declared Governor Smith, "and seem determined by your acts to destroy the very institutions you are pledged and sworn to support. . . . I know you have honest men there, and of sterling worth and integrity; but you have Judases in the camp—corruption, base corruption has crept into your councils—men who, if possible, would deceive their God. . . . Look round upon your flock. Your discernment will easily detect the scoundrels. The complaints, contraction of the eyes, the gape of the mouth, the vacant stare, the hung head, the restless, fidgety disposition; the sneaking, sycophantic look, a natural meanness of countenance, an unguarded shrug of the shoulders, a sympathetic tickling and contraction of the muscles of the neck, anticipating the rope."

The Council, on its part, referred this message to a committee which promptly condemned it as "low, blackguardly and vindictive, and every way unworthy of and disgraceful to the office from which it emanated, and an outrageous libel on the body to whom it was addressed." Then it proceeded to adopt a resolution suspending Governor Smith from office and citing him to appear to defend himself against an enumeration of charges.

Smith then wrote the Council a conciliatory letter, which made no impression upon its members, and the latter proceeded to inaugurate James W. Robinson, the Lieutenant Governor, in Smith's place. Robinson made a bombastic inaugural address, and the Council continued a few days longer to hold sessions. However, after January 17th it was unable to obtain a quorum, and for all practical purposes it ceased to exist.

In the meantime, on January 8th, when Fannin's "call" had appeared, Governor Smith had ordered Houston to proceed to Goliad and other points and take command of the army. Neither Smith nor Houston were aware of the powers that had been bestowed upon Fannin, and it was not until January 21st that Houston learned of them from Johnson at Refugio. Fannin had sailed from Velasco with the "Georgia batallion" and a few Texas volunteers for Copano, where he was later joined by Johnson and Grant and an understanding was reached. Fannin then moved inland to Goliad. He expressed a willingness to serve under Houston, if Houston were

willing to command the expedition against Matamoros. But when Houston came to understand the
situation, and realized that the effect and intention
of the Council's resolution were to displace him, he
returned to San Felipe to report to Governor Smith.

"By remaining with the army," said Houston in a
written report to Smith, "the Council would have
had the pleasure of ascribing to me the evils which
their own conduct and acts will, in all probability,
produce. I consider the acts of the Council calculated to protract the war for years to come; and the
field which they have opened to insubordination and
to agencies without limit (unknown to military usage) will cost the country more useless expenditure
than the necessary expense of the whole war would
have been, had they not transcended their proper duties. Without integrity of purpose and well-devised
measures, the whole frontier must be exposed to the
enemy. All the available resources of Texas are directed, through special as well as general agencies,
against Matamoros; and must in all probability
prove as unavailing to the interests as they will to the
honor of Texas."

While at Goliad, Houston had received an appeal
from Colonel Neill at San Antonio to send him
reinforcements, as he expected an attack from the
enemy, and Houston ordered James Bowie to take a
company of volunteers and proceed to that place. At
the same time Governor Smith, in response to the
letter from Neill, ordered Col. William Barrett
Travis to recruit one hundred "regulars" and go to
Neill's relief. Houston directed Bowie to demolish
the fortifications of the town, and he suggested to

Governor Smith that he be authorized to order an abandonment of San Antonio. He proposed that the Alamo be blown up and the cannon and other equipment there be moved to Gonzales and Copano. "It will be impossible to keep the station with volunteers," Houston wrote to Smith. "The sooner I can be authorized the better it will be for the country." For want of horses and mules, however, the cannon at San Antonio could not be moved, and nothing ever came of Houston's suggestion. Bowie arrived at San Antonio on February 2nd, and he immediately added his own voice to that of Colonel Neill in appeals for reinforcements. Travis arrived a few days later wit thirty men, all he could induce to enlist, and he also joined in the cry for reinforcements.

The Provisional Government, however, had ceased to exist and the people did not respect the authority of either the Council or of Governor Smith. Houston, after reporting to Governor Smith, had asked for a furlough, and had gone to confer with certain Indian chiefs with the object of insuring their good will during the invasion of the Mexican army which was expected. Everything was in a disorganized condition, with no established central authority. The election for delegates to the convention was held on February 1st, however, and the meeting of that body on March 1st now constituted the hope of Texas.

Meantime, Santa Anna was mobilizing an army of more than six thousand men, in five detachments, just below the Rio Grande. He began to move the main body of his army from Saltillo on January 26th and within the next three weeks his plans were complete to begin the invasion of Texas. On February 12th the advance of Santa Anna's main army, under General Ramírez y Sesma, crossed the Rio Grande near Laredo and proceeded toward San Antonio. Five days later, General Urréa, with about one thousand men, including cavalry and infantry, crossed the river at Matamoros, and marched toward San Patricio. The invasion had begun, and Texas was divided and unprepared.

CHAPTER XXXIV

REVOLUTION: THIRD PHASE

IT is a remarkable fact that on the very eve of the Mexican invasion the people of Texas, taken as a whole, had no real comprehension of the imminent danger they faced. Only two weeks before Santa Anna's advance guard crossed the Rio Grande, Travis, on his way to San Antonio, wrote to Governor Smith expressing discouragement over the apathy of the people. "Our affairs are gloomy indeed," he wrote. "The people are cold and indifferent . . . and in consequence of the dissensions between contending and rival chieftains they have lost confidence in their own Government and officers." And on the very day the invasion began, two weeks later, he wrote again in a similar strain from San Antonio. "We hope our countrymen will open their eyes at the present danger and awake from their false security," he said. "I fear it is useless to waste arguments upon them. The thunder of the enemy's cannon and the pollution of their wives and daughters—the cries of their famished children and the smoke of their burning dwellings only will arouse them."

The danger was fully as great as Travis feared. Santa Anna's marching orders, issued at Saltillo on January 23rd, show that his total force amounted to

6,318 men. And at the moment this force began to move across the Rio Grande, there were not more than 800 men under arms in Texas, and more than half of those were volunteers from the United States. Fannin at Goliad had the largest force, but its total was not more than 500 men, consisting of the Georgia Battalion, a Kentucky company, and some Texas volunteers. Johnson and Grant were at San Patricio with about 100 men, including part of the New Orleans Grays under Major Morris. Besides a few scattered men here and there, the only other force was the garrison at San Antonio, and after the arrival of Bowie and Travis the total there was only about 150 men. That was all. Santa Anna's army outnumbered them eight to one, and his orders were that no prisoners should be taken and no quarter given. The Texans faced a war of extermination.

Santa Anna's advance was in accordance with a carefully worked-out plan. The bulk of his forces, after crossing the Rio Grande at San Juan Baustista, northwest of Laredo, were destined for San Antonio, from which point, after reducing the garrison there, he proposed to advance into the settlements. A force of about 1,000 men, under General Urréa, however, crossed the river at Matamoros, and then, keeping near the coast, marched north to San Patricio. The vanguard of the main army, under Ramírez y Sesma, reached San Antonio on February 23rd, and four days later, on the night of February 27th, Urréa reached San Patricio.

Travis was now in command of the garrison at San Antonio, Colonel Neill having gone home on a furlough because of illness in his family. James

Bowie had been elected Colonel of a small contingent of volunteers, but the responsibility of the garrison rested on Travis. With them also was David Crockett, who had arrived at Nacogdoches from Tennessee early in January and had gone directly to San Antonio. Crockett was nationally known in the United States as a backwoods Congressman from Tennessee who had vigorously opposed some of the leading policies of President Jackson. Friends of Jackson managed to defeat Crockett for reelection to Congress in the fall of 1835, whereupon he made a farewell speech to his constituents and characteristically informed them that they could "all go to hell" and that he was going to Texas. Crockett was without question the most prominent American to respond to the appeal of the Texans for help, and he had joined the garrison at San Antonio as being the most likely to provide an early opportunity for action.

It was Travis who sent the first news of the invasion to the settlements, and it was Travis who finally aroused the Texans. As soon as the Mexican vanguard was sighted, he ordered the garrison to occupy the Alamo, the old mission which Cos had used as a fortress during the siege the previous autumn, and he sent Col. James B. Bonham at once with a scribbled note to Andrew Ponton at Gonzales for help. "The enemy in large force is in sight," he wrote. "We want men and provisions. Send them to us. We have one hundred and fifty men and are determined to defend the Alamo to the last." Then the next day, February 24th, after the Mexican army had surrounded the Alamo and had kept up a bombardment for twenty-four hours, Travis sent out an appeal addressed "To the People of Texas and All Americans in the World." It was as follows:

"Fellow Citizens and Compatriots: I am besieged by a thousand or more Mexicans under Santa Anna. I have sustained a continual bombardment and cannonade for twenty-four hours and have not lost a man. The enemy has demanded a surrender at discretion, otherwise the garrison are to be put to the sword, if the fort is taken. I have answered the demand with a cannon shot, and our flag still waves proudly from the walls. *I shall never surrender or retreat. Then,* I call on you in the name of Liberty, of patriotism and everything dear to the American character, to come to our aid with all dispatch. The enemy is receiving reinforcements daily and will no doubt increase to three or four thousand in four or five days. If this call is neglected, I am determined to sustain myself as long as possible and die like a soldier who never forgets what is due his own honor and that of his country. VICTORY OR DEATH,

"WILLIAM BARRETT TRAVIS

"Lt. Col. comdt.

"P. S.—The Lord is on our side. When the enemy appeared in sight we had not three bushels of corn. We have since found in deserted houses eighty or ninety bushels and got into the walls twenty or thirty head of beeves."

Copies of this heroic appeal, which Governor Smith had had printed at once, were being sent broadcast over Texas as the delegates to the convention were gathering at Washington-on-the-Brazos to begin their sessions on March 1st. At the same time news reached the settlements that Urréa had surprised Johnson at San Patricio on the night of February 27th and that nearly all of the men under his command there had been killed. The report was to the effect that Grant and Morris had been killed also. This was not true at the time it was received, for Grant and Morris and fifty of the men were absent from San Patricio on an expedition to round up horses when Urréa arrived at that place. But three days later Urréa overtook them about twenty miles west of San Patricio and slaughtered them without mercy. Santa Anna's orders to take no prisoners and give no quarter were being carried out to the letter. Johnson and three or four others managed to escape from San Patricio, but both Grant and Morris were killed. This news spread over Texas at the same time that copies of Travis's appeal were being circulated and as the convention at Washington-on-the-Brazos got under way. Writing of these events to his wife, Martin Parmer, a delegate to the convention from San Augustine, declared that "the frontiers are breaking up, and Gonzales must be sacked and its inhabitants murdered and defiled without they get immediate aid". "Unless we have a general turn out," he added, "and every man lay his helping hands to, we are lost." A realization of this was now sweeping over Texas at last. Governor Smith issued a call for "a general turn out". "I slight none," he declared. "This call is upon ALL who are able to bear arms to rally without delay, or in fifteen days the heart of Texas will be the seat of war. This is not imaginery. The enemy, from six thousand to eight thousand strong, are on our border and rapidly moving by forced marches for the colonies. The campaign has commenced. We must promptly meet the enemy or all is lost."

The convention opened its sessions on March 1st and its first action was to appoint a committee of five, headed by George C. Childress, to draft a declaration of independence. This committee reported the next day, March 2nd, and the declaration was unanimously adopted. After reciting the reasons for the action, this document concluded as follows:

"We, therefore, the delegates, with plenary powers, of the people of Texas, in solemn convention assembled, appealing to a candid world for the necessities of our condition, do hereby resolve and declare that our political connection with the Mexican nation has forever ended; and that the people of Texas do now constitute a *free, sovereign and independent Republic,* and are fully invested with all the rights and attributes which properly belong to independent nations; and conscious of the rectitude of our intentions, we fearlessly and confidently commit the issue to the supreme arbiter of the destinies of nations."

Fifty-eight delegates, representing every municipality in Texas, signed this declaration, and the convention then proceeded to name a committee to draft a constitution. On March 4th the convention adopted a resolution naming Sam Houston as commander-in-chief of all the Texas forces. This resolution as originally introduced read as follows:

"Whereas we are now in a state of Revolution, and threatened by a large invading army from the Central Government of Mexico; and whereas our present situation and the emergency of the present crisis

render it indispensably necessary that we should have
an army in the field; and, whereas it is also necessary
that there should be one Supreme head or Commander-in-chief, and due degrees of subordination
defined, established and strictly observed.

"Therefore, be it Resolved, that General Samuel
Houston be appointed Commander-in-Chief of all
the land forces of the Texian Army, both regulars,
volunteers and militia, while in actual service, and
endowed with all the rights, privileges and powers
due to a Commander-in-Chief in the United States
of America, and that he forthwith proceed to take
command, establish headquarters and organize the
army accordingly."

By an amendment offered from the floor, the following was added to this resolution and incorporated
in it:

"And that Samuel Houston retain such command
until the election of a chief magistrate of this Government, and to continue in such office unless super-
seded by order of the Government, subject, however,
to the general orders of the Government *de facto,*
until the general organization agreeable to the Constitution, and always amenable to the laws and civil
authorities of the country."

Thus it was that the convention did everything in
its power to make Houston's authority supreme. And
armed with this new authority, Houston took his
leave of the convention on March 6th and departed
for Gonzales, where volunteers were gathering in response to Travis's appeal and Governor Smith's call.

Meantime, on the night of March 1st, Capt. Albert Martin and thirty-one men from Gonzales, con-

stituting every man in the town able to bear arms, got through the Mexican lines into the Alamo, thus bringing Travis's force to about 182 men. Colonel Bonham returned to the Alamo on the morning of March 3rd, running the gauntlet of the enemy's fire to do so, and he was the last man to enter the besieged fortress. On the same day Travis sent a messenger to the convention urging that everything possible be done without delay to get men and supplies to him. He said that the settlements were his only hope, for he had asked Fannin for aid in a message that reached Goliad on February 18th, and then again when the Mexicans first appeared, but had received no response. But unless help came soon, he said, they would have to fight the enemy on his own terms. "I will do my best in the circumstances," he wrote, "and I feel confident that the determined valor and desperate courage, heretofore exhibited by my men, will not fail them in the last struggle; and although they may be sacrificed to the vengeance of a Gothic enemy, the victory will cost the enemy so dear that it will be worse for him than a defeat." That was Travis's last message. And at three o'clock in the morning on March 6th, the same day that Houston left the convention for Gonzales, Santa Anna stormed the Alamo.

Santa Anna had waited for the arrival of heavier artillery and additional forces to bring his total strength to about 2,400 men before attempting the assault. According to the most conservative and reliable estimates, at least that many participated in the storming of the fort. And as Travis had promised, it "cost them so dear" that it was indeed "worse than a defeat". "The Mexican army charged," says an eye-witness, Francisco Antonio Ruiz, alcalde of San Antonio, "and were twice repulsed by the deadly fire of Travis's artillery, which resembled constant thunder. At the third charge the Toluca battalion commenced to scale the walls and suffered severely. Out of eight hundred and thirty men only one hundred and thirty were left alive!" One tragic incident, which also is attested by eye-witnesses, occurred during the final moments of the assault. Lieutenant Dickenson, for some reason that has never been satisfactorily explained, had his wife and little girl in the Alamo, and when all hope was lost he made a desperate leap from the east wall of the chapel with the child in his arms, attempting to escape with her to safety, but both were shot in the act and fell lifeless to the ground. As the Mexicans entered the walls they were met by furious hand to hand fighting. But finally the overwhelming weight of numbers conquered and the last Texan was dead. Bowie, who was ill, was killed in his bed. Crockett died fighting near the west wall. Ruiz, whom Santa Anna required to point out these bodies, is the authority here. "The gallantry of the few Texans who defended the Alamo," says Ruiz, "was really wondered at by the Mexican army. Even the Generals were astonished at their vigorous resistance, and how dearly victory was bought."

"On the north battery of the fortress convent," adds Ruiz, simply, "lay the lifeless body of Colonel Travis, on the gun carriage, shot only through the forehead." Faithfully he had kept his word. He had died "like a soldier who never forgets what is due his own honor and that of his country." And all of his

companions had died with him. There is a tradition
that a few of the Texans, after all their comrades
had been killed, were overpowered and promptly
shot, but Ruiz, whose account is the most reliable
eye-witness record, makes no mention of this. He
does say, however, that 182 bodies of the Texans were
burned in one funeral pyre. In any event, there was
not a single survivor.

The first report of the fate of the defenders of the
Alamo had just been received at Gonzales by the
grief-stricken relatives of the thirty-two men who
had gone from there to Travis's aid, when Houston
reached that place on March 11th. There were weep-
ing and lamentation on all sides and a condition bordering on panic prevailed. Houston proceeded at
once to take hold of the situation. First of all, however, he dispatched orders to Fannin at Goliad directing him to retreat eastward to Victoria without
delay, and then he set about the task of organizing
the volunteers who had gathered at Gonzales into
some semblance of an army. Edward Burleson was
elected Colonel, and Sidney Sherman, who had just
arrived with fifty men from Newport, Kentucky, was
named Lieutenant Colonel. Scouts sent by Houston
toward San Antonio brought in Mrs. Dickenson,
whom they had met on the road, and she confirmed
the report of the Alamo's fall and gave an account of
the heroic defense. But she reported also that a large
Mexican force under Ramírez y Sesma was moving
toward Gonzales. Upon receipt of this information,
Houston told the inhabitants of Gonzales that they
must leave their homes and prepare to move eastward. At the same time he gave orders to the volun-

teers, who numbered about three hundred, to get ready to march. Burleson made an impassioned address to the men, stirring their feelings to a high pitch, during the course of which it is said he first used the famous phrase, "Thermopylae had its messenger of defeat, the Alamo had none!" Then, on the night of March 14th, after setting fire to the town, Houston and his loosely organized army left Gonzales and began a retreat toward the Colorado.

Houston reached the Colorado on March 17th at a point known as Burnham's Crossing and he rested his men on the west bank of the river for two days. Volunteers were joining daily now, and when he crossed the river on March 19th his force had been increased to about 600 men. On the east bank he marched them to Beason's Ferry, almost opposite the site of the present town of Columbus, and here he made camp and began to put the men through a rigid routine of drilling. Volunteers continued to arrive in great numbers and in a few days about 1,500 men were crowded into Houston's camp, but how many of them would be available for active service was a question. They were now on the edge of the most thickly settled region between the Colorado and the Brazos and men came and went daily. Houston felt it would take much training to convert such material into a disciplined army. So he kept up constant drilling at Beason's for a week. And it was while he waited there that he learned that disaster had overtaken Fannin.

Fannin had remained at Goliad, though he had been fully aware since March 1st that he was now between two superior forces of the enemy, with

Urréa only sixty miles south of him and Santa Anna about a hundred miles to the northwest. When on March 14th he received Houston's order to retreat eastward to Victoria, which was in the direction of the Anglo-American settlements, he was caught unprepared to execute it promptly, for two detachments of his force—one of twenty-three men under Captain King and another of 125 men under Colonel Ward—were away at Refugio. He waited four days for their return, only to learn at the end of that time that Urréa had destroyed King's little company and that Ward, finding retreat in the direction of Goliad cut off, was attempting to make his way across country to Victoria. It was not until the morning of March 19th, therefore, that Fannin attempted to retreat to Victoria, and by that time Urréa had reached Goliad, not only with his whole force but with 600 additional men under Colonel Morales, sent by Santa Anna from San Antonio.

Overtaken by Urréa's cavalry in the early afternoon, Fannin made a stand in an open prairie, and presently the Texans were surrounded by a Mexican force that outnumbered them four to one. Fannin put up a stubborn defense during the whole afternoon and well into the night, but next morning, which was Sunday, March 20th, continued resistance seemed futile. So he surrendered with his whole force "as prisoners of war, subject to the disposition of the Supreme Government." Fannin tried to obtain written assurance that his men's lives would be spared, but Urréa insisted that he was without authority to make such terms. He promised verbally, however, to use his personal influence to obtain

clemency for the prisoners, and he did appeal to
Santa Anna in their behalf. The men were disarmed
and marched back to Goliad while Urréa, with a
force of about one thousand, proceeded to Victoria
and took possession of that place. Colonel Ward and
the remnant of his little band reached Victoria shortly after Urréa, and they were promptly made prisoners also and sent under guard to Goliad.

It was news of this disaster that reached Houston
while he was camped at Beason's, and about the
same time (on March 21st) Ramírez y Sesma and
a force of about 700 Mexicans arrived on the opposite bank of the Colorado. Due to heavy rains, the
river was at flood stage, and Houston had taken the
precaution of having all boats moved to the east bank
for several miles in both directions from his camp.
Ramírez y Sesma, finding himself faced by a force
of Texans of superior numbers, sent word back to
Santa Anna, who was still at San Antonio, asking
for further orders and reinforcements. Houston, on
his part, had a difficult time preventing his men from
crossing the river and attacking the Mexicans. Colonel Sherman especially was insistent that with four
hundred men under his command he could put the
Mexicans to rout. But Houston was firm in vetoing
any such move. The news that Fannin's whole force
was in the hands of the enemy made him all the more
determined not to go into battle until he had shaped
the crowd of untrained volunteers into an army. For
he realized that the force under his command was
now the sole hope of Texas.

Meantime, at San Antonio some of the Mexican
officers were becoming alarmed over the manner in

which Santa Anna had divided his forces. He had
sent Morales to join Urréa and at the same time had
dispatched a brigade under General Gaona to Bastrop, which was the northern frontier settlement on
the Colorado, while Ramírez y Sesma had advanced
to the Colorado by way of Gonzales. And he still
had a considerable force at San Antonio. Gen.
Vicente Filisola, an Italian who was second in
command, urged Santa Anna to take steps to concentrate these various detachments without delay, and
when news came from Ramírez y Sesma that he was
confronted by a superior force of Texans on the Colorado, Santa Anna consented. He instructed Ramírez
y Sesma not to cross the river while Houston remained at Beason's, but to await a reinforcement of
600 men he was sending at once. At the same time
he dispatched orders to Gaona to continue toward
San Felipe and he ordered Urréa also to advance in
that general direction. And then Santa Anna prepared to join Ramírez y Sesma himself.

But first he disposed of the question of the fate of
the prisoners at Goliad. Urréa had written him the
circumstances of Fannin's surrender and had suggested that the captives should be shipped to the
United States. In his reply, Santa Anna insisted that
the Government already had decreed the death of all
such prisoners and contended that the indignation of
the nation would fall upon him if he protected such
"highway robbers". "I yield to no one, my friend, in
tender-heartedness," Santa Anna wrote Urréa, "for I
am not aware that I hate any man, and I have never
had a thought of avenging even personal injuries;
but what authority have I to override what the Gov-

ernment of the nation has in specific terms commanded, by remitting the penalty for such criminals
as these foreigners?"

In accordance with Santa Anna's orders, which
Urréa afterwards declared amazed and confounded
every soldier in his division, the prisoners at Goliad,
about four hundred in all, were marched out in three
companies in different directions from the town just
about daybreak on Sunday, March 27th, and
then as they huddled together, unarmed and bewildered, they were all shot down without mercy by
their guards. The lives of the doctors among the
prisoners, who had attended the Mexican wounded,
were spared, and a few others managed to escape
in the confusion of the slaughter. But a total of 390
men, including Fannin himself, gave up their lives
in that bloody massacre.

By the time this terrible news reached the settlements, most of the settlers between the Colorado and
the Brazos were already in flight toward the American border. For on March 26th, the day before the
massacre at Goliad, Houston had ordered his men to
break camp at Beason's and to continue their retreat
eastward to the Brazos. This order nearly broke
up the army, for hundreds of men whose homes were
between the Colorado and the Brazos, especially
those who had joined during the previous week, left
at once to move their families out of the region which
was being abandoned to the advancing Mexicans.
Practically the whole population west of the Brazos
took flight. And when the news of the Goliad massacre spread among them, the flight became a panic.

CHAPTER XXXV

REVOLUTION : FINAL PHASE

THE convention at Washington-on-the-Brazos completed its labors on March 17th, formally inaugurating the officials of an *ad interim* Government at two o'clock in the morning of that day. David G. Burnet was named President of the new republic, with Lorenzo de Zavala as Vice President. The other officials included Samuel P. Carson, Secretary of State; Bailey Hardeman, Secretary of the Treasury; Thomas J. Rusk, Secretary of War; Robert Potter, Secretary of the Navy, and David Thomas, Attorney General. The next day the new officials left for Harrisburg, near the coast, where it was decided to establish the seat of government. They took the precaution of reassuring the people that this decision was not due to "any apprehension that the enemy is near", but that it was resolved upon "before any such report was in circulation" and was not "expedited by such report".

For the moment, such reassurance no doubt served to allay excitement over wild reports of the imminent arrival of the Mexican army in the settlements. But even the wildest reports were soon outstripped by brutal facts, for within two weeks the people were face to face with the realities of a war of extermination. When it became known that Houston's army was the only remaining armed body of Texans, and that it had been withdrawn from the region between the Colorado and the Brazos, there was nothing for the people to do but to move out of that region. And when, in addition to this, there spread among them the almost incredible story of the cold-blooded massacre of Fannin's defenseless men, it was inevitable that a frenzied flight should follow. Within the short period of three weeks all of the armed forces of the Texans had been completely wiped out, nearly all of the 800 men under arms when the Mexican invasion began had been slaughtered ruthlessly, and now the destroyers were advancing into the settlements. The flight was from real dangers, for a Mexican army reached the Colorado by March 21st and within two weeks after Houston left the Colorado, Santa Anna himself had advanced to the Brazos. Indeed, even the officials of the Texas Government, in due course, were fleeing from Harrisburg because of positive knowledge, not mere apprehension, that the enemy was at their heels.

More than three thousand families were living peacefully in the region west of the Brazos at the outbreak of the revolution, and hundreds of them had been settled in the country ten or twelve years. They were mostly farm families and they had established a pastoral and rural society which many who lived among them have described as almost arcadian in character. And now these people were being forced to abandon their homes and flee for their lives.

It was a period of heavy rains. All of the streams were swollen, the rivers were at flood stage, and the roads were almost impassable quagmires. But nothing could check the panic-like exodus of the people. "Wagons were so scarce," writes one eye-witness, "that it was impossible to remove household goods. Many of the women and children, even, had to walk. Some had no conveyances but trucks, the screeching of which added to the horror of the situation. One young lady said she walked with a bucket in hand to keep the trucks, on which her mother and their little camping outfit rode, from catching fire. And, as if the arch-fiend had broken lose, there were men— or devils, rather—bent on plunder, galloping up behind the fugitives, telling them the Mexicans were just behind, thus causing the hapless victims to abandon what few valuables they had tried to save. There were broken-down wagons and household goods all along the road."

"In the road, as far as the eye could reach, east and west," says another account, describing a personal experience, "a motley crowd of suffering, perplexed humanity struggled, uncomplaining, through the mud. Many women and children were walking, some barefooted and bareheaded. A woman whose cart—one of those rude 'truck carts' with wheels sawed from a large tree, into which the spindle of a wooden axle worked, the rough body being fastened to the axle by wooden pegs, and covered with a cotton sheet for tent; you may see many such in old Mexico today—was bogged in one of the numerous *maritas* of the Neches prairie, the oxen lying in the water with only their noses out for air. . . .

"The cry of 'Mexicans', though of daily occurrence, always created a panic. Bedding, provisions, any and every thing, would be thrown off to lighten

the wagons, and the horses whipped into a run. The
prairie at times was white with feathers emptied
from beds . . . . Soon hunger and sickness added their
gaunt forms to the general distress. Women sank by
the roadside from exhaustion, and many little children died."

Most of these people felt they were leaving Texas
forever and the panic continued east of the Brazos
and on to the American border. The great experi-
ment of "redeeming Texas from its wilderness state"
was at an end! For after the Alamo and Goliad and
the rest it would never be possible for Americans to
live in Texas again, if the Mexicans were to rule it.
That was how many of the fugitives felt, and their
one thought was to escape with their lives to their
native land.

Through it all one silent man, helpless to check the
panic, had to bear the brunt of criticism and denunciation as the man responsible for it. Houston, who
was laboring patiently at an effort to create an army,
was widely blamed for the whole situation. Why
had he not stood his ground at the Colorado and
turned back the Mexicans? Why did he not come
out and fight the Mexicans even now? Houston's
own men talked like this among themselves and there
was mutinous intrigue among his officers.

Many writers have repeated the statement that
"why Houston retreated from the Colorado has
never been satisfactorily explained." And yet it is
more than probable that the complete explanation is
the simplest and most obvious. He had just received
news that the only other armed body of Texans, those
under Fannin, had been captured, and that therefore

the little army under his command, which had been brought together hastily only two weeks before, was facing alone a Mexican army of 6,000 men, under trained and seasoned officers. Evidently he did not think his men were ready to do battle with such a force with any assurance of success, and he knew that Texas could not stand another defeat. To fight was to stake all. If he fought and lost, all would be lost. The very panic his retreat from the Colorado caused was proof of this, if proof were needed.

Leaving the Colorado, Houston marched directly to San Felipe, arriving there on March 26th, and the next day he gave orders for the army to move to Groce's Ferry, about fifteen or twenty miles up the Brazos, where he proposed to go into camp. There was sharp disagreement among his officers over these orders, some insisting that the army should move down the river, instead of up, because the bulk of the settlements were down the river and they should be given protection against the advancing Mexicans. Reporting this to Rusk, the Secretary of War, Houston wrote: "Many wished me to go below, others above. I consulted none—I held no councils of war. If I err, the blame is mine." He moved the army on to Groce's Ferry, therefore, though he relented to the extent of detaching two of the chief objectors, Mosely Baker and Wily Martin, each with a small company, and ordering them to guard points on the lower river, directing Baker to remain at San Felipe and sending Martin to Fort Bend.

After a rather uncomfortable march through a heavy rain, Houston's army reached Groce's Ferry on March 31st, and he set to work immediately to reorganize it completely. He created a new regiment and put Sidney Sherman in command of it, promoting him to the rank of Colonel. And this enabled him to make numerous other promotions, thus improving the morale of his officers. But as the Mexicans advanced into the settlements and the flight of the settlers continued, and Houston made no move to break camp and took no measures against the enemy, the grumbling of his men and the discontent of his officers increased. Finally the Government took official notice of what was regarded as his "inactivity", and President Burnet dispatched the following laconic message to Houston:

"Sir: The enemy are laughing you to scorn. You must fight them. The country expects you to fight. The salvation of the country depends upon your doing so."

Houston bore himself with dignity under the ordeal of all this criticism. He betrayed no impatience, indulged in no intemperate language in reply, and confined his comment to an honest statement of the difficulties of his situation. Rusk, the Secretary of War, evidently concluding that, with only one army to look after, he could perform the duties of his office more intelligently on the ground, joined Houston in camp at Groce's Ferry on April 4th and remained. He satisfied himself apparently that Houston knew what he was about, because in due course he was being criticized also by the malcontents among the officers, it being said that he had fallen under the General's "spell".

Meantime, Santa Anna arrived at the Colorado on April 5th, just as Ramírez y Sesma was crossing his men, and placing himself at the head of a brigade which already had crossed he pushed on to the Brazos, reaching it at San Felipe on April 7th. He found that town, the first Anglo-American community established in Texas, in ashes, Mosely Baker having burned it on March 29th. Baker and his company were on the opposite side of the river and had removed all boats to the east bank, so Santa Anna marched down the stream to Fort Bend, where he succeeded in capturing Thompson's Ferry from Wily Martin's company. Being joined by Ramírez y Sesma on April 14th, he crossed the Brazos, after dispatching Cos and 500 men to Velasco, with instructions to march along the coast toward Galveston Bay. Learning that Harrisburg, about thirty miles away, was the seat of the Texas Government, Santa Anna decided to lead a force in person to that place and capture his old enemy, De Zavala, and the other "traitors" constituting that body. With a force of about 750 men, he reached Harrisburg on April 15th, only to learn that the officials of the Government had fled that morning to Galveston Island. Apparently as part of his program of breaking up the Anglo-Amercan settlements in Texas altogether, he burned Harrisburg, and then moved on to New Washington, a small village on Galveston Bay. Before Santa Anna reached New Washington, Houston's army, having crossed the Brazos at last, began a march in the direction of Harrisburg.

Houston had waited until April 11th before showing any sign of leaving Groce's Ferry. On that day John A. Wharton returned to camp with two six-pound cannon, which he had brought up from the coast. These two field pieces, known later as "The Twin Sisters", were a gift from the people of Cincinnati, Ohio, and Houston had sent Wharton from Beason's after them. Upon the arrival of this artillery, Houston dispatched orders to all absent detachments to join the army at Donoho's, a settlement a few miles east of Groce's Ferry, and then he began moving the men across the river on a steamboat he had commandeered for the purpose. He left the banks of the Brazos on the afternoon of April 14th, which was exactly a month from the day he began the retreat from Gonzales, and two days later he started from Donoho's for Harrisburg.

The march to Harrisburg was made doubly difficult by the recent rains. "The prairies were quagmired," Houston said, in describing it afterwards. "The contents of the wagons had to be carried across the bogs, and the empty wagons had to be assisted in aid of the horses. No less than eight impediments in one day had to be overcome in this way." Nevertheless, he added, the march was made with "remarkable success".

Houston arrived opposite Harrisburg in the forenoon on April 18th, and there he rested the army during the afternoon and night. There was a sick list of more than 150 and he spent the afternoon in establishing a hospital camp at Harrisburg, placing it under guard of seventy-five men commanded by Major McNutt. During the afternoon Houston's chief scout, Erastus ("Deaf") Smith, brought in two Mexican couriers who were bearing messages from Filisola and the Central Government to Santa Anna, and thus Houston learned for the first time that Santa

Anna himself was with the Mexican force at New Washington. This meant that he had the dictator, with a Mexican detachment numbering no more than 750 men, between the Texas army and the sea. And he decided to go after him the first thing in the morning.

On the morning of April 19th Houston and Rusk delivered stirring addresses to the men, informing them that they would soon go into battle with the enemy and urging them to avenge the martyrs of the Alamo and of Goliad. Leaving the baggage train in charge of Major McNutt, Houston and the Texas army began the march down the left bank of Buffalo Bayou, crossing it below the mouth of Sims's Bayou. Their destination was Lynch's Ferry at the junction of Buffalo Bayou and the San Jacinto River, a short distance from where the latter flows into the Gulf.

Colonel Almonte, who was with Santa Anna, had been told by some inhabitants of the region that Houston intended to continue his retreat to the Trinity River by way of Lynch's Ferry, and on the basis of this information Santa Anna had resolved to intercept Houston at that point on his return from New Washington, which was only a few hours' march from Lynch's Ferry. With this object in view, he had dispatched orders to Filisola to divert Cos from his expedition to Velasco and have him proceed at once to Lynch's Ferry. Evidently, Santa Anna calculated that Cos could reach that point in time to assist in intercepting Houston. "To cut off Houston from the ferry," wrote Santa Anna in his official report, "and to destroy at one blow the armed force and the hopes of the rebels, was too important to let the opportunity escape. It was my intention to seize the Lynchburg Ferry before he came up, and avail myself of the advantage of the ground."

It required most of the afternoon of the nineteenth to move the Texas army across Buffalo Bayou and it was near nightfall when the crossing was completed. Houston, however, ordered that the march be continued and the Texans moved onward steadily without a halt until nearly midnight. "The troops continued to march," said Houston, "until the men became so exhausted that they were falling against each other in the ranks, and some falling down from exhaustion." Accordingly, a rest of about two hours was taken, and then the march was resumed about two o'clock in the morning. Shortly after daylight on the twentieth, while a brief halt was being made for breakfast, Houston's scouts reported that the enemy was on the move from New Washington. Houston immediately ordered the march resumed, and early in the forenoon the Texans reached Lynch's Ferry. Making a quick survey of the lay of the land, Houston ordered his men to take up a position in an oak grove on the banks of Buffalo Bayou, about a half-mile back from the ferry. To their left was the San Jacinto River, and far to their right was Vince's Bayou, which they had crossed by a bridge in approaching the ferry. Buffalo Bayou was at their back and spreading out in front of them and extending to their right toward Vince's Bayou was a stretch of prairie, about two miles in width, broken by clumps of timber. South of this prairie, on the edge of San Jacinto Bay, was an expanse of marsh land.

Santa Anna had started from New Washington early that morning, after setting fire to the five or six houses which comprised the village, and marched directly to Lynch's Ferry. He arrived shortly after Houston, and he proceeded to take up a position on the opposite side of the stretch of prairie, with the marsh land behind him and on his right, extending to the bay. A deep gully divided his camp from the marsh land.

It was Santa Anna's intention to attack the Texans at once, but their position was so well hidden in the timber that he could not locate it with certainty. To feel them out, therefore, he advanced his one piece of artillery, a six-pounder, protected by a detachment of cavalry, and opened fire. At the same time he made a feint of advancing his infantry as for an attack. Evidently Santa Anna expected this move to be met by musket fire from the Texans, thus giving him a good idea of their position. But instead, and to his surprise, the Texans responded with artillery fire from "The Twin Sisters", compelling his infantry to retreat in a hurry and forcing his artillery and cavalry to take cover in an island of timber on one side of the prairie. From this clump of timber, the Mexican artillery kept up an intermittent firing throughout the afternoon, but did little damage, except that Colonel Neill, who commanded the Texas artillery, was severely wounded.

Late in the afternoon, Colonel Sherman, after obtaining permission from Houston, took a detachment of mounted volunteers and made an attempt to capture the Mexican gun. A lively skirmish with the Mexican cavalry resulted, during which a recruit

named Mirabeau B. Lamar, who had joined the army
at Groce's Ferry as a private, attracted the notice of
all by his gallant conduct. The gun was not captured, but it was withdrawn from its advanced position and Sherman and his men retired in good order,
with two wounded, one fatally. Thus the day ended, with the two armies almost in sight of each other.
A belated Texas norther had blown up and the night
was uncomfortably cold, but Houston's men, who had
been on the march almost constantly from the morning of the nineteenth until nearly noon on the twentieth, got a good rest.

About nine o'clock the next morning, the twenty-
first, Santa Anna was reinforced by the arrival of
Cos with 400 men, thus bringing his force to about
1,150. This gave him a numerical advantage over
Houston, who mustered 783 men that morning. "It
was supposed," says Rusk, in his report on the campaign, "that an attack upon our encampment would
now be made; and, having a good position, we stationed our artillery and disposed of our forces so as to
receive the enemy to the best advantage." Cos had
arrived by the bridge over Vince's Bayou, and, with
the object of preventing further reinforcements using it, Houston sent Deaf Smith to destroy this
bridge. At noon, as Santa Anna had made no move
to attack, Houston called a council of war, the first
since he had taken command of the army, and after
much discussion a decision was reached by his officers to wait until the next morning, and if the Mexicans had made no move by that time, to launch an
attack. Houston always insisted that he took no part
in this decision. The decision proved very unpopular

among the men, however, and a canvas by company showed the army to be in favor of an immediate attack. When Houston learned this, about three o'clock in the afternoon he ordered the army paraded and announced that preparations for an attack would begin immediately. This announcement was received with enthusiasm and the army was put in battle formation.

While the fife and drum corps played "Will You Come to the Bower", the line was formed. The first regiment, with Colonel Burleson in command, was placed in the center, with the second regiment, under Colonel Sherman, on the left. The artillery, with Col. George W. Hockley commanding, was to the immediate right of the first regiment; four companies of infantry, under Col. Henry Millard, were to the right of the artillery; and then on the extreme right was a company of cavalry, consisting of sixty-one mounted volunteers, and commanded by Col. Mirabeau B. Lamar, promoted for gallant conduct the previous day.

The movement was begun by Lamar and his cavalry advancing toward the extreme left of the Mexican camp to engage the enemy's attention, while Hockley moved the artillery to a point within two hundred yards of a breastwork which the Mexicans had thrown up. At the same time the rest of the army moved forward quietly until within musket range of the enemy, and then the attack was launched on all fronts. The Mexicans were taken completely by surprise. Their whole camp was "at ease", and the officers, Santa Anna included, were indulging in an afternoon *siesta,* with no thought of danger from an attack by the Texans. "His Excellency and staff were asleep," says the account of a Mexican officer; "the greater part of the men were also sleeping; for the rest, some were eating, others were scattered in the woods in search of boughs to prepare shelter. Our line was composed of musket stacks. Our cavalry were riding bareback to and from water."

From the very outset the battle was a one-sided slaughter, even the Mexican officers fleeing individually for their lives, after making futile attempts to rally the demoralized men under their immediate command into some kind of formation. "It is a known fact," says our Mexican witness, "that Mexican soldiers, once demoralized, can not be controlled, unless they are thoroughly inured to war." And there were some "recruits" among the Mexicans. "The recruits," Santa Anna reported afterwards, "bunched themselves and confused the tried soldiers, and neither the first nor the second made any use of their weapons." As the Texans advanced upon the Mexican camp, Colonel Sherman called out, "Remember the Alamo!" and this cry was taken up immediately. "Remember the Alamo!" and "Remember Goliad!" was echoed and reechoed in the shouts of the Texans, as they pursued the fleeing Mexicans, "increasing the confusion," says Santa Anna, "with their unfailing rifles." The Texans, he adds, "carried their charge forward rapidly, and shouting madly, secured a victory in a few minutes which they did not dream was possible." As for Santa Anna, our Mexican officer witness says, "I saw His Excellency running about in the utmost excitement, wringing his hands and unable to give an order." And Santa Anna

himself confesses, "All hope lost, with everyone escaping as best he could, my despair was as great as
the danger I was in."

But not "everyone" was escaping. "On the left,
and about musket distance from our camp," says our
Mexican officer, "was a small grove on the bay shore.
Our disbanded herd rushed for it, to obtain shelter
from the horrid slaughter carried on all over the
prairie. . . . Unfortunately, we met, on our way, an
obstacle difficult to overcome. It was a bayou (the
gully), not very wide, but rather deep. The men,
on reaching it, would helplessly crowd together, and
were shot down by the enemy, who was close enough
not to miss his aim. It was there that the greatest
carnage took place."

"Remember the Alamo! Remember Goliad!" the
Texans continued to shout, and the panic-stricken
Mexicans, comprehending at last the meaning of the
words, began to beg for mercy with cries of "Me no
Alamo! Me no Goliad!" And in the end, mercy was
shown. The Texans simply could not carry out the
ruthless policy of "no prisoners and no quarter"
which had been Santa Anna's rule. The action lasted
about twenty minutes in all, but the shooting down
of helpless, bewildered, unarmed men could not be
continued after it became clear that the victory was
complete. Most of the reports of the "battle of San
Jacinto", including the official ones, greatly exag-
gerate the number of Mexicans killed and wounded.
The actual number was great enough, about 380, and
practically all the rest of the Mexicans were captured. The number of prisoners taken was 730, and

only about forty of the Mexicans escaped from the battlefield.

But these prisoners were not all taken the day of the battle. Many managed to escape from the battlefield and scattered over the surrounding country, and searching parties spent most of the next day rounding them up. Among those who escaped from the battlefield was the one who was most wanted, Santa Anna himself. "A servant of my aide-de-camp," reported Santa Anna, "with noble kindness offered me the horse of his master, and earnestly pleaded that I save myself. I looked about for my escort and was told by two dragoons who were hurriedly saddling their horses that their companions and officers had fled. I remembered that General Filisola was at Thompson's Crossing, sixteen leagues distant, and, without hesitation, I tried to make my way to that place through the enemy's ranks. They pursued me and overtook me a league and a half from the battlefield at a large creek where the bridge had been burnt. I turned my horse loose and with difficulty took refuge in a grove of small pine trees. The coming of night permitted me to evade their vigilance. The hope of rejoining the army and vindicating its honor gave me strength to cross the creek with the water above my waist, and I continued on my route afoot. In an abandoned house I found some clothes which I exchanged for my wet ones."

The Texans, of course, searched for Santa Anna from the moment the battle was over, and every new prisoner taken was closely questioned as to his identity. Next day searching parties were sent out to scour the country almost inch by inch, for it was recognized that if Santa Anna could be made captive the war would be over. One detachment of cavalry, under Colonel Burleson, had searched up and down Vince's Bayou all morning without result, when shortly after noon, six members of this party, including Sergeant James A. Sylvester, caught sight of a man on foot about a mile away. As they galloped toward him, he disappeared, but after a careful search they found him lying prone in the tall grass. He tried to feign death, paying no attention to the commands that he get up, and one of the party, levelling a pistol at him, remarked, "I'll make him get up". "Don't shoot!" Sylvester commanded, sternly, and dismounted from his horse. Going over to the prostrate Mexican, he gave him a kick, at the same time sharply command-ing, "Get up, damn you!" The Mexican obeyed, and began to address his captors in Spanish. He said that he was a cavalryman and had abandoned his horse in an effort to escape. He was roughly dressed, but the Texans noted that he wore good shoes and a fine quality of underwear. They felt sure he was no common soldier, and so they took him into camp. As they approached the camp, they passed some Mexi-can prisoners, and at once some of these, on behold-ing the captive, let out the exclamation, *"El Presi-dente!"* And Sylvester knew that they had captured Santa Anna.

Brought before Houston, Santa Anna admitted his identity, and while Moses Austin Bryan, the nine-teen-year-old nephew of Stephen Austin, acted as in-terpreter, he suavely informed "the brave General Houston" that he placed himself at his disposal and that he expected to be treated as a general should be when a prisoner of war. Houston replied that he would be at the disposal of the civil authorities of Texas, and he sent at once for Rusk, Secretary of War, who presently joined the party, accompanied by De Zavala, who acted as interpreter. That Santa Anna did not relish the presence of De Zavala, his ancient enemy whom he had sworn to execute, may be well imagined, and he hailed with delight the suggestion of Rusk that Colonel Almonte, who was also a prisoner, might be present as an interpreter. Santa Anna, without any suggestion from his captors, launched into a defense of the Goliad massacre and the rule of "no quarter" at the Alamo, arguing that he was compelled to obey the orders of the Central Government. Rusk hotly retorted that the less Santa Anna had to say in defense of such crimes, the better it would be for him, if he valued his own life. And that effectively silenced him.

Santa Anna readily agreed to order the other Mexican troops to withdraw beyond the Colorado at once, preparatory to leaving Texas altogether. And he drafted the following dispatch to be sent to Filisola at Thompson's Ferry on the Brazos:

"Your Excellency: The small division under my immediate command having had an unfortunate encounter yesterday afternoon, I find myself a prisoner of war in the hands of the enemy, who have extended to me all possible consideration. Under these circumstances I recommend your Excellency to order General Gaona to march back to Bexar and await orders, as your Excellency will also do with the troops which are under your immediate command; at the same time warning General Urréa to retire with his division to Victoria; since I have agreed with General Houston upon an armistice pending certain negotiations which may put an end to the war forever."

But Filisola had not waited for orders from Santa Anna. A detachment of one hundred cavalry under Colonel García had been left by Cos near Harrisburg when he went to join Santa Anna, and García lost no time after receiving the first news of San Jacinto in joining Filisola on the Brazos. And Filisola had immediately ordered a concentration of all the Mexican troops for a retreat to San Antonio. He needed no orders from Santa Anna to make him realize that the campaign was at an end.

The victory at San Jacinto was indeed complete. And it had been gained with practically no loss to the Texans. Only two Texans had been killed on the battlefield and only twenty-three had been wounded, though six of these died later of their wounds. Houston himself was among the wounded, a ball having lodged in his ankle. When the news of this smashing victory was carried to the fleeing Texans who were still making their way to the American border, there was indescribable rejoicing among the fugitives. Houston had dispatched couriers immediately after the battle to overtake all refugees and to turn them back. And at once these unhappy people were raised from the very depths of despair almost to a frenzy of ecstacy. The caravans which had been terror-stricken at one moment over the approach of hard-riding horsemen seeking to overtake them, at the next were converted into scenes of delirious joy over the glorious news the couriers brought. And soon the fugitives were retracing their steps, and, with lighter hearts than they had ever expected to know again, they were hurrying back to their homes.

And on every tongue, with a prayer of thanksgiving, was the name of Sam Houston. For he had now become "the hero of San Jacinto" and "the savior of Texas."

CHAPTER XXXVI

UNITED STATES SHUTS THE DOOR

IN the city of New York, on April 15th, 1836, six days before the battle of San Jacinto and nearly a month before the first report of the Texan victory would reach the American metropolis, Stephen F. Austin, in desperation over the continued news of disaster from Texas, wrote an open letter to the President of the United States and other leaders of the American Government appealing to them for help.

For weeks Austin had been anxiously reading every scrap of news from Texas and every day had seemed to bring more grievous tidings. The course of events in Texas almost from the day he and his associates had arrived in the United States had been such as to render their mission almost futile, so far as negotiating loans to finance the revolution was concerned. They had obtained $60,000 as the first installment of a loan in New Orleans and had arranged with a New Orleans merchant to accept drafts of the Texas Government for supplies which finally amounted to nearly $100,000. They had been empowered to negotiate the sale of ten bonds of $100,000 each, but after leaving New Orleans the news from Texas was of such a discouraging character that they were unable to obtain another dollar.

Reports of the quarrel between Governor Smith and the Council and of the general disorganized condition existing during January and February spread over the United States, and at the same time news came from Mexico of Santa Anna's preparations to invade Texas. The unpreparedness of the Texans in the face of this impending invasion was common knowledge among the very persons in the United States from whom help might be expected and in consequence there was a general unwillingness to risk money on the outcome. The Texas commissioners did all they could in the circumstances, arousing sympathy for the Texan cause and setting on foot movements to send armed volunteers across the border, but money, which was felt to be absolutely essential to success, was not to be had on any terms.

When the newspapers began to publish accounts of the reverses of the Texans, of the bloody progress of Santa Anna across Texas and of the flight of the whole population to the American border, the feeling became general that their cause was hopeless. The American people were deeply stirred and there was general sympathy for the Texans. But there was no move of consequence in their behalf. To Austin it all seemed the acme of tragedy, for all the results of his life work were being brought to naught by an irresponsible usurper who was running amuck in Texas. It seemed that unless something were done right away, the Anglo-Texans would be driven out of Texas altogether. And the sympathy of the people was so general and apparently so genuine that American intervention and the financial support of the

American Government seemed possibilities. Indeed, at the moment something of this kind seemed the only hope. So Austin wrote an impassioned appeal to Andrew Jackson and other leaders of the Government to come to the aid of the Texans.

"Santa Anna," he wrote, "is now in Texas with about seven thousand men fighting under the bloody flag of a pirate. . . . This is a war of barbarism against civilization, of despotism against liberty. . . . The sympathies of the whole American people *en masse* are with the Texans. This people look to you, the guardians of their rights and interests and principles. Will you—*can* you— turn a deaf ear to the appeals of your fellow citizens in favor of their and your countrymen and friends who are massacred, butchered, outraged in Texas at your very doors? Are not we, the Texans, obeying the dictates of an education received here, from you, the American people, from our fathers, from the patriots of '76—the republicans of 1836? Have not we been stimulated to obey the dictates of this noble education by the expression of opinions all over the United States, and by all parties, that we ought to resist and throw off the yoke of Mexican usurpation, and are we now to be abandoned or suffered to fight alone and single-handed because the cold calculations of policy and party have first to be consulted?"

When President Jackson received his copy of this open letter, he filed it away, without taking public notice of it, after making the following notation on its margin:

"The writer does not reflect that we have a treaty with Mexico, and our national faith is pledged to support it. The Texans, before they took the step to declare themselves independent, which has aroused and united all Mexico against them, ought to have pondered well. It was a rash and premature act. Our neutrality must be faithfully maintained."

This notation, written by Jackson at a time when the outlook for the Texans seemed hopeless and when public sentiment in their favor was at its highest point, may be taken as a fair index of how little chance there would have been of intervention in their behalf by the United States if Houston had failed to stop Santa Anna. And it emphasizes the vital character of the battle of San Jacinto. The stake at San Jacinto was Texas itself: whether the Texans would abandon their homes and property and leave Texas forever, or whether Texas would be completely separated from Mexico. There was no other possibility from the moment Santa Anna and the Centralists decided to conduct a national and racial war against the Texans, treating them as "ungrateful foreigners", and adopted the ruthless policy applied at the Alamo and at Goliad. The victory at San Jacinto and the capture of Santa Anna decided the issue and made effective the declaration of the Texans that their political connection with the Mexican nation was "forever ended". Whatever governmental or political future might lie ahead of Texas, it was now separated from Mexico permanently. The responsibility for its destiny now rested squarely upon the Texans themselves. And this circumstance brought the Texas leaders face to face with immense problems at once.

One of the most pressing of those problems at the moment (and that "moment" lasted seven months) was the proper disposal of their very important prisoner, Santa Anna. And another was the "immigrant volunteers" who now flocked to Texas to swell the size of the army. Santa Anna himself was willing to agree to almost anything, provided his life was spared and he was sent back to Mexico. He readily signed a "treaty" providing for the withdrawal of all Mexican troops beyond the Rio Grande and for the cessation of hostilities on land and sea, and he supplemented this with a "secret treaty" by which he agreed to use his personal influence to bring about permanent peace between Texas and Mexico, with the understanding that the boundary of Texas would not extend beyond the Rio Grande. Santa Anna signed these two documents on May 14th, 1836, at Velasco, to which place he was moved with the *ad interim* Government shortly after the battle of San Jacinto. The condition on which he signed them was that he should be returned to Mexico without unnecessary delay. But six days after the signing of these two "treaties", the Centralist Congress at Mexico City declared "null, void, and of no effect" anything to which Santa Anna might agree while a prisoner. Then the Texas army, greatly increased in numbers by the arrival of "immigrant volunteers" from the United States, addressed a memorial to President Burnet which notified him that the army would not permit Santa Anna's release "until a constitutional Congress and President shall determine that it is expedient". And it added the warning that "should he be liberated without the

sanction of Congress, the army of citizen soldiers
will again assume the privilege of putting down the
enemies of Texas." And finally, when the *ad interim*
Government, on June 3rd, before it had received the
army's memorial, attempted to carry out its bargain with Santa Anna by sending him to Vera Cruz,
the schooner which was to have borne him to that
port was prevented from sailing by a party of "immigrant volunteers" just arriving at Velasco from the
United States. And so Santa Anna's departure was
postponed.

It was postponed indefinitely and the *ad interim*
Government felt compelled to surrender Santa Anna
to the custody of the army for "safe keeping", when
news was received from Matamoros that the Mexican Government had dismissed Filisola from command of the retreating Mexican forces, and that
Urrea had been put at the head of an army of 4,000
men at that place, with orders to begin a new invasion of Texas at once. This "violation" of Santa
Anna's "treaties" enraged the army, and a plot was
hatched among its leaders to arrest President Burnet, seize the Government, and put Santa Anna on
trial for his life. The plot was discovered in time to
frustrate it, but thenceforth Santa Anna became the
prisoner of the army until a constitutional government could be elected and installed. Even then,
however, a new plan was formulated in the army to
bring Santa Anna to trial before a military court, but
about this time Sam Houston, who had been absent
at New Orleans having his wound treated, returned
to Texas, and, assuming again his authority as com-

mander-in-chief, he put a stop in short order to all talk of executing the prisoner.

About the same time Austin returned to Texas, and he lost no time in calling on Santa Anna. He induced the prisoner to write a letter to President Jackson requesting the American President to undertake to prevail upon the Mexican authorities to countermand the order to Urrea and to settle matters by negotiation, on the basis of the Velasco "treaties". Austin then had Houston forward this letter to Jackson. But when Jackson finally replied to it, he pointed out very politely that the Mexican Government had notified the Government of the United States that Santa Anna was without any official status so long as he remained a prisoner and that therefore he could not consider his proposal. Jackson also wrote Houston that a report was current in Washington that Santa Anna was to be shot and cautioned him against such a course. "Nothing could tarnish the character of Texas more than such an act as this," he wrote. . . . "Let not his blood be shed unless imperious necessity demands it, as retaliation for future Mexican massacres. Both wisdom and humanity enjoin this course in relation to Santa Anna." But Houston needed no such counsel, and Santa Anna no longer was in any danger in Texas.

Meantime, Burnet proceeded to insure civil authority by bringing a constitutional government into being. On July 12th he issued an order forbidding the further impressment of private property by the army, and two days later he revoked the commissions of all officers not in active service. Then on July 23rd he issued a proclamation calling an election, to be held on September 5th, for the purpose of choosing a President and Vice President and members of the two houses of the first Congress. He also submitted to a vote of the people the question of whether Texas should apply for annexation to the United States. The submission of this question was in accordance with the opinion of practically all of the Texas leaders that annexation was much more desirable than to attempt to maintain an independent republic. It was known that sentiment for annexation was overwhelming, but a vote of the people was deemed necessary to authorize the new Government to open negotiations on the question.

Houston was elected President by almost a unanimous vote over Austin and Henry Smith. Mirabeau B. Lamar was elected Vice President, and fourteen Senators and thirty-two members of a House of Representatives, constituting the First Congress of the Republic of Texas, were also elected. And the people voted overwhelmingly in favor of annexation. Only 91 votes, out of a total of 6,640 cast in the election, were recorded against annextion, but this question was regarded so much as a matter of course that only a little more than half of those participating in the election took the trouble to vote on it, and the vote in favor of annexation was 3,277. This ratio undoubtedly represented the attitude of the entire population, for there was practically no opposition to annexation.

The First Congress of the Republic of Texas convened for its first session at Columbia, the temporary capital, on October 3rd, and on October 22nd Houston was inaugurated as President. He imme-

diately named Austin as his Secretary of State and
he appointed William H. Wharton as a special envoy to the United States to seek recognition of the
independence of the new republic and to present the
question of annexation. Houston then proceeded to
act on a plan to use Santa Anna in an effort to settle the future status of Texas with the least possible
delay. He was fully informed of the efforts which
Jackson had made through Butler to purchase Texas
from Mexico, and he now proposed that Santa Anna
should go to Washington and negotiate such a deal.
He had a talk with Santa Anna on November 2nd
and as a result the prisoner addressed a letter to
Houston in which he formally proposed such a visit
to Washington. Santa Anna pointed out that the
vote of the people of Texas in favor of annexation
to the United States had changed the whole situation
and had simplified the whole matter.

"Convinced as I am," wrote Santa Anna, "that
Texas will never reunite with Mexico, I am desirous,
on my part, to improve the advantage which may
offer, and avoid the sacrifices which will occur
should an imprudent attempt be made to reconquer
this country, which has hitherto proved more de-
trimental than beneficial; consequently, reducing the
Texas question to this single point—the regulation of
the limits between the United States and Mexico,
which, you are aware, has been pending many years,
and may be fixed at the Nueces del Norte, or any
other boundary, as may be decided at Washington.
Thus disagreeable discussions which might delay the
definite determination of this question, or cause a
difference between two friendly nations, will be

avoided. This, in substance, is a plain, safe and speedy mode of terminating this important matter, and, as all are interested, it becomes necessary that you facilitate my journey to Washington with the least possible delay."

Santa Anna, of course, was interested chiefly in being released from his captivity and getting safely out of Texas. But his proposal probably did not sound altogether impracticable at the time. It was at least plausible to believe that the leaders of Mexico might adopt the plan of "getting something for Texas" by giving the United States a quit claim to it in exchange for a cash consideration. The United States had been trying for six years to buy Texas, and consequently the American Government could be expected to fall in with the plan. And finally the Texans had voted overwhelmingly in favor of annexation.

However, one element of the situation had changed radically, had the Texans but known it. *The United States was no longer interested in buying Texas.* President Jackson and his supporters were busily engaged at the moment in electing Martin Van Buren to the Presidency and the injection into the campaign of such an explosive question as the annexation of Texas would have been highly dangerous. The plan of the opposition was to throw the election into Congress by running a number of regional candidates, each strong in his own section of the country. Daniel Webster was the New England candidate; William Henry Harrison was backed by the Northwest; Ohio put forward Judge John McLean; Jackson's own State, Tennessee, through its Legislature, nominated

United States Senator Hugh L. White, and South
Carolina, under the leadership of Calhoun, supported W. P. Mangum of North Carolina. All of these
men were certain to obtain some electoral votes, and
it was their hope that together they would poll
enough such votes to keep Van Buren from obtaining
a majority. Then there would be a repetition of 1824,
when John Quincy Adams was elected by the House
of Representatives in spite of the fact that Jackson
had been the leading candidate in the election. To
circumvent these plans and elect Van Buren was no
easy task, and all the political skill of the Jacksonians
was being employed to this end. No matter what the
facts might be with respect to Texas, the Abolitionists and certain American politicians had linked it
with slavery, and the strategy of Van Buren's supporters called for keeping the slavery question in the
background as much as possible.

The slavery question had become a much more
prominent issue in American politics since 1820,
when it had compelled Monroe to follow a course
insuring the ratification by Spain of the Treaty of
1819, in order to keep Texas outside the boundaries
of the United States. The opposition to the acquire-
ment of any new territory south of the Missouri Compromise line had increased considerably, and even
Jackson was beginning at last to realize its significance in American politics. It was becoming clear
that even if Anthony Butler had succeeded in negotiating the purchase of Texas during Jackson's administration, it would hardly have been possible to
obtain the ratification of such a purchase by Congress. William Lloyd Garrison had begun the publi-

cation of the *Liberator* in Boston in 1831, the same
year that the country had been shocked by an attempted slave insurrection at Southhampton, Virginia, under the leadership of a negro named Nat
Turner, in which sixty-one white persons had been
massacred. In 1833 England had abolished slavery
in all of its possessions, compensating the owners,
and the same year the American Anti-Slavery Society had been launched at a convention in Philadelphia. The abolitionists were only a small minority
in 1836, but questions related to slavery, such as the
circulation of anti-slavery literature through the
mails and the extension of slavery into new territory,
were beginning to figure prominently in politics. In
his annual message to Congress in December, 1835,
Jackson had recommended the "passing of such a
law as will prohibit, under severe penalties, the circulation in the Southern States, through the mail, of
incendiary publications." Congress not only refused
to follow this recommendation, but it enacted a law
requiring postal officials under heavy penalties to
deliver all matter without discrimination.

While the settlement of Texas and the Texan revolt
had no remote relation to the slavery question in the
United States, there were many who charged that the
"slave power" was at the bottom of both. Only a
month after the battle of San Jacinto, on May 25th,
1836, John Quincy Adams, the former President,
who was now a member of Congress, delivered an
address in the House in which he denounced the
Texan revolt as having for its object the reestablishing of slavery where it already had been abolished.
He pictured Santa Anna and the Mexicans as fight-

ing on the side of liberty and criticized the Jackson administration on the ground that it was making every effort to drive the United States into a war on the side of slavery. And he warned the members of Congress that there was more likelihood of Mexico overrunning the Southwestern States of the American Union than there was of the United States overrunning Mexico. Adams noted later in his memoirs that this speech was greeted by "a universal shout of applause" in the North.

The only ground that Adams had for his charge that the administration was doing all in its power to involve the United States in a war with Mexico was that General Gaines, who had been sent to the Texas border with a detachment of the army, had been instructed that if he found it advisable to cross the border in order to prevent Indian depredations he should do so, though in no case should he advance further than Nacogdoches. The Mexican minister at Washington, Manuel Eduardo de Gorostiza, had engaged in a violent correspondence with the American State Department on this subject, in which he demanded that the instructions to Gaines be recalled.

As for Adams's grotesque description of the struggle of the Texans as being a war waged to reestablish slavery, his sole source of information seems to have been Benjamin Lundy, the former associate of William Lloyd Garrison, who had repeatedly made the charge that the colonization of Texas and the subsequent revolution were the result of a "plot" of Southern slave owners to obtain more slave territory. Lundy never offered any substantial evidence to support this charge, but Adams seems to have swallowed the story whole and he continued to repeat it in speeches in Congress. In due course this became the accepted version of the Texas revolution among the opponents of slavery generally.

But in the face of such a situation, it is not difficult to understand why Van Buren's supporters, chief among whom was President Jackson himself, did not want any question relating to Texas introduced into the campaign. It is true that there was an overwhelming sentiment during the early part of 1836 in favor of recognizing the independence of Texas, and both houses of Congress had acted on this question just before adjourning on July 4th, declaring that Texas independence should be acknowledged by the United States "whenever satisfactory information has been received that it has in successful operation a civil government, capable of performing the duties and fulfilling the obligations of an independent power." But there was no such overwhelming sentiment in favor of annexation, and before the end of 1836 even the sentiment in favor of recognition had cooled off considerably. Jackson adopted a neutral course and meantime he sent Henry M. Morfit to Texas as a special investigator. Morfit spent most of August and September in Texas and the general tenor of his report was favorable, his final conclusion being that the stupidity of the rulers of Mexico and their inability to obtain financial support for a successful war against Texas were the chief guarantees that independence would be maintained. Morfit was in Texas when the election was held, and, of course, he reported the overwhelming vote and universal sentiment in favor of annexation.

Whether Houston was aware of all the obstacles in the way, he was determined, nevertheless, to send Santa Anna to Washington. When he proposed the plan to the Texas Congress, however, strong opposition, headed by Vice President Lamar, developed. A resolution was passed by a majority vote in both houses providing that the prisoner be detained in Texas. Houston promptly vetoed this resolution, and when the opposition, evidently with the idea of trapping Houston into assuming all the responsibility, put through a resolution leaving the disposition of the prisoner entirely in the hands of the President, he accepted the challenge, signed the resolution, and forthwith began making arrangements for Santa Anna's departure. And so at last, accompanied by an official escort composed of Barnard E. Bee, George W. Hockley, and William H. Patton, and with the faithful Colonel Almonte, who was released to act as aide to his chief, Santa Anna left Texas on November 25th, sailing for New Orleans, from which city, in due course, he started on his journey to Washington.

Meantime, Austin, as Secretary of State, had drafted instructions for William H. Wharton, the Texan envoy to the United States, and Wharton left Texas about the same time as Santa Anna. Austin's instructions to Wharton reminded him that, next to obtaining recognition of the independence of Texas, the great object of his mission was to bring about annexation to the United States on the broad basis of equitable reciprocity. He suggested that Texas should have the privilege of becoming a State of the American Union, with the right of dividing into a limited number of new States at the option of the people of Texas. Such details as the disposition of the public debt, the location of Indian tribes and the adjustment of land claims should be worked out, but there should be no limitation placed upon Texas on the question of slavery. As to the boundary, the Rio Grande was suggested, but if this question threatened serious delays Wharton was authorized to agree to a line following the watershed between the Nueces and the Rio Grande, leaving out the settlements east of the Rio Grande in New Mexico.

These were Wharton's official instructions, which he was authorized to divulge to the American Government. But Austin added private instructions in which Wharton was cautioned to take a firm stand and to agree to nothing that might prove unpopular among the people of Texas. There was a strong undercurrent of opinion among the people, Austin said, in favor of continuing as a separate and independent republic, and if peace could be established with Mexico by treaty and the friendship of other powers of the world obtained, public opinion might veer away from annexion. This would be certain to happen if the United States should refuse annexation or should insist on unfavorable terms. If he found any tendency in this direction, Wharton was to talk frankly with the British and French ministers at Washington on the subject of recognition of the independence of Texas by their Governments in exchange for liberal trade and immigration policies. However, within three weeks after Wharton's departure Austin wrote him that sentiment in Texas for annexation was stronger than ever and that he should make every effort to bring it about.

Wharton travelled from New Orleans by way of the Mississippi and Ohio rivers to Wheeling and thence overland to Washington. On the leisurely steamboat journey up the Mississippi he had much opportunity for intercourse with important people along the way, and Wharton made the most of it. He soon came to realize that there were immense obstacles in the way of annexation, and while he continued to believe it to be the most desirable thing for Texas, he was convinced before the Ohio River was reached that it would be practically impossible to obtain it. Writing to Austin he said that the leading newspapers of "the North and East" were everywhere opposed to annexation on the "old grounds of an opposition to the extension of slavery and of a fear of Southern preponderance in the councils of the nation". He added that the friends of Texas to whom he had talked, by which he meant, he said, "those of Louisiana, Mississippi, Kentucky, etc. (for I have seen and conversed with no others as yet)" were opposed to annexing Texas to the United States "on the grounds that a brighter destiny awaits Texas". If Texas became a State in the American Union, they contended, it would be oppressed by "high tariffs and other Northern measures" and would soon be driven to nullification and in the end to civil war. It was their opinion that it would be to the interest of Texas to remain an independent country, thus retaining control of its trade with the nations of the world. "To be plain and candid," continued Wharton, "I believe the recognition of our independence will certainly take place, but I have not at present much hopes of our being annexed. *That question when proposed will agitate this Union more than did the attempt to restrict Missouri, nullification, and abolitionism, all combined."*

The judgment expressed by Wharton in this italicized declaration (though the italics are not in the original), reflecting, as it does, the impression he had received during two weeks travel in the United States in December, 1836, provides a striking picture of the condition of the public mind at that time with respect to Texas. And it certainly did not encourage the hope that Santa Anna would make any headway with his project of interesting Jackson in having the United States acquire a quit claim to Texas. When Wharton reached Washington he found nothing to cause him to change his mind. Indeed, he presently discovered that the outlook even for recognition was not as rosy as he had hoped to find it. Van Buren had been safely elected President, but evidently it was now Jackson's desire to avoid doing anything to commit the incoming administration to any specific course with respect to Texas. Wharton was received by Jackson, unofficially, of course, on December 20th, which was the day before the President submitted Morfit's reports to Congress together with a message on the subject of recognition, and the interview was unsatisfactory, from Wharton's standpoint. And the next day the Secretary of State, John Forsyth, told Wharton bluntly that the vote of the Texans in favor of annexation had greatly embarrassed the American Government in the matter of recognition. Moreover, this view was expressed in Jackson's message to Congress.

Jackson, in his message, used the resolution adopted by Congress in July as a basis for throwing the responsibility of recognition upon Congress, while disclaiming any intent to shirk in the matter and reserving all the powers of the executive in the premises. On this basis also he submitted Morfit's reports. But he then proceeded to express his own "opinions". After reviewing the course followed by the American Government in cases involving recognition of the independence of countries which had thrown off the rule of another, and admitting that Texas had expelled the civil authority of Mexico from its borders, he then called attention to the immense disparity of physical force, in appearance at least, on the side of Mexico.

"The Mexican Republic," Jackson declared, "under another executive is rallying its forces under a new leader and menacing a fresh invasion to recover its lost dominion. Upon the issue of this threatened invasion the independence of Texas may be considered as suspended, and were there nothing peculiar in the relative situation of the United States and Texas our acknowledgment of its independence at such a crisis could scarcely be regarded as consistent with that prudent reserve with which we have heretofore held ourselves bound to treat all similar questions. But there are circumstances in the relations of the two countries which require us to act on this occasion with even more than our wonted caution. Texas was once claimed as a part of our property, and there are those among our citizens who, always reluctant to abandon that claim, can not but regard with solicitude the prospect of the reunion of the territory to this country. A large portion of its civilized inhabitants are emigrants from the United States, speak the same language with ourselves, and are bound to many of our citizens by ties of friendship and kindred blood; and, more than all, it is known that the people of that country have instituted the same form of government with our own, and have since the close of your last session openly resolved, on the acknowledgment by us of their independence, to seek admission to our Union as one of the Federal States. This last circumstance is a matter of peculiar delicacy, and forces upon us considerations of the gravest character. The title of Texas to the territory she claims is identified with her independence. She asks us to acknowledge that title to the territory, with an avowed design to treat immediately of its transfer to the United States. It becomes us to beware of a too early movement, as it might subject us, however unjustly, to the imputation of seeking to establish the claim of our neighbors to a territory with a view to its subsequent acquisition by ourselves. Prudence, therefore, seems to dictate that we should still stand aloof and maintain our present attitude, if not until Mexico itself or one of the great foreign powers shall recognize the independence of the new Government, at least until the lapse of time or the course of events shall have proved beyond cavil or dispute the ability of the people of that country to maintain their separate soverignty and to uphold the Government constituted by them."

Jackson, of course, did not write this message. The general belief at the time, and it was probably correct, was that it was the work of John Forsyth, and it is known that Martin Van Buren was consulted in its preparation. The spirit it manifested was admirable, from the standpoint of Mexico and the nations of the world, but it left Texas out in the cold just the same. Its tone and general attitude came as a surprise—a disappointment to the friends of Texas and a welcome change of front in the view of others. Waddy Thompson, Whig member of the House from South Carolina, who was whole-heartedly for recognition and annexation, was outspoken in his criticism of the President's position, while John Quincy Adams noted in his diary that the message represented "a total reverse of the spirit which almost universally prevailed at the close of the last session of Congress, and in which the President notoriously shared". W. F. Catlett, who had been appointed secretary of the Texas legation under Wharton, wrote Austin that the tone of the message was "coldblooded" and "ungenerous". And Wharton, of course, was keenly disappointed.

It was nearly a month after Jackson had sent this message to Congress, on January 17th, 1837, that Santa Anna arrived in Washington with the object of discussing with the American President the plan to have Mexico give the United States a quit claim to Texas for a cash consideration. Now, none of the objections set forth in the message was quite valid against such a negotiation as Santa Anna had in mind. Indeed, if successfully put through it would remove all of the objections cited. The circumstance

that Santa Anna was in no position to make a
binding bargain was of no consequence, because
he was on his way back to Mexico, and if
Jackson was willing to make a concrete proposition, such as Butler had pressed upon the Mexican Government during six years, Santa Anna
would not be a bad messenger. But Jackson was not
interested. A memorandum on his interview with
Santa Anna among Jackson's papers is the only record of what passed, and according to it Jackson objected that the United States could not act in the
matter without knowing the attitude of Texas toward
it, and inasmuch as the United States had not recognized the independence of Texas it could not hold
any communication with that country to ascertain its
attitude. Indeed, he said, unless Mexico should make
such a proposition through the regular diplomatic
channels, the United States could not discuss the
matter with Texas at all. Jackson was perfectly
aware of the attitude of Texas toward the proposal,
and he had taken official notice in his message of the
vote on annexation without any formal diplomatic
intercourse with Texas. But, of course, these were
not Jackson's reasons for refusing to entertain Santa
Anna's proposal in any way. The real reasons were
identical with those which had impelled Monroe to
keep Texas outside the boundaries of the United
States sixteen years before. They were now affecting
the incoming administration of Martin Van Buren,
and Jackson was going to do nothing to embarrass his
own hand-picked successor. But Jackson did make
a proposition to Mexico through Santa Anna. He
informed the former dictator that if Mexico would

be willing to cede Northern California as well as Texas to the United States it might be made the means of securing permanent tranquility between the two countries. Why it was proper to make this proposition and why the addition of Northern California was necessary to make the proposal desirable to the United States are questions left unexplained in the memorandum. But the impression is unescapable that Jackson simply was not interested in acquiring Texas at that time.

Diplomatic relations between the United States and Mexico at the time of Santa Anna's visit were strained almost to the breaking point, for Gorostiza had finally demanded and been given his passports, after Gaines had sent a small detachment to Nacogdoches and Jackson had refused to disavow the act. And before leaving the country Gorostiza had published a pamphlet in which he discussed the whole controversy and included some of the diplomatic correspondence on the subject. This had infuriated Jackson, who regarded it as a glaring violation of the decorum of diplomatic usage, and a demand had been made that Mexico disavow Gorostiza's whole course. But Mexico stood by its representative, just as the United States stood by Gaines. This was the situation when Santa Anna prepared to depart from Washington. Nevertheless, the United States Government offered him passage home. As guests of the American Navy, therefore, Santa Anna and the ever faithful Almonte set sail on the frigate "Pioneer" and were landed at Vera Cruz on March 1st, 1837. And so at least one object of Santa Anna's trip to Washington was accomplished.

Meantime, very little had been happening in Congress with respect to the recognition of Texas. Senator Walker of Mississippi offered a resolution in the Senate on January 11th, 1837, declaring that inasmuch as there was no longer any reasonable prospect of the prosecution of the war by Mexico, the independence of Texas ought to be recognized, but it was not until March 1st that he succeeded in bringing it to a vote. It was passed by a vote of 23 to 19. The next day, when a larger attendance was present, a motion was made to reconsider the Walker resolution and it failed by a tie vote of 24 to 24, thus showing the Senate equally divided on the question. In the House, after some prodding from Waddy Thompson, the Committee on Foreign Affairs reported out a resolution on February 18th which provided that the independence of Texas ought to be recognized and directed the Ways and Means Committee to provide an appropriation for a diplomatic agent, but three days later this was tabled by a vote of 98 to 86. Then on February 27th, when the House was considering the Civil and Diplomatic Appropriation bill while in Committee of the Whole, Waddy Thompson offered an amendment providing for the salary and outfit of a diplomatic agent to Texas, only to have it defeated by a vote of 40 ayes to 82 nays, more than two to one. Finally on February 28th, when the bill was up for passage, Thompson offered his amendment again in a slightly different form, and this was passed by a vote of 121 to 76, after adding the provision that the appropriation should become available "whenever the President of the United States may receive satisfactory evidence that Texas is an independent power and shall deem it expedient to appoint such minister." On March 2nd the bill, with this amendment unchanged, was finally passed by the Senate without a division.

This left the whole matter up to the President, and Jackson had scarcely twenty-four hours left in that office. But he lost no time in acting, for on the night of March 3rd, while the Senate was holding a night session, he sent in a short message nominating Alcée La Branche of Louisiana as *"chargé d'affaires* to the Republic of Texas", and by this act he formally recognized Texas as an independent nation. Shortly before midnight Jackson summoned Wharton and Memucan Hunt, who had been named the Texan minister to serve in the event of recognition, and after informing them of what he had done he "requested the pleasure of a glass of wine". And thus it came about that almost the last act of Andrew Jackson as President of the United States was to drink to the success of the infant republic.

Wharton dispatched this glad news to Texas at once. But his message was not addressed to Stephen Austin, who would have hailed the event as the culmination of his life's work, for Austin had died on December 27th, 1836. He had not even received the dispatch telling him of the "cold-blooded" and "ungenerous" character of Jackson's message to Congress, and when stricken by his last illness he was very optimistic over the outlook for recognition. His final labor had been the composition of a long letter to Jackson's private secretary, intended for the President's eye, urging additional reasons for prompt recognition. He caught a severe cold about a week be-

fore Christmas, which developed into pneumonia,
and due to a weakened constitution dating back to
his imprisonment in Mexico City, he failed to rally.
It is related that about a half-hour before his death
he awakened from a dream and murmured: "Texas
recognized. Archer just told me so. Did you see it
in the papers?" And so he died in the belief that
the colony he had started in the wilderness had finally
come to be acknowledged by the United States as a
nation among nations.

"Posterity," wrote Sam Houston, many years afterwards, "will never know the worth of Stephen F.
Austin, the privation which he endured, the enterprise which he possessed, his undying zeal, his ardent devotion to Texas and her interests, and his
hopes connected with her glorious destiny."

Recognition of the independence of Texas was only
a step toward the goal the Texans were seeking to
attain, for it was the conviction of most Texas leaders that annexation to the United States was absolutely essential to the welfare of their people. With
the inauguration of Van Buren, however, the situation changed radically for the worse with respect of
Texas. It did not take long for the Texans to discover that his attitude was not over-friendly. He
could not undo what Jackson had done during the
closing hours of his administration, but he was in
no hurry to put it into effect. La Branche's nomination as *chargé d'affaires* was confirmed by the Senate on March 7th, three days after Van Buren's inauguration, but it was not until July 21st, after a delay of four and a half months, that his commission
was issued to him. Likewise, Memucan Hunt, the

new Texan minister, was required to wait around Washington for four months before being officially received by the American Government. Hunt was received by Van Buren on July 6th, 1837, and a month later, on August 4th, he submitted to the State Department the formal proposal that Texas be annexed to the United States, at the same time making an extended argument in support of such action.

Van Buren had retained John Forsyth as Secretary of State, and on August 25th, after careful deliberation and much consultation with his chief, Forsyth handed Hunt a closely reasoned and devastating reply to his proposal. It was not merely a rejection of the proposal, but in effect a refusal to consider it at all. Its purport was summed up in the following paragraph:

"The United States are bound to Mexico by a treaty of amity and commerce, which will be scrupulously observed on their part, so long as it can be reasonably hoped that Mexico will perform her duties and respect our rights under it. The United States might justly be suspected of a disregard of the friendly purposes of the compact, if the overture of General Hunt were to be even reserved for future consideration, as this would imply a disposition on our part to espouse the quarrel of Texas with Mexico; a disposition wholly at variance with the spirit of the treaty, with the uniform policy and the obvious welfare of the United States."

Hunt sent a rather petulant and discourteous rejoinder to Forsyth, but this could not mitigate the crushing effect of the American Government's decision. Texas would have to take care of itself and get along as best it might. A sidelight on what this might mean is provided by a statement made by President Houston in a message to the Texas Congress, just about this time, to the effect that "since the commencement of the present administration, during the first year there was not at the disposition of the executive or in the treasury but five hundred dollars". And Houston added that the finances of Texas from the beginning of the revolution had been "in a more embarrassed situation than any other nation ever experienced".

When the Texas Congress met the following spring, Dr. Anson Jones, a member of the lower house from Brazoria, introduced a resolution directing President Houston to withdraw the proposal of annexation. After reciting the circumstances of the making of the proposal, and of its rejection "for reasons which it is impossible for time or circumstance to invalidate or alter", this measure resolved "that his Excellency the President be authorized and required, so soon as he may think proper, to instruct our minister resident at Washington respectfully to inform the Government of the United States of North America, that the Government of Texas withdraws the proposition for the annexation of Texas to the said United States."

This resolution was passed by the House by a decisive vote, and missed passage in the Senate by a single vote, the argument being urged in the latter body that such questions should be left entirely to the executive department of the Government. A few months later, however, when Hunt resigned his post at Washington, Houston sent for the author of this resolution and asked him to become Hunt's successor. Jones agreed to accept on condition that his first official act on arrival at Washington should be that of formally withdrawing the annexation offer. And so, on October 12th, 1838, Dr. Anson Jones, as the Texan minister at Washington, handed to the American Secretary of State a respectful communication in which it was set forth that although the question of annexation "had been considered by the United States Government as finally disposed of, yet, inasmuch as the impression appeared to remain upon the public mind, in both countries, that the proposition was still pending, he had been instructed by his Government to communicate to that of the United States its formal and absolute withdrawal."

This action was approved and ratified by a joint resolution of the Texas Congress, adopted January 23rd, 1839, and the application of Texas for annexation to the United States became a closed incident.

Meantime, Houston's term as President had expired, and, as the Constitution prohibited him from succeeding himself, Mirabeau B. Lamar had become President of the Republic. And Lamar, who had always opposed annexation, touched on the question in his inaugural address. "I cannot regard the annexation of Texas to the American Union," he declared, "in any other light than as the grave of all her hopes of happiness and greatness; and if, contrary to the present aspect of affairs, the amalgamation shall ever take place, I shall feel that the blood of our martyred heroes had been shed in vain."

And so, with the door of annexation closed, the Republic of Texas proceeded to shift for itself.

CHAPTER XXXVII

A NATION AMONG NATIONS

ANSON JONES, who had the habit of jotting down observations in a memorandum book, made a notation on November 30th, 1839, to the effect that "annexation is the policy for Texas now." "But," he added, "how to obtain it is the question." This probably was the view of most thoughtful men among the Texans at that time. Faced with the task of creating and maintaining a new nation, they felt that it would be much better if Texas could become a State of the American Union. But they recognized that this seemed politically impossible, at least for the time being.

With few exceptions, the advocates of annexation in the United States were Democrats, but the Democratic President, Martin Van Buren, was unalterably opposed to it. As long as he remained in office nothing practicable could be done to further such a measure, and it was a foregone conclusion that at the expiration of his term he would be his party's candidate for reelection. The opposition party, the Whigs, offered no hope, for most of the Whig leaders could be depended upon to do nothing which might seriously offend the anti-slavery faction. And the condition of public opinion generally in the United States was not such as to encourage the belief that the an-

nexation of Texas would become politically possible
in the near future. Nevertheless, the task of successfully maintaining Texas as an independent nation was fraught with such difficulties that thoughtful
Texans could not but realize that annexation would
be more desirable.

There were no supermen among the leaders of the
Texans. The forty-six men who comprised the membership of the first Texas Congress were, for the most
part, just such as one would expect to find among
the leaders of almost any 40,000 average Anglo-
Americans situated as the Texans were when the Republic was established. The same may be said of the
members of each subsequent Congress and of the
Texas leaders generally. There were some exception-
al men among them, to be sure, and some of these
were successful in making their influence felt. But
most of the Texas leaders were men of only average
ability. And yet they did an uncommonly good job in
setting up and maintaining a national government.

The task which faced the Texans would not have
been easy even under ideal conditions, and the conditions were very unfavorable. For one thing, it called
for money. In addition to the ordinary needs of a
new nation, the menace of a Mexican invasion required the maintenance of an army, and this had the
double effect of increasing the need of money and
making money harder to obtain. Besides, a "panic"
had prostrated business of all kinds in the United
States, resulting in the worst depression the country
had ever seen until then, and money was not available
for even the soundest and most attractive enterprises.
The only asset the Texans had to offer was land, but

in order to stimulate immigration and keep up the strength of the army they were compelled to give land away freely to practically all comers, so that this asset had little or no market value. The Texans made the "mistake" of issuing paper money, which quickly depreciated in value and soon became worthless, so that they were no better off with it than they would have been without it, but almost any similar population similarly situated would have made the same "mistake". However, in spite of this and other "mistakes", and in the face of all the unfavorable conditions, the Texans were highly successful in establishing and maintaining a government.

William Kennedy, a distinguished Englishman who arrived in Texas in the spring of 1839, characterized the success of the Texans in maintaining constitutional government as "one of the most remarkable passages in the history of associated man". Kennedy first spent several weeks in the United States, chiefly in New York and Washington, where, he said, he had received alarming accounts of Texas and its people, being warned that if he travelled west of the Sabine he would have a choice of "being eaten by Indians, sliced by bowie knives, or pressed for a soldier". Upon arriving in Texas, however, he was so "astonished to find a condition of things so entirely different" from what he had been "led to expect by the people and press of the Northern States" that he decided to write a book "for the purpose of explaining its true position" to the British public. "I found a stable government," he said, "religion respected, protection afforded to property and person, and the general tone of manners the same as in the United States." Kennedy's comprehensive two-volume work, "Texas: The Rise, Progress, and Prospects of the Republic of Texas", which was published in London in 1841, constitutes today a record of convincing contemporary testimony by an impartial witness, and his appraisal of the Texans undoubtedly expressed the sincere opinion of a competent observer.

Kennedy saw Texas during President Lamar's administration, which was less successful and more expensive than those of Houston and of Anson Jones, chiefly because it was more aggressive and ambitious. Lamar was succeeded by Sam Houston in 1841, and then Anson Jones, who was Houston's Secretary of State, became President in 1844. In a general way it may be said that Houston's policy was to leave the Mexicans alone and to placate the Indians, whereas Lamar's was just the opposite in each case. Jones's policy was very much like Houston's and these two were so succesful that when Jones retired from the office he could say with truth that Texas was in a universally prosperous condition, that it was at peace with all the world, that the frontier was quiet, that the farmer sowed and reaped in security, that industry and enterprise had received new guarantees and a new impulse, and that a large and very desirable immigration was taking place. And he could add: "The expenses of the Government since I have been in office have been paid in undepreciated currency, a very considerable amount of debt incurred by previous administrations has been paid off, and a surplus of available means sufficient to defray the expenses of the Government, economically administered, for

the next two years at least, is left at the disposal of
the State."

The independence of Texas was recognized by
France in September, 1839, by the Netherlands in
September, 1840, and finally by England in November, 1840. Before the end of Lamar's administration,
therefore, the leading nations of the world accepted
Texas as entirely and permanently separated from
Mexico, and in due course they were maintaining
cordial diplomatic relations with its Government as
that of an independent nation. Mexico, however,
continued to regard Texas merely as a rebellious
province and periodically made a great show of an
intention to reconquer it. In this respect Texas was
very much in the same position as that occupied by
Mexico prior to 1836, for it was not until that year,
when the Texas revolution was in full swing, that
Spain finally recognized the independence of Mexico. Packenham, the British minister to Mexico, reported to his Government early in 1839 that Mexican
officials admitted that the reconquest of Texas was
impossible, but that "a feeling of mistaken pride,
foolishly called regard for national honor, deters the
Government from putting an end to a state of things
highly prejudicial to the interests of Texas and attended with no sort of advantage to this country
(Mexico)." Packenham had urged upon Gorostiza,
who was the Mexican foreign minister of the moment, the importance of recognizing the independence of Texas, pointing out the advantage of having
a buffer country between Mexico and the United
States. Gorostiza agreed with this view entirely, as
did other Mexican officials, but he stated frankly

that the recognition of Texas would be so unpopular that it would destroy any Mexican Government that attempted it.

This attitude was greatly encouraged by the activities of a considerable faction in the United States, headed by John Quincy Adams. In spite of Van Buren's complete rejection of the proposal to annex Texas, Adams affected to believe that the administration was following a deep and subtle policy having annexation for its object. And he used every available occasion to denounce and belittle the Texans and their Government. When, for example, Van Buren asked the advice of Congress as to what course should be followed with respect to the vast accumulation of claims by American citizens against Mexico, and toward which a long succession of Mexican Governments had taken an attitude of almost insolent indifference, Adams attacked the administration vehemently on the floor of the House. He declared that "a system of deep duplicity worthy of Tiberius Caesar or Ferdinand of Aragón" had been pursued by the American Government ever since the beginning of Jackson's administration in 1829, and that it had for its object "the breeding of a war with Mexico, in order that, under cover of such a war we might accomplish the annexation of the province of Texas to this Union." He charged that the efforts of the American Government to obtain a consideration of these claims by the Mexican Government were being managed in such a way as to result in "fretting the people of this Union into war with Mexico, and that this object was pursued by indirect means and with a double face."

All of this was the product of Adams's warped imagination. This speech was delivered on July 5th, 1838, at a time when French warships were blockading the port of Vera Cruz in an effort to compel the Mexican Government to make some satisfactory arrangement with respect to claims of French citizens of much smaller amount than those of the United States. Van Buren, in contrast, was following a much more conciliatory course, for he was endeavoring to have the American claims submitted to a commission of arbitration. But Adams had become completely pro-Mexican with respect to every question involving the two countries, and he maintained this attitude with self-righteous fanaticism. Ten or twelve years earlier, when as President he was attempting to buy Texas, he had declared that the "Missouri question" could be "left to Providence", but now he seemed to conceive himself as the instrument of Providence to prevent the annexation of any territory south of the Missouri Compromise line. Recognition of the independence of Texas by Mexico, however, would have taken all the wind out of Adams's sails, so to speak, and with such a friend at court in the United States, Mexican leaders were not likely to do anything to weaken his case. Indeed, some of the dispatches of Mexican ministers at Washington to their Government urged an invasion of Texas in support of Adams's efforts.

Incidentally, the French aggression at Vera Cruz gave Santa Anna the opportunity to stage a comeback, for in a skirmish of no decisive importance with French troops he had the good fortune to be wounded in the foot, necessitating an amputation, and in consequence he was hailed again as a hero by the Mexican populace.

The threatened Mexican invasion of Texas did not materialize, though a force ostensibly intended for such a move was maintained at Matamoros during 1837 and 1838. One reason for this was the constant need of troops in the interior to put down revolts. Bustamante had become President again, being elected by the Centralist Congress in the spring of 1837, and a Centralist Government was being maintained. But the Federalists resumed revolutionary activities almost as soon as the war against Texas was suspended, and they kept the troops of the Government completely occupied most of the time. In Yucatán and Tabasco, the States forming the extreme southern tip of Mexico, the Federalists followed the example of the Texans by separating from Mexico and establishing an independent republic. In the northern States an attempt was made to launch a new federation, under the title of the Republic of the Rio Grande, and the leading military chieftain of the Federalists in that region was none other than Urrea, who had served the Centralists so well in the Texas war. Under the leadership of Gen. Miracle Canales, Coahuila joined the northern federation, and he made overtures to President Lamar with a view of having Texas enter into an alliance with this movement. Lamar declined all formal relationship with the Mexican Federalists, but his attitude was sympathetic and no obstacles were placed in the way of the organization of expeditionary forces among the Texans for service under Canales. Several hundred Texans volunteered and participated in a number of battles south of the Rio Grande before the new "re-public" finally collapsed. Lamar did form an alli-ance with the Republic of Yucatán, however, and loaned it the Texas navy, which, incidentally, was never recovered.

While the Mexicans made no move to invade Texas, the officers in command at Matamoros car-ried on constant intrigue among the Indians and na-tive Mexicans in Texas in an effort to incite them against the Texans. As a result of the activities of Mexican secret agents, Indian depredations became frequent, and for nearly a year, beginning in August, 1838, an armed band of about one hundred native Mexicans from the region around Nacogdoches, led by one Vicente Córdova, with about two hundred Indian allies, terrorized the frontier until it was dis-persed by a force of Texans under Rusk. Finally, a Mexican agent, Manuel Flores, was killed in a fight with Texas rangers, and papers found on his person disclosed plans for a general Indian uprising and campaign. All of this created widespread sentiment among the Texans for a more aggressive policy against the Indians, and the Texas Congress sup-ported Lamar in carrying out such a policy, even to the extent of expelling the Cherokees, who were or-dinarily peaceful, from the borders of the Republic.

Congress refused to support Lamar, however, in another pet policy, that of establishing the authority of the Republic over the area between the traditional boundary of Texas and the Rio Grande, especially the east bank of the river in the region around Santa Fé. Lamar's object in proposing this was to divert the trade existing between Santa Fé and St. Louis to the Texas coast, and this was part of his plan to establish close commercial relations with England as a major policy of the Republic. Lamar had told Kennedy that he would follow such a policy. "Tell your rulers," Kennedy reported Lamar as saying, "to agree to a liberal treaty with Texas, and she will pursue a commercial system by which trade will be freed from its shackles in the valley of the Mississippi and the country beyond the Rio Grande." By bringing Santa Fé under the authority of Texas, and by adopting a low tariff policy, Lamar hoped to establish a condition that would eliminate both Mexican and American tariffs from the Santa Fé trade. If he had been successful, there can be no doubt that this would have been of immense and vital importance in relation to the destiny of Texas as a nation, and Lamar would have been hailed for his wise statesmanship. But the plan failed, and in consequence Lamar was widely condemned by his contemporaries, and historians have continued to heap ridicule upon his head.

The plan failed chiefly because Lamar was misinformed as to the attitude of the people and the authorities of Santa Fé toward it. Moreover, due to the opposition of Congress, the expedition which he authorized was practically a private undertaking, and consequently it was not properly equipped and many of the three hundred men who participated in it were unsuitable for such an enterprise. When the expedition finally arrived at Santa Fé, after narrowly escaping starvation in a mountainous wilderness, its members, including several American citizens who accompanied it as prospective traders, were promptly taken into custody. They were treated with extreme cruelty, and then were sent, on foot and in chains, to Mexico City as captured invaders. They were paraded as exhibits through the principal streets of every town and village between El Paso and Mexico City. Many of them died on the way and they all underwent great hardship. All of this was reported in detail in the American newspapers and caused much public indignation. The incident became the subject of a warm controversy between the United States and Mexico, but ultimately those of the prisoners who had not died during their captivity were released.

The Santa Fé expedition, the activities of the Texas volunteers with the Federalists in Coahuila, and the lending of the Texas naval vessels to Yucatán were all interpreted by Mexican leaders as acts of aggression calling for reprisals, and when Houston succeeded Lamar he found that he had a more belligerent Mexico to deal with. He had returned to the office of President scarcely a month when Gen. Mariano Arista issued from Monterrey a proclamation to the people of "the department of Texas" announcing the intention of the Mexican Government to reoccupy the "department" and offering full amnesty to all residents who received the Government's troops without opposition. The struggle for independence, he said, was hopeless, and he warned that while Mexico held out "the olive branch of peace in one hand, she would direct with the other the sword of justice against the obstinate".

This preposterous document was received in Texas in the latter part of January, 1842, just about the time that the first news of the fate of the Santa Fé expedition reached the Texans. Congress was in session and the members were unanimous in the conclusion that "something should be done about it" at once. So they proceeded to enact a bill formally annexing to the Republic of Texas the two Californias, all of Chihuahua, Sonora, and New Mexico, and parts of Tamaulipas, Coahuila, Durango, and Sinaloa. Houston promptly vetoed this fantastic measure, but the gentlemen of Congress then proceeded with great enthusiasm to pass it over his veto.

Evidently, this was their idea of impressing Arista with the fact that they could match him at making jokes. Arista, however, was not through. During the first week of March, 1842, detachments of Mexican troops advanced across the Rio Grande and captured San Antonio, Goliad, and Refugio. Houston immediately issued a proclamation calling the militia to arms, and by March 15th more than three thousand armed Texans were gathered at San Antonio. The Mexicans were already gone, however, for after holding the captured towns for two days they withdrew and marched back beyond the Rio Grande as suddenly as they had come. The Texas militia wanted to retaliate with an invasion of Northern Mexico, but Houston forbid anything of the kind and then proceeded to call a special session of Congress to meet on July 27th.

Houston recommended to the special session of Congress that an invasion of Mexico be authorized and the means be provided to finance it. He expressed the belief that Mexico could never conduct a successful campaign against Texas, but declared that its leaders should be made to understand that they could not invade Texas without retaliatory consequences. Congress passed a bill authorizing an expedition against Mexico, all right, but it provided for the expense merely by appropriating ten million acres of land for the purpose. Houston, who had acted largely in deference to public opinion, and who really preferred to leave Mexico alone, accepted the chance to place the blame for inaction upon Congress and vetoed the bill, pointing out that such an expedition could not be financed in the manner provided. And so the war scare subsided. But not for long, for on September 11th, 1842, a Mexican force of about fourteen hundred men, under Gen. Adrian Woll, descended upon San Antonio, took fifty-three prisoners, including the judge of the district court, which was in session, and several members of the bar, and three days later, after a few skirmishes with Texan forces, retired again with the prisoners beyond the Rio Grande.

This exasperating method of warfare aroused such a demand for a retaliatory invasion of Mexico that Houston could not ignore it, and he issued a call for volunteers to assemble at San Antonio. About twelve hundred men responded to this call, but before a start was made for the Rio Grande a month later fully five hundred of them had returned to their homes. General Somervell, whom Houston had ordered to command these volunteers, decided after reaching the Rio Grande that this force was inadequate for such an expedition and he ordered the men to return to Gonzales and disband. About one-third of them, however, refused to obey this order and undertook an attack on the Mexican town of Miér, which was defended by a force of fifteen hundred Mexican regulars under Gen. Pedro Ampudia. The inevitable result was that they were captured in a body. Then they were ordered to march, under guard, to Mexico City, in much the same fashion as the Santa Fé prisoners had done a year before. Because of a daring but futile attempt to escape which the prisoners made on the way, it was decreed that one in every ten of them should be executed, the choice to be made by lot. There were now one hundred and seventy prisoners, so that seventeen were condemned to death. Each of the Texans was required to reach into a jar of beans, blind-folded, and to withdraw one bean. Seventeen of the beans were black, and each man who drew one of these was shot. The rest of the prisoners were continued on their journey to Mexico City, where they were imprisoned for several months before being released.

These events, while causing public excitement in Texas, affected directly only a very small percentage of the population. Most of the people went about their daily business undisturbed, sowing and reaping their crops, clearing away the wilderness and placing new land under cultivation each year, and otherwise laying the economic foundations of civil society. This whole period was one of continued growth for Texas and within ten years after San Jacinto the population was more than doubled. And when Anson Jones, in 1846, spoke of "the universally prosperous condition of the country" he described a state of affairs that was clearly apparent to all. It was undeniable that Texas was on the way toward becoming an important nation.

The Mexican raids were interpreted by the statesmen of the leading countries as conclusive evidence
that Mexican leaders themselves had no faith in the
ability of Mexico ever to reconquer Texas. But at
first it was believed that they were the beginning of
a campaign to reestablish Mexican authority between
the Rio Grande and the Sabine. The first reports
of the invasion in the spring of 1842 aroused great
interest in the United States and friends of the Republic arranged public meetings in the principal
cities for the purpose of creating sympathy for the
Texans and of urging volunteers to go to their assistance. These demonstrations caused much resentment among Mexican leaders, and the Minister of
Foreign Relations, Bocanegra, made them the subject of complaining notes to the American Secretary
of State. In reply to one such note, the American
Secretary, under date of July 8th, 1842, made the
following declaration:

"M. de Bocanegra would seem to represent that,
from 1835 to the present time, citizens of the United
States, if not their Government, have been aiding
rebels in Texas in arms against the lawful authority
of Mexico. This is not a little extraordinary. Mexico may have chosen to consider, and may still choose
to consider, Texas as having been at all times since
1835, and as still continuing, a rebellious province;
but *the world has been obliged to take a very different view of the matter.*"

Considering its source, this was a very significant
declaration. For the signature attached to this note
was that of Daniel Webster!

CHAPTER XXXVIII

ALL BECAUSE OF "TYLER TOO"

WHEN Martin Van Buren ran for reelection to the Presidency of the United States in 1840, his attitude toward Texas did not figure in the campaign at all. It was one of the most noisy campaigns in American political history, and while Van Buren was denounced for almost every conceivable reason, his rejection of the annexation proposal was not even mentioned.

That was the campaign of "Tippecanoe and Tyler too", the first in which spectacular methods were used to "get out the vote". The Whig candidate for President was Gen. William Henry Harrison of Ohio, Indian fighter and veteran of the War of 1812, and John Tyler of Virginia was his running mate. There were no dominant "issues", for the various elements comprising the Whig "party" were in agreement on nothing except a mutual hatred for Andrew Jackson and a common desire to beat Van Buren, and in consequence it was largely a campaign of personalities. The Whigs heralded Harrison as a log-cabin hero and ridiculed Van Buren as a darling of the rich who put perfume on his whiskers. But they did this noisily and with tumultous enthusiasm. "The Whig campaign", says Muzzey, "was a continuous festival of oratory, pageant, song, and shout-

ing. . . . Log cabins were erected for Whig headquarters, with the coonskin nailed to the wall and the
latchstring hung out. Mass meetings gathered around
the cider barrel." There was no serious discussion.
"The immense multitudes who gathered at the meetings," says another observer, "came to be amused, not
to be instructed. They met, not to think and deliberate, but to laugh and shout and sing."

The result of all this was that an unprecedented
number of voters thronged the polls on election day,
the total vote reaching 58 per cent above that of the
previous election. Van Buren's popular vote was 48
per cent greater than his vote of 1836, and yet he was
badly beaten. He carried only seven States—Virginia, South Carolina, Alabama, Arkansas, Missouri,
Illinois, and New Hampshire. He lost his own State
of New York and Jackson's State of Tennessee, and
even such States as Mississippi and Louisiana. However, it was not the spectacular campaign alone that
was responsible for this. The "panic" had much to
do with it. The unprecedented hard times, which
had lasted for three years and from which no relief
seemed in sight, were blamed on Van Buren and on
Jackson by a large portion of the public. Every bank
in the United States had suspended specie payments,
factories were closed, great numbers of workmen
were thrown out of employment, and the price of
cotton dropped in 1839 to the lowest point on record
until then. Van Buren had no quick cure for these
conditions. He attempted to talk dignified common
sense during the campaign, but he was drowned out
by the noise of the opposition.

The Texans watched all this with interest, but with little hope that it had any meaning for them. They had not much sympathy for Van Buren, but the Whig victory held out little promise, so far as their own interests and destiny were concerned. And when it became known that the President-elect had named Daniel Webster as his Secretary of State, it was taken for granted that Texas would have to shift for itself for another four years. Moreover, it was an open secret that Harrison would not be much more than a figurehead, and that the policies of the administration would be directed from the Senate by Henry Clay.

Then there occurred one of those political accidents which occasionally have such far-reaching and unexpected consequences as to modify the very destiny of the nation. Exactly one month after his inauguration, General Harrison died of pneumonia, and John Tyler became President of the United States. In due course, Henry Clay and the other Whig leaders came to learn that this had completely upset all their plans and had brought their smashing victory to naught. For Tyler was a dyed-in-the-wool States' rights Democrat, absolutely opposed to most of Clay's pet measures on principle, and entirely out of sympathy with the Whig majority in Congress. He had been nominated by the Whigs to catch Southern votes and because of prominence he had attained by resigning from the Senate rather than to obey the instructions of the Virginia Legislature to vote in favor of expunging from the record a resolution censuring Andrew Jackson, with whom he had quarrelled over nullification and the tariff. The

Whigs had expected that as Vice President he would merely preside over the Senate and have nothing whatever to do with the policies of the administration. But having taken the oath as President faithfully to execute the duties of that office and to "preserve, protect, and defend the Constitution of the United States", Tyler proposed to observe that oath in accordance with his own conscience and in the light of his own deep-seated convictions.

If, as has been asserted by many historians, the annexation of Texas marked a turning point in the history of the United States, then there have been few similar events since the adoption of the Constitution of such vital consequence as was the sudden death of William Henry Harrison and the resulting elevation of John Tyler to the Presidency. For Tyler believed that the most fundamental interests of the United States as a nation required the annexation of Texas, and while he deplored slavery, his convictions were such that its existence in Texas did not constitute for him an obstacle in the path of annexation. He believed the Missouri Compromise to be unconstitutional and he had little of the politician's caution which expressed itself in fear of the anti-slavery sentiment. In addition to this, he had the energy, resourcefulness, and dogged persistence essential to success in putting through such a measure in the face of strong opposition.

At first, however, it did not appear, either to the Whig leaders or to the Texans, that the change would make any difference. Harrison had called a special session of Congress for May 31st, 1841, to enact Whig reforms into law, and when it convened Tyler's message gave no hint of the coming storm. By the middle of September, however, Tyler had vetoed most of the major measures proposed by Clay and all of Clay's friends in the cabinet, who had been appointed by Harrison and were left undisturbed by Tyler, resigned in a body. Webster, however, remained in the State Department, partly because he did not choose to play the tail to Clay's kite, but chiefly because he desired to complete the negotiation of the northeastern boundary treaty with England. And finally, on March 31st, 1842, Clay resigned from the Senate to devote all his time to rebuilding the Whig party and to insuring his own nomination for the Presidency in 1844.

As long as Webster remained in the State Department, any move in the direction of the annexation of Texas was out of the question, and his continuance in office left the Texans in doubt as to the attitude of the administration. Tyler had spoken to Webster on this subject, however, as early as October, 1841, immediately following the resignation of Clay's friends from the cabinet, and he subsequently put his proposal in writing. "I gave you a hint," he wrote Webster, "as to the probability of acquiring Texas by treaty. I verily believe it could be done. Could the North be reconciled to it, could anything throw so bright a lustre around us?" Webster gave the President no encouragement to develop this theme, and meantime he was attaining a brilliant success with the British treaty, so the matter rested. He followed a firm policy in dealing with Mexico, however, making it very clear that the United States regarded Texas as an independent nation and protesting vigorously against the kind of warfare represented in the Mexican raids of 1842. His correspondence with the Mexicans, it should be said in passing, was marked by several exchanges of threats of war, and when he resigned, as he finally did on May 8th, 1843, the relations between the two countries were in much worse shape than Van Buren and Forsyth had left them. It is also to be noted that at the time of his resignation he was the only member of Tyler's cabinet who was opposed to the annexation of Texas.

The Texas Government, in the meantime, had taken steps to further the project of annexation. When Houston began his second term as President on December 12th, 1841, he adopted a policy having one of two alternatives for its object. Either Texas must be annexed to the United States or peace with Mexico, on a basis of full recognition of Texan independence, must be obtained through the agency of other nations, which meant chiefly England. Anson Jones, whom Houston had appointed Secretary of State, developed this policy in such a way that it finally took the form of furthering the cause of annexation in the United States by creating among American leaders a fear of British influence over the policies of the Republic of Texas. Jones recognized early that the problem of effecting annexation resolved itself into giving it an aspect of vital interest to the United States, so vital as to overcome all the objections urged against the measure on anti-slavery grounds. "It had always been my prime object, in procuring the interference of these European powers," wrote Jones afterwards, "to arouse the slumbering jealousies of the people of the United States."

The circumstance that it would require more than the support of the President to bring about annexation, that the attitude of Congress was at least quite as important, was recognized by the Texans from the first, and they shaped their policy accordingly. During the first two years of his administration, Tyler was at war with the Whig Congress, and its disposition was to oppose anything the President favored. James Reilly, whom Houston had sent to Washington as the Texan minister, reported on March 25th, 1842, that "nothing can be done here in the way of any negotiation for Texas". But three weeks later he wrote that he felt "satisfied fully" that the administration was "decidedly in favor" of annexation. Then, under date of July 11th, 1842, he wrote that he had had a frank talk with President Tyler on the subject, and that "the President would act in a moment if the Senate would concur." He expressed the fear, however, that there was not sufficient support of the project in that body to warrant the negotiation of a treaty.

Reilly was succeeded at Washington in August, 1842, by Isaac Van Zandt, and within a few months Van Zandt was writing the Texan Government that as soon as Tyler could be convinced of adequate support in the Senate he would act. He expressed the belief that the time would soon arrive when he would be able to negotiate an annexation treaty and suggested that he be given full authority to settle the terms of such a treaty. A little later, however, Van Zandt wrote that the other branches of the Government, especially the Senate, were not disposed "to aid Mr. Tyler in his views upon any important question; therefore, his efforts, no odds how laudable they may be, will meet with more or less opposition."

In this situation, the Texans began to apply the policy of playing England against the United States, and vice versa, as the best means of furthering their interests. For example, under date of January 24th, 1843, Houston wrote to Capt. Charles Eliot, the British minister to Texas, informing him that the subject of the annexation of Texas to the United States was being much talked about, both in Texas and in the United States, and that the American people were rapidly becoming a unit in favor of this policy. "To defeat this policy," wrote Houston, "it is only necessary for Lord Aberdeen to say to Santa Anna, 'Sir, Mexico must recognize the independence of Texas.' Santa Anna would be glad of such a pretext." Then in March, Anson Jones made a notation on a letter from Van Zandt as follows: "I no longer think it policy to maintain an attitude of supplication towards the United States, but will try a different course. We have begged long enough—too long, indeed." And about the same time (under date of March 15th, 1843), Van Zandt wrote Jones from Washington as follows:

"Some of the people of this country are disposed to think that they can claim what they please at our hands, and we will yield it, of course; that there is no danger of our going to Europe to make commercial arrangements to their prejudice. Now, I think it our policy, at this time, to endeavor to alarm them to some extent on this subject. . . . The late view I

have presented to the President on the subject of
English efforts in Texas has aroused him very considerably, and if matters were settled here, he would
undoubtedly make a move. Mr. Webster will leave
the State Department very soon. Though friendly
to us, he is very much in the way at present; he is
timid and wants nerve, and is fearful of his abolition
constituents in Massachusetts. . . . The President,
though much abused, is gaining ground; the Democrats and moderate Whigs are falling into his ranks,
and coming to his support. Our principal strength
in this country is with the Democrats. Our own success here depends much on the political turns in this
country. The President said to me the other day,
'Encourage your people to be quiet, and not to grow
impatient. We are doing all we can to annex you to
us, but we must have time.' "

Certain happenings during the summer of 1843
served to further considerably the policy of arousing
"the slumbering jealousies of the people of the
United States" with respect to the "danger" of
British influence in Texas. First of all there
came news that an armistice between Texas and
Mexico had been declared, pending the negotiation
of a peace treaty, and that this had been arranged
through British influence. Houston had issued a
proclamation declaring such an armistice on June
13th, following a communication from Santa Anna,
who was again President of Mexico, transmitted
through Captain Eliot, the British minister resident
in Texas. This was the result of activities of James
W. Robinson, who had been Lieutenant Governor of
the Provisional Government of Texas in 1835, and

who was one of the prisoners carried off in Woll's raid on San Antonio in 1842. Robinson was imprisoned in the castle of Perote, and with the idea of obtaining his freedom he wrote to Santa Anna that he believed if he should be permitted to return to Texas he could bring about a reconciliation between Texas and Mexico. Santa Anna ordered his release and provided him with a statement of terms upon which Mexico would consent to make peace with Texas. These terms consisted of six proposed articles, including (1) that Texas should acknowledge the sovereignty of Mexico, (2) that a general act of amnesty for past acts in Texas be enacted, (3) that Texas should form an independent department of Mexico, (4) that Texas should be represented in the General Congress, (5) that Texas should institute or originate all local laws, rules, and regulations, and (6) that no Mexican troops under any pretext whatever should ever be stationed in Texas. There was no chance, of course, that the Texans would ever acknowledge the sovereignty of Mexico again, but Houston, while objecting to the terms, had Captain Eliot to write to Packenham, the British minister at Mexico City, suggesting that he procure an armistice, pending negotiations. The armistice was the ultimate result of this, and Houston named George W. Hockley and Samuel Williams to act as commissioners to discuss its conditions, while in the meantime hostilities were suspended.

The news of this armistice was received at Washington just prior to the installation of A. P. Upshur as the American Secretary of State, and he and President Tyler interpreted it as new evidence of the growth of British influence in Texas. Then in a few weeks there came more disturbing news, this time from London. The World Convention of Abolitionists was opened at London on June 13th, under the auspices of the British and Foreign Anti-Slavery Society, and among the delegates was Stephen Pearl Andrews of Galveston, who was registered as the representative of the abolitionists of Texas. One of the subjects discussed at the convention was the abolition of slavery in Texas, and Andrews reported a growing sentiment among Texan slave-owners in favor of such a course and expressed the opinion that all that was necessary to accomplish this was money to reimburse the owners. A committee from the convention called on Lord Aberdeen, the British Foreign Minister, and proposed that the British Government guarantee the principal of a bond issue the proceeds of which would be used to purchase the slaves in Texas. And it was reported that Lord Aberdeen gave the committee a sympathetic hearing and agreed to recommend such a course to the Government. Lord Aberdeen later denied that he ever made such a promise, but not before a highly colored report of the whole incident had reached Washington and convinced Tyler and Upshur that unless Texas was annexed to the United States without delay it would soon be too late.

This incident also attracted the attention of Ashbel Smith, the Texan minister at London, and he made it his business to ask Lord Aberdeen about it point blank. Lord Aberdeen assured Smith that while England was interested in seeing slavery abolished everywhere, "there was no disposition on the part of the British Government to interfere improperly on this subject, and that they would not give the Texan Government cause to complain." But Lord Aberdeen disclosed to Smith that the British minister at Mexico City had been instructed to suggest to the Government of Mexico the advisability of offering Texas full recognition on condition that it abolish slavery. Writing to Jones about the attitude of the British Government, under date of August 2nd, 1843, Smith said:

"It has been a work of some difficulty for me to convey a correct idea of the course of conduct of the British *Government* in relation to slavery in America, at the same time that I have desired not to attribute to that Government any sinister or covert purposes against Texas. The abolition of slavery is their open and avowed policy, and they have invariably pursued it for a long period, in favor of their own commerce, manufactures, and colonial interests. They will persevere in this policy, and employ all means for its accomplishment. Should money be necessary, they will give it, as they have done to Spain; because they anticipate, and, in my opinion, justly, that more than counterbalancing pecuniary advantages will accrue to Great Britain from abolition. In persuance of this policy, so far as regards Texas, the British Government and its officers very naturally, and perhaps properly, study the interests of *their own country alone,* in entire disregard of its influence upon the prosperity of Texas, without, however, any hostile or unfriendly feeling towards our country; but, on the contrary, with as much prac-

tical good will for us as may be consistent with the
vigorous perseverance in their abolition policy."

Smith already had written Van Zandt at Washington a circumstantial account of the sentiment in England for the abolition of slavery in Texas. "Rely on
it as certain," he wrote, "that in England it is intended to make an effort, and that some things are
already in train to accomplish if possible abolition
of slavery in Texas. And might not Texas, exhausted
as just described, listen in a moment of folly to such
overtures of the British Government?" Van Zandt
had shown this letter around in Washington, thus furthering the process of arousing "the slumbering jealousies" of a number of the gentlemen of Congress.

Meantime, William S. Murphy, the American
chargé d'affaires in Texas, wrote the American State
Department that he was sure that something was
going on between Texas and England, but that he
could not discover what it was. "What steps are in
progress I know not," he wrote, under date of July
6th, 1843, "nor can I know until they shall develop
themselves to the world. England may at this time
be setting on foot a negotiation of vast consequence
to the United States, and in all probability such is the
case."

A few weeks after this, Van Zandt reported to
Jones a conversation he had had with Secretary of
State Upshur. "The Secretary is fully alive to the
important bearing which our institutions have upon
this country," he wrote. "He expresses some alarm
lest England is attempting to exercise some undue influence upon our affairs. His inquiries upon this
subject I waived by replying, I knew nothing of the

measures of England towards Texas, except that she professed and evinced a desire to secure us peace; but if she did intend, or was trying to obtain an undue influence over Texas, the better way to counteract her efforts was for the United States to act promptly and efficiently, and show her disposition to afford to Texas every facility which she might expect to obtain from England."

Upshur wrote to Murphy in much the same tone as he took in this conversation with Van Zandt. He expressed the fear that England was seeking to obtain undue influence over Texas, and that Texas, in its extremity, would be compelled to consent to it. "If she should receive no countenance and support from the United States," he wrote, "it is not an extravagant supposition that England may and will reduce her to all the dependence of a colony, without taking upon her self the onerous duties and responsibilities of the mother country." Upshur reminded Murphy that "the United States have a high interest to counteract this attempt, should it be made."

All of these suspicions seemed to be confirmed when Lord Brougham, in asking a question of Lord Aberdeen in Parliament, declared that he looked forward most anxiously to the abolition of slavery in Texas, because he was convinced that it would ultimately end in the abolition of slavery throughout the whole of America. He felt, he said, that Texas would do much toward abolishing slavery if Mexico could be induced to recognize its independence, and he desired to know what the British Government was doing to that end. Lord Aberdeen replied that he was quite as anxious as Lord Brougham to see slav-

ery abolished in Texas, and while he must decline
to give specific information on the subject, this was
not due to indifference, but quite otherwise. In any
event, he said, "he could assure his noble friend that,
by means of urging the negotiations, as well as by
every other means in their power, Her Majesty's
ministers would press this matter."

In this connection, it should be said that as early
as June 20th, 1843, Ashbel Smith sent a note to Lord
Aberdeen by which he placed on record "the explicit
disapproval of the Texas Government of all proceedings having for their object the abolition of slavery in Texas." And Anson Jones took notice of this
in a communication to Smith, dated September 30th,
1843, and observed that "the subject, as you are already aware and as you have properly stated to Lord
Aberdeen, can not and will not be entertained in any
shape by this Government". This was not known
in the United States at the time, however, and besides it had no effect upon the British purpose to
work for the abolition of slavery, in Texas and elsewhere.

But aside from the question of slavery entirely, the
British policy with respect to Texas was, to quote
Anson Jones, "to build up a power independent of
the United States," which could "raise cotton enough
to supply the world", and it was the intention that
this power should maintain a free trade policy. This
in itself was a menace to the interests and the welfare
of the people of the United States, and if this policy
had succeeded it would have exerted such economic
pressure on the cotton-growing States as would have
tended in time to promote their secession from the

Union to a compelling degree. It is well to remember that it was the tariff, and not anti-slavery agitation, that occasioned the nullification movement. That episode so thoroughly convinced some of the South Carolina leaders that their State and the South generally were condemned forever to an inferior economic position in the Union that at all times after 1832 they were ready to favor secession on any plausible pretext. The competition of the Republic of Texas, as an independent nation with a system of free trade, would have been felt to an ever-increasing degree by the cotton-growing States, and this inevitably would have been reflected in the political struggles within the United States.

Be all this as it may, when newspaper reports of Lord Aberdeen's statement in Parliament reached the United States about the middle of September, 1843, Tyler and Upshur decided that the time had come for action. Upshur dispatched notes to both the American *chargé d'affaires* in Texas and the American minister in London on the subject of British intentions in Texas. But even before doing this, he informed Van Zandt that the American Government contemplated a definite change of policy and early action on the matter of annexation. He suggested that Van Zandt inquire of his Government whether it still desired to negotiate a treaty of annexation and that he ask for full powers to act in connection with such a treaty. Van Zandt replied that the proposal for such a treaty should first be made by the American Government and that he was quite certain he would not be authorized to act unless the United States made a definite proposal. Upshur said that he was not prepared to make a definite proposal, and furthermore he did not think it would be proper to make one unless Van Zandt was possessed of full power to negotiate. Van Zandt reported all this to Anson Jones, adding that Upshur had expressed the opinion that an annexation treaty could be safely submitted to the next Senate because of the growing sentiment in all sections of the country in favor of annexation.

This was on September 18th, 1843. Four weeks later, before Van Zandt had time to hear from his Government, Upshur informed him definitely that the American Government was ready to negotiate a treaty of annexation whenever he was possessed of the necessary powers. Upshur admitted that he could not give Texas positive assurance that such a treaty would be acceptable to all branches of the Government, but declared that the President was ready to present the matter to Congress with the strongest kind of recommendations.

When Houston and Anson Jones received Van Zandt's dispatch reporting this definite proposal from the American Government, they soon came to the conclusion, after discussing all the considerations involved, that it would be extremely hazardous for Texas to enter into such a negotiation without greater assurance that an annexation treaty would be ratified by the United States Senate. They decided, therefore, to decline the proposal, and instructions in line with this decision were sent to Van Zandt under date of December 13th, 1843.

"In the present state of our foreign relations," wrote Jones to Van Zandt, "it would not be politic to abandon the expectations which now exist of a speedy settlement of our difficulties with Mexico, through the good offices of other powers, for the very uncertain prospect of annexation to the United States, however desirable that event, if it could be consummated, might be. Were Texas to agree to a treaty of annexation, the good offices of these powers would, it is believed, be immediately withdrawn, and were the treaty then to fail of ratification by the Senate of the United States, Texas would be placed in a much worse situation than she is at present." The Texas Government, Jones said, was duly sensible of the friendly feeling shown by the President of the United States in offering to conclude such a treaty, but at the same time it was of the opinion that approval of such a treaty by other branches of the American Government would at least be very uncertain. "At this particular time, therefore," Jones concluded, "and until such an expression of their opinion can be obtained as would render this measure certain of success, the President (of Texas) deems it most proper and most advantageous to the interests of this country to decline the proposition for concluding such a treaty."

So it was that Texas ceased to "maintain an attitude of supplication towards the United States" and adopted a "different course".

Meantime, the probability of the annexation of Texas to the United States was made the subject of a heated correspondence between Upshur and the Mexican minister at Washington. This post was now occupied by Santa Anna's faithful Almonte, who had attained the rank of General. Almonte had arrived

in Washington in the latter part of 1842, and he had
started almost at once to bombard the Mexican foreign office with fervent exhortations to begin an invasion of Texas without delay. As early as January
25th, 1843, he predicted that the question of annexation would be a leading topic of discussion at the
next session of Congress, which convened the following December. By that time, he sincerely hoped,
Texas would be garrisoned by Mexican troops, and
thus it would be made clear that annexation would
mean war with Mexico. He returned to this subject
again and again, and one can hardly escape the suspicion that somebody in Washington was coaching
Almonte, somebody who needed the argument that
annexation would mean war. On February 7th, for
example, he urged that good use be made of the time
that would elapse between adjournment of the then
current session of Congress on March 4th and the
first Monday in December, when the new Congress
would meet. "It is important that by that time, if the
conquest of Texas is not complete," wrote Almonte,
"at least operations will be well advanced." Then
on March 4th, in transmitting to the Mexican Government a copy of the latest public manifesto of
John Quincy Adams, which made the startling proposal that the Union be dissolved in the event of annexation, Almonte expressed the hope that some part
of Texas would be occupied before Congress met
again, so as to show that the United States could not
annex Texas, except at the cost of war. This formula—that the annexation of Texas would mean war
with Mexico—became the keystone of Mexican
diplomacy, and it first appeared in Almonte's dis-

patches from Washington. Inasmuch as the failure of Mexico to conduct a successful war against Texas during a period of seven years made a threat of war against the United States, including Texas, sound rather empty, Almonte, either as a result of his own deductions or on the advice of somebody in Washington, coupled this formula with urgent insistence on the importance of active Mexican operations against Texas before the question of annexation should come up in Congress. Later, when no such invasion had materialized, this formula took the form of vehement threats, made directly to the American Government.

Incidentally, the Adams document which Almonte transmitted to his Government was in the form of a joint declaration, signed by Adams himself and by Joshua R. Giddings of Ohio and twelve other members of Congress. It was issued on March 3rd, 1843, and was widely printed in the newspapers. Besides rehashing the Lundy story of a Southern "plot" to colonize and detach Texas from Mexico and annex it to the United States, in order to insure that "the undue ascendency of the slave-holding power of the Government shall be secured and riveted beyond all redemption", it declared that annexation would be a violation of the Constitution and therefore "identical with dissolution". It set forth that this would be so unjust and so inimicable to the interests of the free States as to justify fully a dissolution of the Union. The doctrine thus declared was more extreme than Calhoun's "nullification" and on a par with that of the most rabid secessionist. This document was promptly translated into Spanish and circulated in Mexico, where it had a determining effect upon public opinion and national policy. It was among the chief influences which resulted in the decision of the Mexican Government to adopt Almonte's formula before the Tyler administration had made any move in the direction of annexation.

The first enunciation of this formula by the Mexican Government was made in a note from the Minister of Foreign Relations to the American minister in Mexico, Waddy Thompson, on August 23rd, 1843. It announced bluntly that the enactment of any measure by the American Congress having for its object the annexation of Texas would be regarded by the Mexican Government as equivalent to a declaration of war against Mexico. This was a poor substitute for the invasion which Almonte had insisted upon, but it had to serve. At the same time the Mexican Government jumped at the opportunity to discuss an armistice with Texas, which provided an excuse for its inaction, though nearly a year had elapsed between Woll's raid on San Antonio and the armistice, and no preparations had been made for a campaign against Texas. Thompson sent the kind of a reply to the Mexican note that its contents called for. The threat of war, he said, precluded any discussion of the subject. The American Government wanted no war with Mexico, but the constant repetition of such threats was calculated to change that attitude. He asked that such threats be not repeated. Upshur approved this reply, but instructed Thompson that if the Mexican Government addressed him again in such terms to demand an apology.

Almonte repeated this threat in a note directly to the State Department on November 3rd, basing his complaint on common report that annexation would be considered at the next Congress, and a heated correspondence with Upshur resulted. Finally, Upshur made it perfectly clear that the American Government did not feel that it was under any obligation to discuss Texas with Mexico at all. He pointed out that Texas had successfully resisted Mexico's authority for eight years, which was ample proof of the ability of Texas to maintain its independence. "This proof," wrote Upshur, "has been satisfactory to many of the most considerable nations of the world, that have fully acknowledged the independence of Texas, and established diplomatic relations with her. Among these nations the United States are included, and indeed they set the example which other nations have followed. Under these circumstances, the United States regard Texas as in all respects an independent nation, fully competent to manage its own affairs, and possessing all the rights of other independent nations. The Government of the United States, therefore, will not consider it necessary to consult any other nation in its transactions with the Government of Texas." This, it should be noted, was simply a restatement of the American position as it had already been defined by State Department officials, particularly by Daniel Webster.

This position was clearly stated again by President Tyler, when he sent his annual message to Congress on December 5th. If Almonte had any idea of intimidating the administration, he soon had his answer. For Tyler transmitted the whole of the correspondence to Congress with his message, at the same time remarking that "the representatives of a brave and patriotic people will suffer no apprehension of future consequences to embarrass them in the course of their proposed deliberations, nor will the executive department of the Government fail for any such cause to discharge its whole duty to the country."

The President declared boldly that the "predatory incursions", which constituted the sum total of Mexico's efforts to reconquer Texas, must cease. "There must be a limit to all wars," said the President, "and if the parent State after an eight years' struggle has failed to reduce to submission a portion of its subjects standing out in revolt against it, and who have not only proclaimed themselves independent, but have been recognized as such by other powers, she ought not to expect that other nations will quietly look on, to their obvious injury, upon a protraction of hostilities. These United States threw off their colonial dependence and established independent governments, and Great Britain, after having wasted her energies in the attempt to subdue them for a less period than Mexico has attempted to subjugate Texas, had the wisdom and justice to acknowledge their independence, thereby recognizing the obligation which rested on her as one of the family of nations. An example thus set by one of the proudest as well as most powerful nations on earth it could in no way disparage Mexico to imitate. While, therefore, the executive would deplore any collision with Mexico or any disturbance of the friendly relations which exist between the two nations, it cannot permit that Government to control its policy, whatever it may be, toward Texas, but will treat her—as by the recognition of her independence the United

States has long since declared they would do—as entirely independent of Mexico. The high obligations of public duty may enforce from the constituted authorities of the United States a policy which the course persevered in by Mexico will have mainly contributed to produce, and the executive in such a contingency will with confidence throw itself upon the patriotism of the people to sustain the Government in its course of action."

This was Tyler's answer to Almonte's formula to the effect that "annexation means war". The message was interpreted generally to indicate that not only had President Tyler decided on the annexation of Texas, but that he was ready to go to war with Mexico, if this should be the inevitable consequence of such a course. If Almonte was perturbed in any degree by President Tyler's frankness, he was quickly reassured, for within a week after the delivery of the message, on December 11th, he wrote the Mexican Minister of Foreign Relations that there really was nothing to fear. He had had a long talk with John Quincy Adams, he said, and that gentleman had assured him that nothing would come of Tyler's move. The newly elected House of Representatives, to be sure, might have a majority in favor of annexation, but the Senate would never vote for it. Almonte felt certain that this could be depended on, and that while there would be a lot of talk about annexing Texas, it would amount to nothing in the end. President Tyler was very unpopular, he concluded, and all sensible people in the United States were against annexation. Between the lines, this dispatch of Almonte's boiled down to an assurance from John Quincy Adams that there was no danger that Mexico would be called upon to make good its threats.

Houston and Anson Jones took very much the same view of the matter as that expressed by Adams, but when copies of President Tyler's message reached Texas and its contents became generally known, the pressure of public opinion in favor of negotiating a treaty made it difficult for them to maintain this attitude. The Texas Congress was in session, and it soon became apparent that an overwhelming majority of its members favored a treaty. And meantime pressure was being exerted from Washington to convince Houston that the risk was not as great as he believed. Van Zandt took the liberty of delaying formal notification of the Texas Government's decision, and wrote Jones to this effect. At the same time he informed Jones that the American Government would be willing to provide adequate military and naval protection to Texas from the moment a treaty was signed. Van Zandt had told Upshur privately of the instructions he had received, and the latter undertook to supply Murphy in Texas with arguments calculated to cause Houston to change his mind. "Measures have been taken," Upshur wrote Murphy on January 16th, 1844, "to ascertain the opinions and views of Senators upon the subject, and *it is found that a clear constitutional majority of two-thirds are in favor of the measure.* This I learn from sources which do not leave the matter doubtful; and I have reason to know that President Houston himself has received the same information from sources which will command his respect."

The pressure of public opinion in Texas, however, was great enough to cause Houston to change his policy, in spite of his private doubts, without this pressure from Washington. He had ventured, for example, to speak disparagingly in a public address of the manner in which the United States had treated Texas during the previous eight years, contrasting it with the efforts of England to induce Mexico to make peace, and immediately there was a chorus of criticism in Texas newspapers of his "pro-British" attitude. Apparently Anson Jones was more thoroughly convinced than was Houston that an annexation treaty would fail in the American Senate, in spite of all assurances to the contrary, and he seems to have sought to hold Houston in line. But the prospect of annexation to the United States took hold of the feelings of the mass of the people of Texas in a way that brooked no opposition, and Houston was compelled to yield. Accordingly, on January 20th, 1844, Houston sent a special message to a secret session of Congress in which he discussed the whole situation frankly and recommended that a special commissioner be sent to Washington to discuss a treaty of annexation and that Congress make an appropriation for the expenses of such a commissioner. Then, without waiting for the Texas Congress to act on this recommendation, Houston directed Anson Jones to send instructions to Van Zandt to begin negotiations for a treaty, provided he was convinced that the United States Senate would ratify it. These instructions were sent to Van Zandt on January 27th, 1844. Just before adjournment, the Texan Congress appropriated five thousand dollars for the expenses of a special commissioner, and on February 10th Houston named J. Pinckney Henderson as commissioner.

Meantime, Upshur had been having interviews with Almonte in an effort to reconcile Mexico to annexation. He sought to make clear to the Mexican minister that the situation was such that the United States was compelled to choose between annexation and British ascendency in Texas of a character that would be greatly inimicable to the interests and safety of the United States. And he suggested that the United States would be willing to pay an indemnity to Mexico in exchange for its consent to annexation. Almonte was not impressed. He did ask his Government for instructions on the proposal of an indemnity, however, and pointed out that it might be advisable to use this as an excuse to delay the negotiations, but nothing ever came of the proposal. Incidentally, Almonte expressed the opinion to Upshur that England might object to the annexation of Texas, even though Mexico consented to it, whereupon Upshur informed him that President Tyler was willing even to go to war with England over the matter, if that should become necessary, so vital to the interests of the United States did he consider the future status of Texas.

During all this time, at Sabinas, Mexico, the conditions of the armistice between Texas and Mexico, to prevail while a treaty of peace would be negotiated, were being discussed in good faith by the Texas commissioners, Hockley and Williams, with General Woll, who represented Mexico. Even after instructions had been sent to Van Zandt to proceed on an annexation treaty, Houston continued to write

Hockley and Williams in an encouraging tone, and finally on February 18th, 1844, an agreement setting forth the conditions of an armistice was signed. It referred to Texas as a "department" of Mexico, however, and Houston subsequently rejected it on this ground. But he failed to notify Mexico of this decision and it was not disclosed even to Eliot, the British minister in Texas, until he inquired definitely about annexation rumors on March 22nd, 1844, and it was no longer possible to withhold from him the fact that an annexation treaty was contemplated.

The instructions to Van Zandt to proceed with negotiations for an annexation treaty had just reached Washington, when a terrible tragedy interrupted the whole proceeding. On February 28th, 1844, during an inspection by Government officials of the new United States man-of-war *Princeton,* a pivot gun exploded, killing Secretary of State Upshur and four other persons. The tragic accident shocked the whole country, and the Texas negotiations, of course, were suspended. Upshur's death was a great loss to the cause of annexation, especially with respect to the delicate task of getting the Senate to ratify such a treaty. Tyler appointed John C. Calhoun to succeed Upshur, but he sought to have the negotiations concluded by Attorney General Nelson, who temporarily acted as Secretary of State, before Calhoun arrived in Washington to assume the duties of his office. Van Zandt, however, preferred to have Henderson, the special commissioner, to sign the treaty for Texas, and as Calhoun and Henderson reached Washington within a day of each other, it was these two gentlemen who completed the final negotiations.

The treaty, providing for the annexation of Texas to the United States, was signed by them on April 12th, 1844.

Both before and after the signing of the treaty, Calhoun had interviews with Almonte and renewed the proposal to indemnify Mexico, if it would consent to the annexation. He explained, as Upshur had done, that the action was forced upon the United States by the British policy toward Texas, and that no affront of any kind to Mexico was intended. He said that he would send a special messenger to Mexico City to explain this to the Mexican Government. Almonte took the position that his Government had been ignominiously treated, and refused to receive any proposal connected with the annexation treaty.

Calhoun also addressed a note to Packenham, who was now the British minister at Washington, having been transferred from Mexico, in which he replied to a British note which had been delivered to Upshur, just prior to the latter's death. The British note had been occasioned by certain references to alleged British interference in the affairs of Texas contained in President Tyler's message to Congress, and it sought to explain fully Great Britain's policy with respect to the abolition of slavery everywhere. Calhoun could not resist the opportunity to write an extensive criticism of that policy and an elaborate defense of the institution of slavery. The note was addressed to Packenham, but it was intended chiefly for the United States Senate, to which body a copy of it was sent in due course. And the circumstance that Calhoun should have thought it proper to compose such a document in connection with the treaty of annexation illustrates why Tyler desired to conclude the negotiations before he reached Washington.

The treaty was sent to the Senate on April 22nd, 1844, together with a message from President Tyler which set forth at length why, in the opinion of the President, the most vital interests of the country required the incorporation of Texas within the boundaries of the United States. There was only slight reference to slavery in the message, other considerations being stressed by Tyler, and advantages which would accrue to all sections being described in some detail. He emphasized particularly that if the annexation were not consummated without delay, the opportunity might be lost forever. Texas had often before made advances to the United States, he said, but until now these had been repelled. "The hazard of now defeating her wishes," he declared, "may be of the most fatal tendency. It might lead, and most probably would, to such an entire alienation of sentiment and feeling as would inevitably induce her to look elsewhere for aid, and force her either to enter into dangerous alliances with other nations, who, looking with more wisdom to their own interests, would, it is fairly to be presumed, readily adopt such expedients; or she would hold out the proffer of discriminating duties in trade and commerce in order to secure the necessary assistance. Whatever steps she might adopt looking to this object would prove disastrous in the highest degree to the interests of the whole Union."

The treaty had no sooner been submitted to the Senate than the opinion became general that it would not be ratified. For one thing, both Henry Clay and Martin Van Buren, the outstanding leaders respectively of the Whig and the Democratic parties, declared at once against its ratification and against the annexation of Texas by any other means. Both of these men were expected to be nominated for the Presidency in a few weeks, Clay by the Whigs and Van Buren by the Democrats, and their opposition to the treaty was taken to mean that strict party men of both parties would oppose it. Another unfavorable feature of the situation was that Tyler's friends, just about this time, announced him as an independent candidate for reelection, with the slogan "Tyler and Texas". And Calhoun's pro-slavery argument in the treaty's support had not helped matters, either.

Even before Clay and Van Buren declared against the treaty, C. H. Raymond, secretary of the Texas legation at Washington, wrote Anson Jones that he had "scarcely any hope of its ratification". He said that the coupling of Tyler's candidacy with annexation had been injurious to it, and he complained also of Calhoun's pro-slavery note. "I have just been informed," wrote Raymond, "that Mr. Calhoun has, in his letter to the Senate, placed the question almost solely on the ground of British interference with the institution of slavery, and presents this as the grand argument for the measure. Such a position may answer with the South, but it will only create and strengthen opposition North and West. Indeed, I have heard this morning that the views of Mr. Calhoun have brought the Ohio Senators into opposition. They say that if this Government rests the policy of the measure upon the alone fact, as Mr. Calhoun's letter does, of the question of slavery, they can not,

in justice to the State they represent, and the interests
of even the whole country, vote for the treaty."

This letter was written two days after the submission of the treaty to the Senate. Four days after this,
on April 28th, 1844, W. D. Miller, secretary to Hen-
deson, the special Texas commissioner, wrote Anson
Jones as follows: "Both Clay and Van Buren are out
against annexation *in extenso*. . . . You may now be
fully assured that the treaty will be lost; I verily believe it will not receive ten votes in its favor. Mr.
Tyler's strength amounts to nothing, and with the
exception of two or three friends who are fully identified with the measure, both of the rival parties,
Whigs and Democrats, will be united against us. . . .
You may rely upon it that we shall *never* be annexed
to this country—they will never receive us. Everything here goes according to party organization, and
no party will probably ever be able to command two-
thirds of the Senatorial branch of Congress to ratify
a treaty."

These appraisals of the situation were fairly accurate. The Texas treaty was doomed to defeat, and it
really looked as if Texas, to quote further from Miller's letter, was "in a bad predicament". However,
Raymond reported to Jones that he had had a talk
with Packenham, the British minister, who assured
him that "if the treaty should be rejected, the fact
of its having been made would not change Great
Britain's friendly policy to Texas".

"We must, of course, look to ourselves," wrote
Miller, "and to some line of policy which may best
suit our condition. What that is must in a great degree depend upon circumstances."

CHAPTER XXXIX

A MANDATE FROM THE PEOPLE

CLAY and Van Buren both planned to keep the annexation question out of the Presidential campaign of 1844, and there is basis for the belief that privately they made some sort of an agreement on the subject. But they reckoned without a due respect for the resourcefulness of John Tyler in arousing public sentiment and for the power of such sentiment in the United States to determine political issues.

The Clay and Van Buren statements were published the same day, though this was probably a coincidence, and, while it is certain they were prepared independently of each other, the arguments they presented were very similar. Both gentlemen affected to be greatly concerned over Mexico's alleged rights in the matter, though each of them, when occupying the office of Secretary of State, had been entirely unmindful of Spanish rights with respect to Texas by offering to purchase the province from Mexico at a time when Spain continued to assert sovereignty over it. Clay had made such an offer to Mexico in 1825, which was only four years after American ratification of a solemn treaty with Spain fixing the boundary at the Sabine, and Van Buren had made a similar offer in 1829, when a Spanish army was actually on Mexican soil for the purpose of reestablishing Spain's sovereignty over that country. The truth was, of course, that the concern for Mexican rights which they professed to feel was not the impelling reason for their attitude. The impelling reason was their mutual desire to avoid all discussion of slavery during the campaign, and because, in common with most American politicians of the time, they both regarded everything pertaining to Texas as having become inextricably entangled with the slavery question. Indeed, Clay rather incautiously let the cat out of the bag by citing as one of the reasons for his position the circumstance that annexation would be "in decided opposition to the wishes of a considerable and respectable portion of the confederacy", and that consequently it would introduce a new element of discord and distraction.

Clay was very much peeved that the issue should be raised at all, and as early as December 5th, 1843, the day Tyler's annual message was read to Congress, he wrote to a friend that he did not "think it right to allow Mr. Tyler, for his own selfish purposes, to introduce an exciting topic, and add to the other subjects of contention which exist in this country". Just whom Clay blamed for "allowing" Mr. Tyler to introduce this "exciting topic" and how, in his opinion, Mr. Tyler might have been prevented from doing whatever he chose "for his own selfish purposes" it would be difficult to imagine. The attitude of both Clay and Van Buren was characteristic of a time when "leading statesmen" arrogated to themselves the right to determine precisely what issues should be passed on by the electorate. Clay's peevishness was easily understandable, however. He was perfectly familiar with all of the issues for which Van Buren stood, and knew his attitude on all public questions, and he had full faith in his own ability to deal with all this in the campaign and to win the election. But Tyler had impertinently introduced a new and "exciting" topic, and this disturbed the outlook to which Clay's plans had been adjusted. The two statements on this new topic, showing substantial agreement on the part of the two prospective candidates, were intended to meet this situation effectively.

Van Buren, however, recognized that this might not dispose of the matter, and that his position on annexation might endanger his nomination. He declared frankly that he was aware of the risk he ran. The probable truth is that Van Buren had concluded that a nomination on a platform declaring for the annexation of Texas would be worthless and would lead to defeat at the polls. Clay's situation was entirely different. He would have endangered his own nomination by favoring annexation, and if he took any stand at all it had to be against the treaty. He would have preferred to remain silent on the subject, but Tyler's boldness in sending the treaty to the Senate on the very eve of the Presidential campaign rendered such a course politically impossible.

The Whig convention met at Baltimore on May 1st. It was entirely harmonious and Clay was nominated by acclamation. It adopted a short statement of Whig "principles", which was simply a condensation of Clay's well known views, but it carefully refrained from making any mention of the annexation of Texas. This, of course, was in line with the plan.

to keep that subject and everything pertaining to slavery out of the campaign.

The Democratic convention was scheduled to meet on May 27th, also at Baltimore, and meantime President Tyler saw to it that the annexation question was kept before the public in a way to increase sentiment in favor of the treaty. He played a trump card on May 16th, just eleven days before the Democratic convention would meet, by transmitting to the Senate a copy of a letter written by Andrew Jackson to a friend, accompanied by a special message emphasizing its significance. In this letter Jackson declared that "the present golden moment to obtain Texas must not be lost, or Texas might from necessity be thrown into the arms of England and forever lost to the United States." Tyler called the Senate's attention to the fact that this letter was written after Jackson had had an interview with a confidential messenger from Sam Houston, and that consequently his statement was made "with a full knowledge of all circumstances, and ought to be received as conclusive of what will be the course of Texas should the present treaty fail." "I entertain not the least doubt," Tyler added, "that if annexation should now fail it will in all human probability fail forever. Indeed, I have strong reasons to believe that instructions have already been given by the Texas Government to propose to the Government of Great Britain, forthwith on the failure, to enter into a treaty of commerce and an alliance offensive and defensive."

Tyler declared in this message that since the submission of the treaty to the Senate the question of annexation had been "much agitated". And this sort of thing was infallibly calculated to keep it "agitated" until the Democratic delegates gathered at Baltimore. By the time the convention met it was the dominant topic of political discussion throughout the country. And as the delegates exchanged views it became evident that there was general agreement among them that Van Buren's statement was a "fatal blunder", and yet a majority of them were under instructions from their constituencies to vote for Van Buren. The burning question was, "What will the convention do about it?" It was a perplexing question, and its answer was not made any simpler when the friends of President Tyler descended upon Baltimore the very day the convention was called to order, held a nominating gathering of their own, and invited the voters of the country to rally under the banner of "Tyler and Texas".

As the Democratic convention proceeded to organize, the question arose almost immediately as to whether the two-thirds rule should be adopted. This rule was then only twelve years old, for the 1844 meeting was only the fourth nominating convention of the party. It had not been really important at the three previous conventions, for all of them had been without contests for the nomination. But at this convention Van Buren's chances for the nomination were at stake. If the two-thirds rule should not be adopted, Van Buren probably would be nominated on the first ballot; if it should be adopted, Van Buren probably would lose the nomination. And yet, in spite of the fact that a majority of the delegates were under instructions to vote for Van Buren, the two-thirds rule was adopted by a vote of 148 to 118. With 266 votes in the convention, this meant that 178 votes would be necessary to nominate.

The convention proceeded to vote, and on the first ballot Van Buren's total was 146, a majority of 26 votes over all the other candidates together, but 32 votes short of the necessary two-thirds. Gen. Lewis Cass of Michigan, who had declared in favor of annexation, was in second place with 83 votes, and the rest of the votes were scattered among five other candidates. On the second ballot Van Buren's vote fell to 127, seven votes less than a majority, and that of Cass rose to 94. On the third ballot Van Buren lost another six votes, his total falling to 121, and at the same time the Cass vote fell to 92. From that point Van Buren's vote fell off with each ballot, and Cass continued to gain. The fourth ballot gave Van Buren 111 and Cass 105; Cass passed Van Buren on the fifth ballot, the result being 103 for Van Buren to 107 for Cass; the sixth ballot stood 101 for Van Buren and 116 for Cass, and the seventh showed 99 for Van Buren and 123 for Cass.

By this time it had become clear that more than one-third of the delegates, chiefly Van Buren supporters, would not vote for Cass under any circumstances, and no other candidate had developed much show of strength. On the seventh ballot, the last of the first day's session, only two other candidates received any votes, these being James Buchanan of Pennsylvania with 22 votes, and Richard M. Johnson of Kentucky with 21 votes. Johnson had received 38 votes on the third ballot, but had lost ground on every ballot thereafter. Buchanan's greatest strength had been shown on the fifth ballot, but even then he had received only 26 votes. When the first day's session adjourned, therefore, the convention seemed hopelessly deadlocked. And the cause of this was the Texas annexation issue. President Tyler had succeeded in blocking Van Buren's nomination.

No such situation had ever arisen before in a political convention, and most of the delegates were completely at a loss as to what should be done. During the night, however, there was much conferring, and when the eighth ballot was taken the next day it showed 104 for Van Buren, 114 for Cass, and 44 for James K. Polk of Tennessee. Prior to this ballot Polk had not received a single vote. His was an entirely new name on the list of candidates, and the first time it appeared his vote was greater than any other candidate, except the two leaders, had received on any ballot. Polk, a former Governor of Tennessee, had served in Congress and had been Speaker of the House, but he also had been twice defeated for Governor. He was not counted among the important leaders of the party, his abilities were not more than ordinary, and he had been thought of only as one among many candidates for second place on the ticket. But he was known as an ardent advocate of the annexation of Texas, and it was said that Jackson was favorable to his candidacy if Van Buren could not be nominated. During those night conferences his friends had won over the New Hampshire delegation and seven votes from Massachusetts, and these had been joined by the Tennessee and Alabama delegations and a few scattering delegates from other States. In the existing situation, the effect of his unexpected show of strength was immediate. On the ninth ballot the New York delegation withdrew Van Buren's name and voted for Polk and the stampede was on. When it was over it was found that the Democratic Party had nominated its first dark horse by acclamation.

George M. Dallas of Pennsylvania was named as the party's nominee for Vice President and the convention then adopted the platform, which included a declaration in favor of the "re-annexation" of Texas. This declaration was coupled with another asserting an American title to the "whole of the territory of Oregon" in a resolution reading as follows:

"Resolved, that our title to the whole of the territory of Oregon is clear and unquestionable; that no portion of the same ought to be ceded to England or any other power; and that the re-occupation of Oregon and the re-annexation of Texas at the earliest practical period are great American measures which this convention recommends to the cordial support of the Democracy of the Union."

This was the "Fifty-four forty or fight" plank of the platform, and while an effort was made by means of this slogan to emphasize the Oregon part of the recommendation, the real issue of the campaign was the annexation of Texas.

Congress had recessed during the period of the convention, and when it reconvened the Senate proceeded at once to take up the Tyler treaty of annexation. With Tyler out as a candidate for reelection, using the treaty as his platform, both Whig and Democratic Senators had resolved to dispose of it as quickly as possible. Accordingly, a direct vote on ratification was taken on June 8th, 1844, with the result that only sixteen Senators voted in favor of it, and thirty-five voted against it. And so the Tyler treaty was rejected by a vote of more than two to one.

The resourceful Tyler was fully prepared for this, however, and three days later he sent a message to the House of Representatives, submitting all the correspondence and other papers bearing on the matter to a consideration of its members, and recommending that annexation be effected through the action of a majority of the two houses of Congress. "While the treaty was pending before the Senate," he said in this message, "I did not consider it compatible with the just rights of that body or consistent with the respect entertained for it to bring this important subject before you. The power of Congress is, however, fully competent in some other form of proceeding to accomplish everything that a formal ratification of the treaty could have accomplished, and I therefore feel that I should but imperfectly discharge my duty to yourselves or the country if I failed to lay before you everything in the possession of the Executive which would enable you to act with full light on the subject if you would deem it proper to take any action upon it." Tyler emphasized the national character of the proposal to annex Texas, avoiding entirely the question of slavery. "I have regarded it as not a little fortunate," he said, "that the question involved was no way sectional or local, but addressed itself to the interests of every part of the country and made its appeal to the glory of the American name." He then proceeded to discuss the principal objections which had been urged against the treaty in the Senate, setting forth that none of them stood up under impartial examination. And he emphasized again the neccessity of prompt action.

"With the views which I entertain on the subject," he said, "I should prove faithless to the high trust which the Constitution has devolved upon me if I neglected to invite the attention of the representatives of the people to it at the earliest moment that a due respect for the Senate would allow me so to do. I should find in the urgency of the matter a sufficient apology, if one was wanting, since annexation is to encounter a great, if not certain, hazard of final defeat if something be not *now* done to prevent it." On this point he directed the attention of the members to his message to the Senate of May 16th and to Jackson's letter, and he concluded by saying that while he would have preferred to accomplish annexation by means of a treaty, the object could be attained through another constitutional method. "The great question," he said, "is not as to the manner in which it shall be done, but whether it shall be accomplished or not. The responsibility of deciding this question is now devolved upon you."

This message was sent to the House within a week of the adjournment of Congress, so that its object could not have been that of obtaining any immediate action. What it did, and what Tyler undoubtedly intended it should do, was to keep the annexation question alive before Congress during the Presidential campaign, in spite of the rejection of the treaty.

During the early days of the campaign the Democrats were not very confident of victory. Van Buren's defeat in the convention had left much soreness, and there was no enthusiasm for Polk. It was recognized that Clay was by far the abler man of the two, and with Tyler in the race on a platform similar to that of the Democrats it was feared that a divided vote would result in Clay's election. Democratic leaders, including even Jackson, set to work to bring about Tyler's withdrawal from the race and the return of his followers to the Democratic fold. Tyler was assured that they would be received with open arms. Tyler recognized fully that his continued candidacy might result in the defeat of the cause of annexation and the election of Clay, and he finally yielded. On August 21st he issued a statement announcing his withdrawal from the race and his support of Polk. About the same time the extreme anti-slavery men assembled in the convention of "the Liberty Party" and nominated James G. Birney of Ohio for the Presidency. These two events heartened the Democrats considerably, and as Van Buren set a good example to his followers by getting behind the ticket, they were soon conducting an enthusiastic campaign.

Clay and the Whigs sought to avoid the annexation issue, but it soon became evident that it was the dominant question of the campaign, so far as the interest of the public was concerned, and Clay was compelled to write no less than six restatements of his stand on the question, "explaining" his original statement. In the end he left himself unguarded from the charge that he was against annexation in the North and for it in the South. While Birney and the Liberty Party were opposing annexation on the ground that it would enhance the "slave power", Clay, anxious to give the impression that under cer-

tain conditions he might favor annexation, was finally
forced into a declaration that he did not think "the
subject of slavery ought to affect the question, one
way or the other."

Texas leaders observed all these events in the
United States with mixed feelings. They rejoiced
over Van Buren's defeat in the Democratic convention, of course, and they hoped to see Clay meet the
same fate in the election, but they did not relish the
spectacle of Texas being made a political football
by American politicians. They feared it would all
result in no good for Texas. Houston and Anson
Jones had been compelled to consent to a treaty by the
pressure of public opinion, and it was poor consolation to them to be able to say "I told you so" when
events justified their fears. Houston's first impulse
was to call the whole thing off as soon as he learned
of Clay's and Van Buren's opposition, and he immediately sent instructions to Henderson, the special
commissioner, to make no further effort in the matter.
Henderson expressed regret that Houston should
take this attitude, because, he said, he thought the
friends of Texas could elect Polk, "provided the
question of annexation remained a pending question,
to be decided by the result of the Presidential election." Houston evidently was of the opinion that a
policy of offended pride would be more effective, for
when Van Zandt asked to be relieved of his post at
Washington, Houston decided not to replace him for
the time being. "I am led to believe," he wrote Jones,
"that our minister's leaving Washington City will
have a favorable influence on the general concerns
of Texas. We shall have to be as sharp-eyed as

lynxes, as wary as foxes, for we are not yet out of the woods."

As Houston's term of office neared its close, Anson Jones became a candidate for President, and, as if to add insult to injury, the latter's political enemies charged him with being opposed to annexation. Occupying the post of Secretary of State, Jones felt that the condition of the Republic's foreign relations made it inadvisable for him to reply publicly to this charge, and in consequence it was widely reported in the United States that annexation was the leading issue in the Texas campaign and that Jones was the candidate opposed to it. When Jones was elected, therefore, near the close of the Presidential campaign in the United States, American newspapers reported the result as an expression against annexation by the people of Texas. This really tended to help Polk by stressing the importance of prompt action by the American Government, if the opportunity to annex Texas was not to be lost forever.

A wait-and-see policy was adopted by England, after the British minister at Washington succeeded in convincing Lord Aberdeen that the surest way to cause the American people to elect Polk and to annex Texas would be for England to make a definite move of some kind against annexation. When it first became clear that Tyler intended to negotiate an annexation treaty, England and France agreed to file a joint protest with the American Government against such action, but they soon abandoned this plan as likely to defeat its object. Lord Aberdeen did, however, inform Ashbel Smith, the Texan minister at London, that if Texas would refuse annexation, England and France would be willing to become parties to a "diplomatic act", under the terms of which Texas would be guaranteed its independence, recognized by Mexico, and Mexico would be protected against any armed action by the United States. Smith received this proposal without comment, and communicated it to Anson Jones and Houston for their information. "Should any circumstances occur," Smith wrote Jones, "which may render annexation not desirable by Texas, I believe, nevertheless, the present occasion a favorable one for making advantageous commercial arrangements with Great Britain and France. We may also insist on a treaty with Spain in reference to our commerce with Cuba; for it is believed that the word of the king of the French is all potent with the Spanish Government. I have not omitted to urge the importance we attach to the commerce of Cuba in my conversations with these Governments. If deemed best to give me any instructions relative to this subject, I think no time should be lost in transmitting them to me."

The proposal of a "diplomatic act" was not unattractive to Houston, and, after thinking it over a few weeks, he actually sent a written order to Anson Jones to instruct Smith to proceed with negotiations for such a compact. Jones, who already had been elected President, and who believed that such a pact would have meant war between England and the United States, with great injury to Texas regardless of its outcome, took the liberty of pigeon-holing this order. Instead of obeying it, he sent instructions to Smith to return home. Jones had decided to make Smith his Secretary of State, which he did in due course, and to send George W. Terrell, an uncompromising opponent of annexation, to Europe in his place. Houston seems to have leaned, during the closing months of his administration, in the direction of keeping Texas an independent nation, and even Jones would not have regarded this as the worst fate that could befall Texas. Moreover, Terrell was not by any means the only Texan of ability and influence who strongly opposed annexation.

The Texans watched the progress of the Presidential campaign in the United States as closely as the existing means of communication permitted. Raymond reported from Washington that "the Democracy were never in finer spirits, and they certainly have cheering indications of success from all quarters of the Union." "Our Democratic friends in this country," he added, "are anxious that Texas should await the issue of the pending election, before she resolves against annexation." Others thought it would have a better effect to keep the United States guessing. Col. James Morgan, in congratulating Jones on his election to the Presidency, wrote: "A hint in your message at a reduction of the tariff will create a favorable alarm in the United States." Some of the correspondence of the Texans on the subject of the campaign showed remarkably accurate knowledge of the trend it was taking. Barnard E. Bee, for example, wrote to Jones from Charleston, South Carolina, that Silas Wright of New York was of the opinion that the Democrats had "everything to hope" in that State. "And New York, you know, decides the question," added Bee. "It is thought that, at the last moment the abolitionists will abandon their own candidate, and rally upon Mr. Clay. This may elect him; but all is uncertainty." Bee's letter was written late in October, only three weeks before the election. A month earlier than this, W. B. Ochiltree wrote to Jones from San Augustine as follows: "Mr. Tyler has withdrawn from the canvass. . . . Mr. Clay has come out emphatically denying his opposition to annexation. There is a strong showing, I think, on the part of the abolitionists to cast their vote for an independent candidate; if they do, it may seriously affect Mr. Clay's prospects, as a very slight waver in New York, Ohio, and Pennsylvania would produce most important results."

The outcome of the election proved this to be almost a precisely correct analysis of the situation. The election was held on November 12th, and Polk was elected. And it is a fact that if Clay had received 16,000 votes which were cast for Birney in New York the result would have been reversed. For Polk's plurality over Clay in that State was only 5,000, and without New York's electoral vote he would have lost the election.

Nevertheless, Polk's victory was decisive, his electoral vote being 170 to Clay's 105. And there was nothing sectional about it. Besides New York, Polk carried the "free" States of Maine, New Hampshire, Pennsylvania, Michigan, Illinois, and Indiana. Clay, on the other hand, carried four of the slave States—Maryland, North Carolina, Kentucky, and Tennessee. But it was in the Congressional races that the most smashing victory was scored. The Democrats won 120 seats in the House to only 72 won by the Whigs. And Democratic leaders, including President Tyler, now back in the fold, interpreted this vote as an emphatic mandate from the American people in favor of the annexation of Texas.

Three weeks after the election, President Tyler, in his annual message to the "lame duck" session of Congress, called upon the representatives of the people to carry out their will with respect to the annexation of Texas. "The decision of the people on this great and interesting subject has been decisively manifested," he declared. "The question of annexation has been presented nakedly to their consideration. . . . A controlling majority of the people and a large majority of the States have declared in favor of immediate annexation. It is the will of both the people and the States that Texas shall be annexed to the Union promptly and immediately."

The President's proposal, of course, was that the annexation should be effected by means of a joint resolution of Congress, and without a treaty. This would require only a majority vote in each house of Congress. But it also meant that the United States would have to act without committing Texas, and the Texas officials, headed by Anson Jones, conceived it to be their best policy to manifest a receptive attitude, but without giving any assurance that an annexation proposal from the American Government would be accepted. They sought to give the impression that the terms of the proposal would be important, and that certainly it was not true that Texas would accept annexation "regardless of the terms". No new minister had been sent to Washington by the Texans, and their affairs at the American capital were still cared for by the secretary of the legation,

Charles H. Raymond. A good idea of the Texas attitude may be had from a letter written by Raymond to Anson Jones on December 17th, 1844, in which he said:

"Members of Congress, and others, are continually making inquiries and seeking information from me relative to Texas, and I am thus kept continually employed. I am frequently asked, what are the present views of our Government in regard to annexation? I answer, that having been repeatedly repulsed and rejected, we do not feel disposed to place ourselves in a condition to be similarly treated again. That we have not, however, interposed any obstacle to the measure, but, on the contrary, avoiding all entangling alliances, have kept the question open and free for the action of both countries; and that when the necessary provision for an admission into this Union has been made, then it will be time for our Government to declare its disposition and mark its course."

Several resolutions providing for annexation, each embodying a different plan, had been introduced in the House, but the chief point of difference was with respect to Texas's public debt. The rejected Tyler treaty had provided for the assumption of the Texas debt by the Government of the United States, and those who still favored such a provision argued that it was a small price to pay for such a rich region, and that the public lands of Texas would more than reimburse the United States. There were those who, while favoring annexation, opposed assuming this debt, however, and who declared they were willing for Texas to keep its public lands, provided it also kept its debts. It was argued that Texas might not be willing to accept annexation unless its public debt was assumed by the United States, that the prospect of such assumption was one of the chief objects of annexation from the standpoint of the Texans. But it became apparent that the inclusion of such a provision in the resolution would endanger its passage in the House, and so the plan of having Texas to keep both its public lands and its debts was adopted. A joint resolution embodying this plan was finally passed by the House on January 25th, 1845, by a vote of 118 to 101. The text of this resolution was as follows:

"*Resolved by the Senate and House of Representatives of the United States of America in Congress assembled,*

"That Congress doth consent that the territory properly included within, and rightfully belonging to, the Republic of Texas, may be erected into a new State, to be called the State of Texas, with a republican form of government adopted by the people of said Republic, by deputies in convention assembled, with the consent of the existing Government, in order that the same may be admitted as one of the States of this Union.

"*And be it further resolved,* That the foregoing consent of Congress is given upon the following conditions, to-wit:

"*First:* Said State to be formed subject to the adjustment by this Government of all questions of boundary that may arise with other Governments, and the Constitution thereof, with the proper evidence of its adoption by the people of said Republic of Texas, be laid before Congress for its final action, on or before the first day of January, 1846.

"Second: Said State, when admitted into the Union, after ceding to the United States all public edifices, fortifications, barracks, ports and harbors, navy yards, docks, magazines and armaments, and all other means pertaining to the public defense, belonging to the said Republic, shall retain all the public funds, taxes and dues of every kind which may belong to or be due and owing to said Republic; and shall also retain all vacant and unappropriated lands lying within its limits, to be applied to the payment of the debts and liabilities of said Republic of Texas, and the residue of said lands, after discharging said debts and liabilities, to be disposed of as said State may direct; but in no event are said debts and liabilities to become a charge upon the Government of the United States.

"Third: New States of convenient size, not exceeding four in number, in addition to said State of Texas, and having sufficient population, may hereafter, by the consent of said State, be formed out of the territory thereof, which shall be entitled to admission under the provisions of the Federal Constitution; and such States as may be formed out of that portion of said territory lying south of thirty-six degrees thirty minutes, north latitude, commonly known as the Missouri Compromise Line, shall be admitted into the Union with or without slavery, as the people of each State asking admission may desire; and in such State or States as shall be formed out of said territory north of said Missouri Com-

promise Line, slavery or involuntary servitude (except for crime) shall be prohibited."

The "third" provision in the above resolution, which is frequently cited as endowing Texas with special rights and powers, merely embodies the method decided upon to extend the Missouri Compromise line to the western boundary of Texas, a provision insisted upon by some members of Congress, inasmuch as a considerable part of Texas as it was then constituted was north of the line. The right to divide into two or more States and to seek admission to the Union for such States "under the provisions of the Federal Constitution" is possessed by every State to an equal degree with Texas. If anything, this provision placed a limitation on Texas by providing that the new States shall not exceed four in number, though it is doubtful that one Congress possesses power to bind succeeding Congresses in this way. Be this as it may, the object of this condition in the resolution was to extend the Missouri Compromise line to the western boundary of Texas. Like the Compromise itself, which was subsequently repealed by mere Congressional enactment, it amounted to a gentlemen's agreement limiting the number of States that might be carved from the new territory.

When the resolution reached the floor of the Senate, the question was again raised as to whether Texas would accept annexation on such terms. It was urged that the refusal to assume the public debt of Texas might endanger annexation for all time. To meet this objection and to provide for the contingency of a rejection of the terms by Texas, an amendment was

adopted empowering the President, should he deem
it more advisable, to negotiate with the Republic of
Texas for its admission into the Union on such terms
and conditions as might be mutually agreed upon by
the two Governments. The resolution, thus amended,
was adopted by the Senate on February 26th, 1845,
by a vote of 27 ayes to 25 noes. The change of a
single vote would have defeated the resolution by a
tie. The division, however, was not along sectional
lines. The slave States were almost equally divided
in the vote. The Senators from Virginia, Louisiana,
Kentucky, and Tennessee voted solidly against the
resolution, and those from Alabama, Georgia, North
Carolina, and Maryland were divided. Only four
of the slave States—Missouri, Arkansas, South Carolina, and Mississippi—gave a solid vote in favor of
the resolution. On the other hand, the Senators from
New Hampshire, New York, Pennsylvania, Ohio,
and Illinois voted solidly for the resolution, and
Maine and Connecticut each gave one vote in its
favor. The truth was that the division was strictly
along party lines, with two exceptions. Two Whig
Senators voted for the resolution, but all the other
votes in its favor were those of Democrats. All of
the votes against the measure were Whig votes. The
Whigs were smarting under the recent defeat of their
idol Henry Clay, and they simply would not vote for
a measure sponsored by that "double renegade", John
Tyler.

As for Tyler himself, he was finishing his term as
President with much reason for satisfaction. The
House promptly accepted the Senate amendment to
the annexation resolution, and on March 1st, three

days before James K. Polk would be inaugurated,
Tyler signed the measure. Then on March 3rd, his
last day in office and the eighth anniversary of American recognition of Texas independence, he dispatched instructions to A. J. Donelson, the American
chargé d'affaires in Texas, to propose to the Texas
Government its acceptance of the terms of the original House resolution. The new President, Mr. Polk,
would have to complete the job of bringing Texas
into the Union, but Tyler had the satisfaction of
knowing that if annexation should be consummated,
the glory of that achievement would belong to him
more than to any other man.

On March 6th, 1845, Almonte, who had believed
almost to the last that the Senate would never vote
for annexation, filed a vehement protest with the
State Department against the resolution and asked
for his passports. In reply, James Buchanan, the new
Secretary of State, informed him that it was too late
a day "to reopen a discussion which has already been
exhausted, and again to prove that Texas has long
since achieved her independence of Mexico."
"Neither Mexico nor any other nation," he said,
"will have just complaint against the United States
for admitting her into this Union." At the same time
he expressed the President's regret that Mexico
should choose to take offense, and assured Almonte
that every effort would be made to adjust amicably
all differences between the two countries.

Almonte kept a belligerent attitude to the last, but
the invasion of Texas, which he had urged upon the
Mexican Government for more than two years, never
materialized. Santa Anna had done much talking

about reconquering Texas, but he had not sent a single soldier across the Rio Grande. Some show of belligerency was made at the time of the signing of the Tyler treaty, but the American Government then warned Santa Anna in no uncertain terms that it would not sit idly by and see Texas attacked on account of that treaty. However, Santa Anna was really convinced that Texas could not be reconquered, and there was good ground for the charge, made by his enemies, that he used the constant promise of a Texas campaign as an excuse to lay new and heavy burdens on the people.

At the moment that Almonte was asking for his passports at Washington, Santa Anna had come to the end of his rope and was in prison, awaiting the verdict of the Mexican Congress, which was considering impeachment charges against him and deliberating upon his fate. During the previous three years Santa Anna had ruled Mexico with a high hand. Not even in the reign of the Emperor Augustín I had there been such lavish public show of luxury and extravagance. It was during this period that there occurred one of the most fantastically extravagant and bizarre incidents of Santa Anna's extraordinary career: the ceremony of burying the foot which he had lost in his skirmish with the French at Vera Cruz. The amputated foot was brought to the capital and was given a gorgeous military funeral, which was attended by all the members of the cabinet and the general staff of the army; it was honored by a salute of artillery, and a funeral discourse was delivered over it by a dignitary of the Church. This was a characteristic public show of "pomp and glory" in a period of corruption in high places and neglect of the general welfare.

The time came, however, when patriotic Mexicans began to say that this sort of thing had to end. When Santa Anna asked Congress to levy additional burdensome taxes for a war against Texas, it became common gossip that he really wanted money for new extravagances, and that the talk about Texas was subterfuge. And then when a member of the House of Deputies arose during a debate on this measure and declared that the man who had lost Texas by going to sleep in the face of the enemy had no right to lay grievous burdens on the people, under the pretext that he would reconquer that province, this declaration was wildly cheered in the galleries. That was the beginning of the end. In due course angry crowds were making insulting demonstrations around Santa Anna's statues in the capital, and, at the suggestion of some leader with a sense of poetic fitness, the coffin containing the honored foot of the hero of Vera Cruz was taken from its tomb and dragged by a wildly yelling mob through the streets of Mexico City. In the course of a few months things reached a point where Santa Anna concluded it would be best for him to flee the country, but on January 15th, 1845, while he was attempting to make his way to the coast, he was captured. He was brought back to the capital and imprisoned in the castle of Perote. Congress finally ordered his banishment from Mexico, and he left the country on June 3rd, 1845, to reside in Cuba. In March, therefore, he was still in prison, and Gen. José Joaquin Herrera was President *ad interim* and Luis Gonzago Cuevas was Minister of Foreign Relations.

The Mexican Government, as thus constituted, formally severed diplomatic relations with the United States on March 28th, by handing the American minister at Mexico City his passports. But more than a week before taking this action, Cuevas had informed the British minister at the Mexican capital that Mexico was prepared to receive overtures from the Republic of Texas, with a view to Mexican recognition of its complete independence, on condition that Texas agree not to annex itself or become subject to any other country! And before this information could reach Texas (and twenty-four hours before Donelson officially presented the annexation offer of the United States), the Texas Government had authorized Captain Eliot to make a similar proposal to Mexico, with the understanding that the people of Texas should be given the opportunity to accept or reject any resulting agreement.

This almost simultaneous action by the Mexican and Texan Governments was the result of eleventh-hour activities of both the British and French ministers at Mexico City and in Texas, acting under instructions from home. It was too late, of course, for anything of this kind, for there was never the shadow of a doubt about the attitude of the people of Texas toward the proposal contained in the resolution of the American Congress. The news of the adoption of the resolution was received with universal rejoicing in Texas, and whatever the attitude of the Texas officials might have been, it was clear, without a referendum, that public opinion was so emphatic and overwhelming as to amount to a mandate. Nevertheless, the proposal to have Mexico formally recognize the independence of Texas, even conditionally, was of genuine importance to Texas, and when Captain Eliot and Count A. de Saligny, British and French ministers to Texas, presented to Secretary of State Ashbel Smith the instructions of their respective Governments to proffer their good offices in negotiating with Mexico, President Anson Jones instructed Smith to enter into an agreement with them. Accordingly, on March 29th, 1845, a document was signed by which the Texas Government agreed to proclaim the conclusion of preliminaries of peace with Mexico upon receipt of the signature of a duly authorized official of the Mexican Government attached to certain agreed conditions. The Texas Government also agreed that for a period of ninety days it would not "accept any proposal, nor enter into any negotiations to annex itself to any other country." The conditions, to which it was proposed both countries should agree as "preliminary to a treaty of peace between Mexico and Texas", were set forth under four heads, as follows:

"1. Mexico agrees to acknowledge the independence of Texas.

"2. Texas agrees that she will stipulate in the treaty not to annex herself or become subject to any country whatever.

"3. Limits and other conditions to be matter of arrangement in the final treaty.

"4. Texas will be willing to remit disputed points, respecting territory and other matters, to the arbitration of umpires."

Captain Eliot was provided with a copy of these conditions, formally signed "Ashbel Smith, Secretary of State", and he left at once for Mexico City. The proposal was laid before the Mexican Congress on April 21st, 1845. In due course it was approved by the Chamber of Deputies by a vote of 41 to 13, and subsequently by the Senate by a vote of 30 to 6, and President Herrera signed the measure accepting the proposal on May 19th, 1845. Captain Eliot delivered an official copy of this document to the Texas Government on June 4th, 1845, and President Anson Jones immediately issued a proclamation declaring the conclusion of a preliminary peace with Mexico.

Meantime, on April 15th, President Jones had issued a call for a special session of the Texan Congress, to convene on June 16th, and then on May 5th he issued a proclamation providing for a convention of representatives of the people of Texas, to begin its sessions on July 4th. The special session of the Congress was called so that "the consent of the existing Government" could be given (or denied) to the annexation proposal. The convention, in addition to acting on the proposal, would have the duty of drafting the State Constitution, in the event annexation was accepted.

There was not the slightest doubt about annexation being accepted. All the successive steps necessary to annex Texas to the United States and to admit it as a State into the Union were taken in routine order. The special session of the Texan Congress opened when the "preliminary peace" with Mexico had been in effect less than two weeks. President Jones submitted the "treaty" to the Senate, but privately he asked his friends in that body to postpone action on it, so that the "peace" might continue in effect until after the action of the convention. But the members could see no point to this. The Congress voted unanimously in favor of giving consent to annexation on the terms set forth in the resolution of the American Congress, and it also rejected the preliminary treaty with Mexico without a dissenting vote. The truth was that in the existing condition of public excitement President Jones was widely suspected of desiring the defeat of annexation, and of conspiring with the British minister to that end. That he had gained a great advantage for Texas by bringing about a situation in which it could make a free choice between annexation and independence under a peaceful arrangement with Mexico, was not acknowledged by the members of Congress. All they wanted was annexation, and they rejected the Mexican treaty almost angrily. And then they proceeded to vote down a resolution thanking President Jones for his services in connection with the whole matter.

When the convention met on July 4th, the same story was repeated. One delegate, Richard Bache of Galveston, a great-grandson of Benjamin Franklin, voted against the ordinance of annexation, but, having registered his opinion, he later joined in making it unanimous by signing the measure. The ordinance of annexation embodied the text of the resolution of the American Congress, and then concluded with the following enacting clause:

"Now, in order to manifest the assent of the people of this republic, as is required in the above recited portions of said resolutions, we, the deputies of the people of Texas, in convention assembled, in their name and by their authority, do ordain and declare that we assent to and accept the proposals, conditions and guarantees contained in the first and second sections of the resolution of the Congress of the United States aforesaid."

And so Texas was formally annexed to the United States. There remained the task of drafting a State Constitution, of having this ratified by a vote of the people, and of otherwise complying with the conditions attendant upon the admission of Texas into the Union as a State. All this was carried out in regular order and in due course, and finally on February 16th, 1846, J. Pinckney Henderson, Governor-elect, and the other State officials of the new State of Texas were inaugurated. President Anson Jones hauled down the Lone Star flag of the Republic, and hoisted the Stars and Stripes of the United States in its place. "The Republic of Texas is no more," he said simply. And so the story ends.

CHAPTER XL

INSTEAD OF AN EPILOGUE

THE Mexican War, chiefly because it started in 1846, is usually associated with the annexation of Texas. And yet, the connection was only superficial. Certainly the annexation of Texas was not the "cause" of the Mexican War. The war was not merely the working-out of the Almonte formula. A moment's reflection is sufficient to make this clear. It is necessary only to subject the formula "annexation means war" to a little analysis. Who would start such a war? Mexico? During more than nine years Mexico had been unable to conquer Texas alone. Would it attempt to conquer Texas and the United States together? Would the United States start such a war? Why would it start such a war over Texas? Texas was safely in the Union. *If the Mexican war was an unavoidable war, this must have been due to something other than the annexation of Texas.*

A brief description of the incidents leading up to the outbreak of the war makes it perfectly clear that annexation was not the "cause" of it. After the acceptance of the annexation proposal by the Texas Congress, a detachment of American troops, under command of Gen. Zachary Taylor, moved into Texas. These troops were stationed at Corpus Christi on the Nueces River, which stream was the tradi-

457

tional southern boundary of Texas. Texas, to be sure, had set up a claim to the Rio Grande as the boundary, but this boundary had never been occupied by Texans and had never been established by treaty. The annexation resolution provided that the State of Texas would be formed "subject to the adjustment by this Government (the United States) of all questions of boundary that may arise with other Governments." Verbal assurance was given that the United States would contend for the Rio Grande boundary, but that was something to be adjusted with Mexico. As long as the Republic of Texas continued to exist and President Anson Jones's authority was effective, he required that no troops should cross the Nueces River.

The troops remained on the Nueces River for several months, and their presence there was not made an issue by Mexico. But on March 8th, 1846, three weeks after Jones had hauled down the Lone Star flag of the Republic of Texas, General Taylor began to move his army from the Nueces to the Rio Grande, acting under orders from the United States War Department. He arrived on the Rio Grande, opposite Matamoros, on March 28th, and proceeded to establish camp. Two weeks later, on April 11th, a Mexican force under Gen. Pedro Ampudia reached Matamoros, and the next day Ampudia sent a formal demand to Taylor that he withdraw his troops from the soil of "the Department of Tamaulipas" within twenty-four hours. The text of this demand is interesting, for it required Taylor "to break up your camp and retire to *the other bank of the Nueces River,* while our Governments are regulating the

pending question in relation to Texas." "If you insist on remaining on the soil of the Department of
Tamaulipas," continued Ampudia, "it will clearly
result that arms, and arms alone, must decide the
question; and in that case I advise you that we accept
the war to which, with so much injustice on your
part, you provoke us."

The substance of Ampudia's demand was that
Taylor return to the soil of Texas, where he had been
stationed for several months, in which event the negotiations between the two Governments on "the
pending question" would continue peaceably. But if
Taylor failed to comply with this demand, and remained on the "soil of the Department of
Tamaulipas", as the region between the Nueces and
the Rio Grande was designated under Mexican law,
and as abstracts of title to lands in the region show
to this day, then war would result.

Well, Taylor failed to comply with this demand
and this was the occasion of the outbreak of the war.
If war could have been avoided by his withdrawal to
the Nueces, or by his having remained at the Nueces
in the first place, then certainly the war was not
"caused" by the annexation of Texas.

Anson Jones said afterwards that he had insisted
that no troops should cross the Nueces as long as his
authority over Texas remained because he was determined that if Mr. Polk wanted a war, he would
have to make it himself, that he was resolved to deliver Texas to the United States "without a war".
General Taylor acted under orders from Washington when he moved to the Rio Grande, and if those
orders had for their object the starting of a war with

Mexico, that object had nothing to do with the annexation of Texas. Texas was already safely in the Union.

George Lockhart Rives, whose work, "The United States and Mexico: 1821-1848", includes an exhaustive study of the causes of the Mexican War, has the following to say on this point:

"For the American Government, . . . the question of Texas was settled and done with from the spring of 1845. There was no fear of serious Mexican aggression; and if the question of Texas stood alone, affairs with Mexico might very well have been left to settle themselves. But the Texan question by no means stood alone. The unpaid claims of American citizens against Mexico constituted a very substantial and very real grievance which remained to be disposed of, along with the adjustment of the new boundary. Here, it was hoped, was a lever which might serve to move the Mexican Government to make territorial concessions, precisely as Spain had been moved twenty-six years before to yield the Floridas. A settlement of the spoliation claims and an adjustment of a disputed boundary, by yielding all the peninsula of Florida, were what Monroe had obtained from the Spanish monarchy. It was a precedent complete in all particulars, and Polk looked to make a similar bargain, only this time there was to be a surrender of land on the shores of the Pacific Ocean. His ambitions did not concern themselves any longer with Texas. That had been acquired by his predecessor. What he looked to was California."

It would be interesting, of course, to examine the evidence and attempt to determine whether the order to move to the Rio Grande was given with the deliberate object of starting a war. But that really is another story.

What came of the oft-repeated threat to dissolve the Union in the event of annexation is also another story. But it should be noted that the admission of Texas did not increase the influence of the "slave power" in Congress to any great extent. As a matter of fact, Sam Houston, as one of the Senators from Texas, fought the Kansas-Nebraska bill from its inception to the end. He was the only Democrat in the Senate, whether from the North or the South, who did this. But aside from this, it should be noted that the only alternative to annexation was the continuance of Texas as an independent republic. Even Mexico recognized this in the end, but regardless of Mexico's attitude, the choice was between annexation and an independent Texas. And an independent Texas, with free trade, would have exerted immense economic pressure on the American cotton-growing States, trading with the world from behind a tariff wall in competition with free-trade Texas. This would inevitably have been reflected in the political struggles within the United States.

However, the manner in which the annexation of Texas was received by the extreme opponents of slavery may be illustrated by quoting from a speech delivered by William Lloyd Garrison before an anti-slavery convention at Concord, Massachusetts, on September 22nd, 1845, which was shortly after the Texas convention completed the work of drafting the State Constitution. "An overwhelming majority of the people," said Garrison, "are prepared to indorse this horrible deed of Texan annexation. The hearts of the few who hate it are giving way in despair; the majority have got the mastery. Shall we therefore retreat, acknowledge ourselves conquered, and fall into the ranks of the victors? Shall we agree that it is idle, insane, to contend for the right any longer? Sir, I dreaded, almost, when I heard this convention called. I will be frank with you. I am afraid you are not ready to do your duty; and if not, you will be made a laughingstock by tyrants and their tools, and it ought to be so. . . . I am for revolution were I utterly alone. I am there because I must be there. I must cleave to the right. I cannot choose but obey the voice of God. Now, there are but few who do not cling to their agreement with hell, and obey the voice of the devil. But soon the number who shall resist will be multitudinous as the stars of heaven."

This reflects the reaction of the extreme radical. A more philosophical attitude was that taken by Ralph Waldo Emerson, who, when he heard that the annexation resolution had been adopted by the Senate, wrote the following in his journal:

"The annexation of Texas looks like one of those events which retard or retrograde the civilization of ages. But the World Spirit is a good swimmer, and storms and waves cannot easily drown him. He snaps his finger at laws."

Mr. Emerson used different terms from those of Mr. Garrison, but he was quite as naive in identifying his own views with the eternal purposes of Diety. Today it requires a lot of explaining to make clear why these gentlemen, and many who shared their opinions, regarded the annexation of Texas as

a crime against civilization, and why they characterized the Mexican War, which resulted in adding
the area of California, Arizona, and New Mexico to
the United States, as "a war fought for the extension
of slavery".

However, none of this is an essential part of the
story unfolded in these pages. That story, which began with an accidental meeting of two obscure men
on the plaza of old San Antonio, two days before
Christmas in the year 1820, ended on February 16th,
1846, when Anson Jones hauled down the Lone Star
flag and remarked, "The Republic of Texas is no
more".